ASP.NET
Core
for Jobseekers

---

*Build Career in Designing Cross-Platform
Web Applications Using Razor and Entity
Framework Core*

Kemal Birer

www.bpbonline.com

FIRST EDITION 2022
Copyright © BPB Publications, India
ISBN: 978-93-91392-581

To View Complete
BPB Publications Catalogue
Scan the QR Code:

Dedicated to

My beloved Wife: Emine Bektaş Birer

About the Author

Kemal Birer has a bachelor's degree in Mathematics and Computer Science. He has been working as a developer in the industry for 15+ years in different domains such as ERP, health care, GIS, and e-government.

About the Reviewer

Prajeesh Prathap is an experienced technologist specializing in building web scale, cloud-native applications with special interest in event-driven and distributed systems. He is currently working for the IT and Care industry in Netherlands as a product owner for the platform team specializing in setting up the containerized environments, CI/CD using Azure DevOps, observability platforms, and so on. He is a regular speaker at numerous technology conferences and has authored various video courses on Reactive Microservices in .NET Core, Continuous Delivery with VSTS, and PowerShell DSC.

Acknowledgement

My gratitude goes to Shali Deeraj and other dear people involved with the development of the book at BPB Publications for providing me with great support and Prajeesh Prathap for the technical review.

Preface

This book covers the different aspects of the ASP.NET Core framework and fundamentals of web application development from the perspective of applying jobs that need ASP.NET Core knowledge. Not only does it provide the theory and principles of ASP.NET Core, but also useful practical tips about general software development so the reader can have self-confidence while applying for a job that requires ASP.NET Core skills. It teaches backend development as the main subject but also shows the basics of frontend development.

This book is for individuals who are new to the software world and would like to make a start with ASP.NET Core or developers who have experience with other technologies and would like to learn and switch to ASP.NET Core.

This book is divided into 14 chapters. They will cover general information about basic knowledge of the .NET Core framework, basics of web development with HTML, CSS and JavaScript, server-side development, asynchronous programming, security, optimization techniques, accessing data, software architectures with ASP. NET Core, and learn them for preparing for a job interview.

Chapter 1, introduces the ASP.NET Core framework along with its features and evolution of the ASP.NET framework.

Chapter 2, covers setting up the development environment for Windows, Linux, and MacOS by introducing .NET CLI and various integrated development environments such as Visual Studio and Visual Studio Code.

Chapter 3, covers running and debugging ASP.NET Core applications along with deploying them to a running environment with different operating systems and server options. It also introduces reverse proxies and their roles in an environment.

Chapter 4, introduces the fundamental web technologies like HTTP, HTML, CSS, JavaScript and gives basic information about them using useful libraries and tools such as Twitter Bootstrap, Fiddler, and Postman.

Chapter 5, covers the server-side UI development with ASP.NET Core by introducing Razor pages and MVC by using tag helpers and HTML helpers. It also covers routing, model binding, validation, layout pages, and the MVC pattern work.

Chapter 6, covers the server-side web service and API development by implementing REST principles. It also shows how to configure ASP.NET Core applications in different ways.

Chapter 7, covers easy asynchronous programming by the async/await pattern of .NET Core and teaches how to program the ASP.NET Core pipeline by middlewares.

Chapter 8, covers dependency injection in the ASP.NET Core framework by explaining fundamental principles of IoC and configuring the DI container along with lifetimes of service instances. It also covers developing action filters and implementing built-in filters like authorization, resources, etc.

Chapter 9, explains different ways of managing the state in ASP.NET Core by cookies, query strings, hidden fields, and session framework. It also shows how to utilize identity management in ASP.NET Core and authentication.

Chapter 10, covers accessing data in ASP.NET Core and its evolution from Ado. NET to the Entity Framework. It also teaches concepts like repository pattern, lazy, eager loading, and how to manage transactions.

Chapter 11, covers optimizing ASP.NET Core applications by implementing principles such as response caching, cache tags, content minification, and bundling. It also explains how to measure and debug performance problems by diagnostic tools and other useful tips for optimization.

Chapter 12, introduces possible security flaws in a web application such as SQL injection, CSRF, man in the middle, XSS, open redirect attacks, and how to avoid them in ASP.NET Core. Alongside those, it also shows how to use the data protection framework to protect sensitive data shared with clients.

Chapter 13, covers software architectures in general and helps choose the right architecture. It does so by explaining monolithic, layered, service-oriented, and microservices architectures by comparing them. It also covers CQRS and backend for frontend patterns, eventual consistency, and API gateways to explain microservices.

Chapter 14, covers how to prepare for job interviews and answers to possible interview questions that require ASP.NET Core knowledge.

Downloading the code
bundle and coloured images:

Please follow the link to download the
Code Bundle and the *Coloured Images* of the book:

https://rebrand.ly/a509a8

Errata

We take immense pride in our work at BPB Publications and follow best practices to ensure the accuracy of our content to provide with an indulging reading experience to our subscribers. Our readers are our mirrors, and we use their inputs to reflect and improve upon human errors, if any, that may have occurred during the publishing processes involved. To let us maintain the quality and help us reach out to any readers who might be having difficulties due to any unforeseen errors, please write to us at :

errata@bpbonline.com

Your support, suggestions and feedbacks are highly appreciated by the BPB Publications' Family.

Did you know that BPB offers eBook versions of every book published, with PDF and ePub files available? You can upgrade to the eBook version at www.bpbonline.com and as a print book customer, you are entitled to a discount on the eBook copy. Get in touch with us at :

business@bpbonline.com for more details.

At **www.bpbonline.com**, you can also read a collection of free technical articles, sign up for a range of free newsletters, and receive exclusive discounts and offers on BPB books and eBooks.

BPB is searching for authors like you

If you're interested in becoming an author for BPB, please visit **www.bpbonline.com** and apply today. We have worked with thousands of developers and tech professionals, just like you, to help them share their insight with the global tech community. You can make a general application, apply for a specific hot topic that we are recruiting an author for, or submit your own idea.

The code bundle for the book is also hosted on GitHub at **https://github. com/bpbpublications/ASP.NET-Core-for-Jobseekers**. In case there's an update to the code, it will be updated on the existing GitHub repository.

We also have other code bundles from our rich catalog of books and videos available at **https://github.com/bpbpublications**. Check them out!

PIRACY

If you come across any illegal copies of our works in any form on the internet, we would be grateful if you would provide us with the location address or website name. Please contact us at **business@bpbonline.com** with a link to the material.

If you are interested in becoming an author

If there is a topic that you have expertise in, and you are interested in either writing or contributing to a book, please visit **www.bpbonline.com**.

REVIEWS

Please leave a review. Once you have read and used this book, why not leave a review on the site that you purchased it from? Potential readers can then see and use your unbiased opinion to make purchase decisions, we at BPB can understand what you think about our products, and our authors can see your feedback on their book. Thank you!

For more information about BPB, please visit **www.bpbonline.com**.

Table of Contents

CHAPTER 1
Introduction to ASP.NET Core

Introduction

In this chapter, we will introduce you the ASP.NET Core framework. We will learn the benefits and fundamentals of the framework. This chapter is for individuals who would like to start to learn ASP.NET Core and are not required to have any knowledge about the framework.

Structure

In this chapter, we will discuss the following topics:

- Knowing ASP.NET Core
- Benefits of ASP.NET Core
- Future of ASP.NET Core
- Fundamentals of ASP.NET Core

Objectives

After reading this chapter, you should be able to have an idea of ASP.NET Core and the benefits you can get from it by learning its features and fundamental parts.

Knowing ASP.NET Core

ASP.NET is a server-side framework designed and developed by Microsoft to build dynamic web pages. It is the successor of **Active Server Pages (ASP)**. ASP.NET Core is a cross-platform redesign of the framework of ASP.NET combined with different frameworks like the Entity Framework.

If we take a look at its history, ASP.NET was first released in the early 2000s as a rival framework of Java. It could be hard to start a new project back those days. We had to configure memory and CPU usages with care. When they were set a bit high, the applications would start keeping CPU 100% and let nothing else run; if they were set too low, then the applications started stalling and become unstable. We had to create codebases and frameworks that required too much groundwork and managing configuration could be quite a mess.

ASP.NET came with web forms which had capabilities that we could start developing web applications without worrying too much about code base and too much groundwork. It allowed us to develop web pages in an event-based way like developing a desktop application.

The authentication, authorization, and basic security came as built-in features of ASP.NET. Even making an application with a few web pages got very simple; thanks to Sql DataSource!

Then, ASP.NET MVC was released in around the year 2010. It allowed separation of concerns with the Model View Controller pattern so that frontend developers could make web pages with Razor and backend developers could make development simultaneously in parallel. It introduced Razor so we can create HTML web pages with the merging server-side C# code and HTML.

Microsoft continues to minimize the efforts of developers to make them write less code for groundwork and concentrate on the domain and business of the job itself with ASP.NET Core. Now, we can take advantage of the Linux operating system and run our ASP.NET applications on Linux without changing our code.

ASP.NET Core comes with strong features such as:

- We have a unified way for making web applications. We can use MVC and web API frameworks in the same project.
- We can use razor pages to develop web pages by putting the server-side logic in HTML.
- Develop, debug, and run your applications on macOS, Windows, and Linux. We have cross-platform development and runtime environments with containerization support for docker.
- Host your applications on popular web servers.

- Develop cloud-ready applications.

- Consume services with gRPC.

- Write applications using built in dependency injection for achieving inversion of control, easily managing dependencies, and creating better testable code.

- Create rich applications by utilising bidirectional communication with SignalR.

- Write maintainable and readable asynchronous code easily with the async/await pattern.

- Intercept requests and responses by programming the pipeline with middleware or using built-in extensible filters made for different purposes such as exception handling, authorization, caching, and many more.

Benefits of ASP.NET Core

In this section, we will explain possible reasons of choosing ASP.NET Core for developing web projects.

Open source

We can review the code of the framework on GitHub (**https://github.com/dotnet/aspnetcore**), download and make changes to it as we see fit, compile, and use it. We can even make contribution to it or seek help and counsel from a huge open-source community.

Great programming features

There is a tradition and experience behind the framework that comes from its previous ASP.NET versions. The developers should do less groundwork to start, configure, and develop a new project. This tradition continues as the same with the ASP.NET Core, so it is not just some kind of new framework. It has got its past and roots evolved in many years. This heritage and principles allow the framework to have great features such as:

- Simplified package management with NuGet

- Easy asynchronous programming

- Independence of programming languages

- Fast automated memory management by garbage collection

- Short learning curve

- Fast development

Cross-platform support

This is the most breaking changes made to the framework. Windows was officially the only way to run the previous versions of ASP.NET. Now, we can choose our preferred platform and run our application without changing our code and paying operating system licences.

Performance

According to framework benchmarks, ASP.NET Core is way ahead of the many known frameworks with the features it provides:

- **Garbage Collection**: By the ASP.NET Core version 5.0, the framework is optimized in a refined way that it assures fast running applications. Thanks to solid improvements made to garbage collector (gc) and memory management. Many efforts have gone into applying state-of-the art algorithms to memory allocation and garbage collection.

- **JIT Compiler**: Developers experience less compiling time in any platform. Thanks to the .Net Compiler Platform referred as 'Project Roslyn' and JIT (Just in time compiler).

- **Networking**: There are improvements for networking primitives, security infrastructure, sockets, HTTP, and HTTP/2.

- **Intrinsic**: If you are developing a performance sensitive application, you may use CPU target instruction sets in C# such as SSE4 (Streaming session extensions), or instructions for Arm brand CPUs.

> TIP: Previous .Net frameworks were optimized for the Windows platform but .Net Core is optimized to a server-centric model for different platforms. Redesigning the framework with open-source philosophy for cross platform unlocked many things possible.

Simplified development

We can write code with the comfort of C# and start developing enterprise projects by making the configuration and writing a codebase in a few days. Some provided advantages are:

- Use already built-in features. Many of the key functionalities such as authentication, form submission, model binding, configuration, and many more things are already present in the framework. You do not have to write your own modules, but if you need to, you can modify necessary parts of existing components easily and use them or write your own from scratch.

- Separate the concerns. While backend developers create business of the application, frontend developers can develop the user interfaces with razor or any other front-end framework.

- Use MVC and apply *Convention over configuration* to your code which allows you to map the URL to action methods and binds JSON data to your model classes without effort.

- Configure the inversion of control with the built-in dependency injection framework and control their lifetimes and creation easily.

- Write more testable code by using dependency injection. Use integrated test tools for unit testing.

- Write asynchronous code easily by the async/await pattern and make your application more scalable.

- Deploy your code on the Docker or any cloud environment.

Razor web pages

Increase your control over HTML by mixing your server-side code with HTML. Generate the HTML output using common HTML helpers or encapsulate, create, and reuse your own HTML helpers as you see fit.

Here is an example of a simple razor page:

```
@using some_namespace
@{
var isAdministrator=Model.CheckIfAdministrator();
Layout="~/Views/Shared/_Layout.cshtml"
}
<section class="content">
@if(isAdministrator){
        <div>your admin panel here</div>
}
else{
        <div>your non-admin panel here</div>
}
</section>
```

Web API development

Restful services are the most common used method in cross-platform client server communication. You can create any web API service with any maturity model you want easily. We will cover these in *Chapter 6: Developing Restful Services with ASP. NET Core.*

SignalR

SignalR is an open-source library that allows a bidirectional communication between the server and client browser by choosing the best method based on the capabilities of the server and client browser. It is a well-encapsulated library, and you usually do not have to write any specific code for the chosen method.

Flexible deployment

Deploy your application as framework-dependent so only your code files are deployed along with the referenced libraries. This method requires the ASP.NET Core runtime installed on the server.

Or deploy your application as self-contained by containing the framework runtime files along with your application so your customers can run your application without installing ASP.NET Core runtime.

Interoperability

Function pointers are a new addition to C# 9.0; a special kind of delegate to call unmanaged code methods in an efficient way. Also, .Net introduces interoperability with Swift, Objective-C, and Java.

The legacy Windows forms framework ported to .NET 5 and it is enhanced. You can migrate to your legacy desktop applications written in Windows forms to .NET 5.0 without changing your code and take advantage of the .NET 5.0 performance.

Benchmarking

BenchMarkDotNet is an outstanding benchmarking framework. You can generate benchmark reports, track metrics, any kind of measurements, and so on. It is as easy as writing unit test code by allowing you to design your benchmark experiments and scenarios. You can also benchmark your methods against different versions of the framework.

Here is a simple template code for using BenchMarkDotNet:

```
//specify your targets to run benchmark your code
[SimpleJob(RuntimeMoniker.Net48)]

[SimpleJob(RuntimeMoniker.NetCoreApp30)]

[SimpleJob(RuntimeMoniker.NetCoreApp20)]
```

```
[SimpleJob(RuntimeMoniker.NetCoreApp50)]
[RPlotExporter]
public class BenchmarkTest
{
    [GlobalSetup]
    public void Setup()
    {
        //setup your benchmark test
    }

    [Benchmark]
    public void DoSomething(){
        //do something that it's performance measurable
    }
}
```

Diagnostics

There are many improvements made to the diagnostic system. The tools are available without .NET SDK. You can diagnose assembly loading and trace your applications initialization also. We will cover these in the *Chapter 11: Optimizing ASP.NET Core Applications.*

Blazor

Blazor is an exciting addition to the ASP.NET Core. It allows you to create interactive web UIs without writing JavaScript, and it does not require plugins like Silverlight did a decade ago. It is a fairly new addition, and we will not cover it in this book.

Job roles that ASP.NET Core is used for

You may be employed by varying development roles such as Junior, mid-career, senior software developer, team leader, and so on.

Future of ASP.NET Core

By the time this book is written, .NET 5.0 is the latest .Net Core version in the market and .NET 6.0 preview versions were released. It is clear from the roadmap that Microsoft has long term plans for .NET and committed to make continuous improvements.

According to .NET release cadence:

- .NET Core 3.1: Dec 2019
- .NET 5: Nov2020
- .NET 6: Nov 2021
- .NET 7: Nov 2022
- .NET 8: Nov 2023

When we take a look at the roadmap for .NET 6, we notice important updates such as (subject to change):

- HTTP/3 and QUIC support
- Hot Reload for ASP.NET Core
- Blazor enhancements
- OpenAPI support for developing minimal APIs
- Long running activity support in SignalR

Fundamentals of ASP.NET Core

We will give a summary of the framework in this part. We will discuss the following in the book with detail:

Host

At the start up, every ASP.NET Core application builds its host. An object that encapsulates all the resources includes the following:

- Http Server
- Registered services in the dependency injection container
- Registered middleware components
- Configuration of your application

The host is configured on the entry point of your application. The **CreateHostBuilder** method in the **Program.cs** file.

The Startup class

This is the class that services, and the request pipeline are configured:

```
public void ConfigureServices(IServiceCollection services)
{
//configure ioc
```

```
}
```

```
public void Configure(IApplicationBuilder app)
{
//configure request pipeline
}
```

The **ConfigureServices** and **Configure** methods are called by the ASP.NET Core runtime when your application starts.

> NOTE: You should avoid unhandled exceptions in the startup class. If not, your application may fail to initialize, and your action methods may not execute.

Dependency injection

ASP.NET Core comes with built in dependency injection. Services, and their lifetimes are configured in the **ConfigureServices** method of the **Startup** class:

```
public void ConfigureServices(IServiceCollection services)
{
// configure lifetime of the services.
services.AddScoped<IDependencyInterface,DependencyImplementation>();

}
```

After registration, you can inject your instance to the controller, model classes, and so on. The dependencies will be resolved automatically:

```
public class IndexModel:PageModel
{

    public IndexModel(IDependencyInterface service)
    {
    }

    public void OnGet(){}
}
```

If the built-in IoC container doesn't meet your applications needs, you can always integrate and use a third-party container. We will cover di in the *Chapter 8: Dependency Injection and Action Filters in ASP.NET Core*.

Middleware

After configuring IoC in the **ConfigureServices** method, you can configure the pipeline by the Configure method in the **Startup** class. An ASP.NET Core Middleware is simply a delegate that allows you to perform operations on the incoming Http request; you can redirect it by the URL rewriting, pass execution to the next middleware component or short circuit, and terminate the request:

```
app.Use(async (context, next) =>
{
var request = context.Request;
// do something with the request
…

…

// Call the next delegate/middleware in the pipeline
await next(context);
// do something with the response
});
```

Routing

A route in ASP.NET Core is simply a URL pattern matched to a resource on the server. This resource can be a middleware, a razor page, or an action method of a web API controller.

Server

After the Startup class methods are called and the host is built, a server implementation is created and encapsulated into **HttpContext**. ASP.NET Core supports the following server implementations:

- **Kestrel**: A cross-platform web server often runs under reverse-proxy configuration with IIS, Apache or Nginx but can be run as a standalone web server since ASP.NET Core 2.0 also.

- **IIS**: Internet information services server is a server application for the Windows platform.

- **HTTP.sys**: A non-cross-platform alternative to Kestrel that only runs on the Windows platform and offers some security features that Kestrel does not.

We will cover them in *Chapter 3: Running, Debugging, and Deploying ASP.NET Core Applications*.

NOTE: If you plan to use Kestrel and make your application accessible from Internet, you really should consider placing it under a reverse proxy such as Nginx, Apache, or IIS and expose only the reverse proxy to the Internet for the sake of security of your application.

Configuration

ASP.NET Core provides a configuration framework that can load name-value pairs from many different types of sources such as .xml files, .json files, command line arguments, environment variables, or custom configuration sources. These can be combined and merged to a unified key-value paired configuration data.

Environment

ASP.NET Core reads the ASPNETCORE_ENVIRONMENT environment variable value and stores its value in the **IWebHostEnvironment** implementation, you can use dependency injection to inject this interface and access the properties and methods.

You can set the ASPNETCORE_ENVIRONMENT value to anything you like meaningful such as Development, Test, Staging, Production and write conditional code based on the environment.

Here is an example of using it. If the environment is development, there is no harm in viewing the detailed error, exception message, and stack trace:

```
public void Configure(IApplicationBuilder app, IWebHostEnvironment env)
{
// checks if ASPNETCORE_ENVIRONMENT variable is Development
if (env.IsDevelopment())
{
//if it is development show exception detail on the page
app.UseDeveloperExceptionPage();
}
else
{
//Redirect to custom error page if environment production
app.UseExceptionHandler("/Error");
}
}
```

You can create different startup classes by environment in the form **Startup{environment name}** like **StartupDevelopment.cs** or **StartupProduction.cs**, and so on.

You can also create configuration files based on the environment name in the form **appsettings.{environmentname}.json** like **appsettings.Development.json**, **appsettings.Production.json**, and so on.

We will discuss these topics in the upcoming chapters in detail.

Logging

ASP.NET Core has an internal logging framework that can write logs to many targets. Available providers are:

- Console
- Debug Output
- Event Tracing on Windows
- Windows Event Log
- Azure Application Insights
- Azure App Service

If these are not sufficient, then you may write your own logging provider.

Using it is easy. Simply inject it to anywhere possible and use the respective log method:

```
public class SomeController : ControllerBase
{
    private readonly ILogger _logger;

    public TodoController(ILogger logger)
    {
      _logger = logger;
    }

    [HttpGet()]
    public ActionResult GetById([FromQuery]string id)
    {
      _logger.LogInformation("GetById", "Getting item {Id}", id);
     // do something and return
```

```
    }
}
```

Conclusion

We introduced ASP.NET Core and learned the fundamental parts of the framework. We will cover these in detail in the upcoming chapters.

Questions

1. If we are starting a new project, when should we prefer using ASP.NET Core?

2. When should we use reverse proxy for deploying our ASP.NET Core applications?

3. Where do we configure our applications service container and request pipeline?

4. What could we use for intercepting and modifying requests?

CHAPTER 2

Setting up the Development Environment

Introduction

In this chapter, we will show you how to set up your development environment and use various integrated development environments.

Structure

In this chapter, we will learn the following topics:

- Setting up the development environment in Windows
- Setting up the development environment in Linux
- Setting up the development environment in MacOS
- .NET Command line interface
- Understanding integrated development environments for ASP.NET Core
- Introducing Visual Studio
- Introducing Visual Studio Code

Objectives

After reading this chapter, you should be able to set up the development environment for ASP.NET Core and start using various tools and IDEs. You can use a simple text editor such as notepad for quick editing of source code, but you really should use an integrated development environment for easy development and get the best from the .NET framework.

Setting up the development environment on Windows

There are mainly two ways to set up .NET SDK on the Microsoft Windows Platform. We can install .NET SDK first and then use the preferred IDE for our development, or you can install .NET SDK along with Visual Studio.

We can download SDK as zipped binaries or executable installer by visiting the web page at **https://dotnet.microsoft.com/download/dotnet** and choosing the version and Windows platform we want.

We can install .NET SDK along with Visual Studio also. Please follow the instructions on **https://visualstudio.microsoft.com/**. You can download the free community edition or commercial version such as Professional or Enterprise. In the set up dialog box, you can choose any .NET SDK version on the `Individual components` tab:

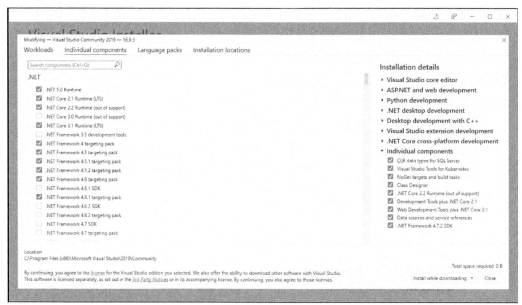

Figure 2.1: *Install .NET SDK along with Visual Studio*

Setting up the development environment on Linux

.Net Core is supported on many different Linux distributions such as Alpine, Debian, CentOS, openSUSE, Ubuntu, Red HAT, Fedora, and SLES. We will cover how to install on Ubuntu.

We can install .Net Core on Ubuntu by performing the following steps:

1. Install the package key to your package repository:

```
wget https://packages.microsoft.com/config/ubuntu/{your ubuntu
version here}/packages-microsoft-prod.deb -O packages-microsoft-
prod.deb


sudo dpkg -i packages-microsoft-prod.deb
```

2. Update your package repository:

```
sudo apt-get update; \
sudo apt-get install -y apt-transport-https && \
sudo apt-get update
```

3. Install .Net Sdk 5.0:

```
sudo apt-get install -y dotnet-sdk-5.0
```

If we want to set up the runtime environment on our server, we need to install ASP. NET Core runtime with the following command without installing the SDK:

```
sudo apt-get install -y aspnetcore-runtime-5.0
```

For other Linux distribution, please refer to the documentation at **https://docs.microsoft.com/**. Installation is like setting up the sdk on Ubuntu.

Setting up the development environment on macOS

We can download .NET SDK from **https://dotnet.microsoft.com/download/dotnet** like setting up on Windows and follow the instructions. We must also set the environment variables for the dotnet file.

We can choose to install SDK along with Visual Studio for macOS by downloading the installer on **https://docs.microsoft.com/visualstudio/mac/installation?view=vsmac-2019**. It is like installing on Windows and can be installed by following the instructions.

.NET Command line interface

.NET CLI is a cross-platform toolchain used for creating new projects, building, running, and publishing .NET applications. It comes along with .NET SDK.

The common format of commands usually is as follows. We put the necessary statements inside the parts with curly braces:

```
dotnet {command name} {arguments} {options}
```

Let us take a look at the common commands used:

- For getting help:
  ```
  dotnet {command name} -h
  ```

- For creating new projects:
  ```
  dotnet new {project template short name}
  ```

For ASP.NET Core projects, you can supply the following template names:

- ○ **web**: For empty ASP.NET Core project.

- ○ **mvc**: For default ASP.NET Core project set up with MVC and razor pages. There are some options that we can use for configuring the project creation:

- **-au** or **--auth**: Used to configure authentication of the project:

  - ○ **None**: No authentication (it does not mean completely no authentication. If you would like to develop your custom authentication from scratch, you choose this.)

  - ○ **Windows**: Windows authentication.

  - ○ **SingleOrg**: Authentication for a single tenant.

  - ○ **MultiOrg**: Authentication for multi-tenant.

  - ○ **Individual**: Authentication combined with the Identity Server using open ID connect.

- **-f** or **--framework**: Specify the .NET framework version.

  - ○ **angular**: For the default ASP.NET Core project set up for Angular.

  - ○ **react**: For the default ASP.NET Core project set up for React.js.

  - ○ **webapi**: For the default ASP.NET Core web API project set up.

  There are more templates for creating components to existing ASP.NET Core projects such as razor pages, viewstart files, and so on. Please refer to the documentation at **https://docs.microsoft.com/dotnet/core/tools/**.

We can even create our custom templates for our specific needs and install them on our machine or publish them to NuGet for worldwide availability.

- To install the custom template, use the **-i** option:

```
dotnet new -i {path to custom template or nuget id}
```

- To list installed templates, use the **-l** or **--list** option:

```
dotnet new -l
```

- To set up the project with specified programming language, use the **-lang** or **–language** option. You can choose one of the c# ,f# ,vb languages by default but not every project type supports every language mentioned, so please refer to the documentation.

```
dotnet new webapi -lang {language name}
```

- To give a name to our project, we will use the **-n** or **--name** option. If not specified, the current directory name is used:

```
dotnet new webapi -n {project name}
```

- To specify the output folder of the generated files, we will use the **-o** or **--output** option:

```
dotnet new webapi -o {path to output folder}
```

- For building a project (must be run on the directory of the project file):

```
dotnet build
```

We can specify the output folder for build files with the **-o** or **--output** option. If not specified, the default output folder is **{path of your project file}/ bin/{configuration}/{framework version}**.

We can specify the build configuration with the **-c** or **--configuration** option; it can be Debug, Release, or any custom build.

The .NET framework version can be specified in the **-f** or **--framework** option.

If we have some pre or post build actions, sometimes we can get into trouble while building our project and we would require more detailed info of building stages. We can achieve this **-v {level}** or **--verbosity {level}** option. The values of the level determine the detail level and they can be quiet, minimal, normal, detailed, and diagnostic. The default value for the verbosity option is minimal.

We can use **--version-suffix** to specify our projects' version number.

> **NOTE: Many of these settings are set in project files. We will cover project files and build configurations in detail in *Chapter 3: Running, Debugging, and Deploying ASP.NET Core Applications.***

- For restoring a project, use the following command:

```
dotnet restore
```

This command instructs the NuGet package manager to download the necessary dependencies added as references or required by the project. Usually, it is not required to execute restore; this command is automatically executed when the dotnet build command is executed, but it may be required for continuous delivery/deployment scenarios.

- For adding a package to a project, use the following command:

```
dotnet add package {package name}
```

To add a package with the specific version, the -v or –version option is used. This command checks whether the package's framework version is compatible with our project's framework version.

- For running a project, use the following command:

```
dotnet {path to dll file that .NET application entry point
located. It is the dll file which Main method located which is by
default Program.cs file}
```

- For publishing a project (must be run on the directory of the project file), use the following command:

```
dotnet publish
```

- Check changes in files and execute a command on a change:

```
dotnet watch {run/test args}
```

The **watch** command starts a watcher that listens for changes in files and runs the project or executes tests in the project accordingly. **dotnet watch run** also launches a browser for the ASP.NET Core applications and refreshes it when the files in the project are changed and built successfully. This is a helpful tool that improves productivity for implementing quick trial and error cases.

> **TIP: You can keep a watcher for running unit tests with the dotnet watch test command and do your development in parallel. This way you can immediately get the result of the tests as you write the code.**

- To run tests in a project, use the following command:

```
dotnet test
```

This command executes unit tests in a project based on the testing framework used (MSTest, xUnit, NUnit) and displays the results on the command line. It has so many features which can come in handy for continuous integration scenarios.

Integrated development environments for ASP.NET Core

The dotnet CLI is useful for setting up production or test environments. But for development, it can be painful because usually we must manage many types of different projects in a solution together.

Therefore, you need a software that has user interfaces to assist your development. You simply cannot use a text editor and dotnet CLI commands for developing medium to large scale projects. That is where **Integrated Development Environments (IDE)** come to the rescue.

Here are some of the benefits of using an IDE:

- Manage our application's projects at the same time.

- Switch between source files as we wish and write our code.

- Handle different types of source files such as JavaScript or C# with the syntax highlighting specific to them and format our code easily.

- Take advantage of automatic code completion while coding.

- Search a package or manage our references and packages by a user interface not by the command line.

- Use themes and customize the style of our code editor as our eyes feel comfortable.

- Build, debug, and publish our application with just clicking on a button.

- Run our unit tests with just clicking on a button and get results of the tests as a report.

- Monitor our application resource usages such as CPU, memory, network, and hard disk as we debug.

- Manage our source code files for source control. It is easy to merge conflicts, send our changes, get the latest changes, and view history of a source code file from source control.

- Take advantage of templates while creating new projects, classes, interfaces, etc. and start with minimal code required that is already generated for us.

- Take advantage of background compilation and realize our errors while coding.

- Measure our code quality by analysis.

- Refactor and rename our variables that is referenced everywhere in our code.

There are powerful IDEs for developing ASP.NET Core projects which may be a rest service or a razor application:

- **Microsoft Visual Studio**: An IDE developed and supported by Microsoft that has great capabilities for developing .NET applications. It has free community, professional, and enterprise editions. It can be used on Windows and macOS.

- **Visual Studio Code**: A cross platform and free editor that can run on Windows, Linux, and macOS. It is known for its speed and simplicity. It has a plugin system and supports many different types of computer languages, not just .NET languages.

- **OmniSharp**: This adds cross-platform development support for popular editors such as Atom, Vim, Emacs, Sublime Text, and Brackets. Visual Studio Code uses the OmniSharp server plugin to support autocompleting the code.

- **JetBrains Rider**: A cross-platform IDE comes with free and paid versions. It has as many features as Visual Studio.

We will introduce Visual Studio and Visual Studio Code in this book, so please feel free to use any IDE you see fit for yourself.

Introduction to Visual Studio

Visual Studio is the official IDE from Microsoft. It has originated from the 90s before the first .NET was born. With the release of the first .NET in 2002, it primarily focused on .NET. It evolved in many years together with the .NET framework.

Visual Studio has free community editions that can be used by individual developers or companies having fewer than 5 developers and an annual revenue less than 1 million $ (these license terms may change so please refer to the web site at (**https:// visualstudio.microsoft.com/vs/compare**). It is possible to write commercial applications with the community edition by complying with its license.

It has paid versions such as Visual Studio Professional and Enterprise. They have more features compared to the community edition. Please refer to the web site in the previous paragraph for comparison.

If you are an individual developer, the community edition will be enough for you.

Let us introduce some of its features in detail:

- **Create a new project**: We can create our ASP.NET Core or any other type of projects by clicking on **New** -> **Project** from the menu and using the **Create New Project** wizard.

  We can create custom project templates of our own or download and install custom project templates to Visual Studio from the Internet:

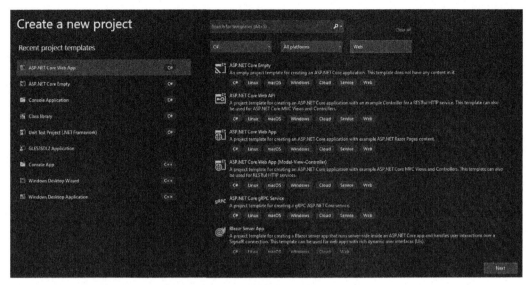

Figure 2.2: Create a New Project Wizard

- **Solution Explorer**: A .NET solution is simply a collection of related projects that is desired to be managed together. For separation of the concerns and allowing better code re-use, we put our code in different projects.

TIP: If you are developing a medium to large scale enterprise project, you should never put all your code in a single ASP.NET Core project. We will cover these concepts in the upcoming chapters.

For example, in a typical three-layer architecture, we usually have a presentation project (in our case, it is ASP.NET Core project), a business layer project (a class library project) and a data access layer project (again a class library project):

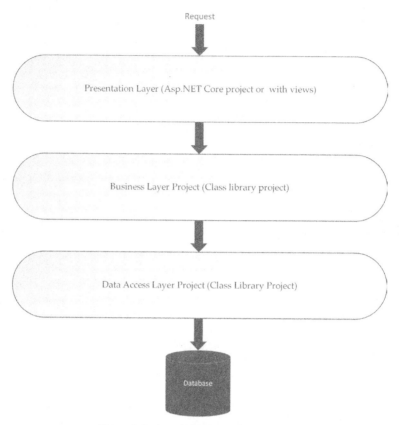

Figure 2.3: *A typical 3-layered architecture*

In this classic three-layer architecture, the request arrives at our presentation layer and triggers some code (action methods in ASP.NET Core projects). Then, we will call methods from objects in the business layer, and then from the business layer objects, we will call data access layer object methods.

As seen, we must access source code files in every project at once while developing because we write the code in a layer that depends on other layer.

We can achieve this by grouping our projects into a solution. It is nothing but a human-readable text file with the extension of **.sln**.

Luckily, Visual Studio provides a solution explorer to us like many other IDEs do. It lists projects and source files under   in a tree. The second level in the tree hierarchy is the projects (a folder contains source code files and the project file of the project) and the third or next hierarchy levels are folders, source code files, or other types of files.

We can navigate easily and open them as tabs in the source code editor. You can use the search bar on the top for filtering the solution to find the file you are looking for:

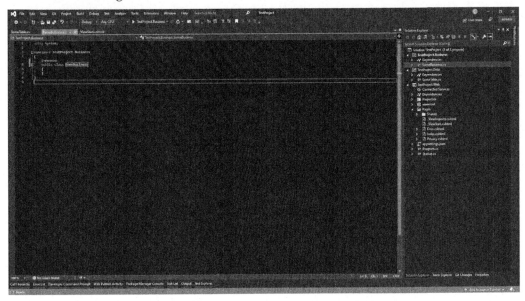

Figure 2.4: *A simple project in solution explorer*

- **Team Explorer**: We can connect to a source control system and manage code changes by accessing the features source control presents. Visual Studio officially supports the Azure DevOps Server (formerly, the TFS team foundation server) or Git through the plugin. You can open Team explorer pane from `View` -> `Team Explorer` from the menu and drag it anywhere on the screen.

  We can access the features of our source control whether it is Git or the Azure DevOps Server from the options on Team explorer. There may be options specific to Azure DevOps such as include, exclude, check in, or specific to Git such as push, pull, stage, and unstage.

  Visual Studio 2019 comes with a powerful Git integration. We can manage many features of Git from basic things such as cloning a repository to more advanced operations like resolving conflicts. Usually, developers deal with Git by executing commands from the command or shell prompt, but from now on, we have a tool with a user interface in Visual Studio that eases our source control operations for Git:

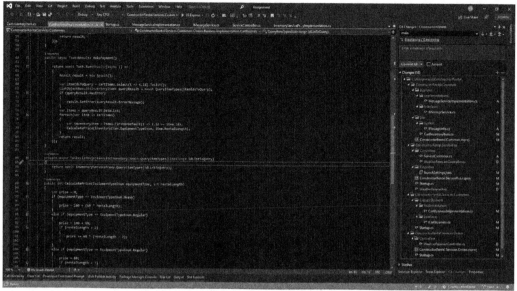

Figure 2.5: Team explorer with Git options

The source code or other files that we modified in the solution is shown with red tick marks next to them, which means we have written something in them and now they are different from their source control version.

> **NOTE: Refactoring with renaming variables, methods, and generating properties may also modify the source code files without your attention!!!**

- **Building, debugging**: We can simply build our entire solution from the menu by clicking on **Build** -> **Build solution** or build a single project from the Solution Explorer by right clicking on the project file and selecting the build from the context menu.

  We can debug our entire solution similarly by clicking on **Debug** -> **Start Debugging** from the menu or debug a single project in our solution by right clicking on it and selecting the debug from the context menu.

> **TIP: You may encounter many solutions with tons of projects. Your development experience can be hindered because of compilation and building time of the solution depending on your computer's hardware.**
>
> **To reduce compilation and building time you may do the following:**

- **Group related small number of projects into multiple solutions. You can always run multiple instances of Visual Studio and work on multiple solutions. This method gives a great development experience if you have multiple monitors.**

- **Unload the projects that are not required for your development at that time by right clicking on the project in the Solution Explorer and clicking on Unload Project from the context menu. For example, they may be test projects or projects giving build errors that do not interest you at that time.**

- **Configuring Build**: We can configure building of our application by right clicking on our solution and clicking on properties. Visual studio displays a pop-up window.

  On the left-hand side column, by selecting **Common properties** -> **Start-up project,** we can select:

  o Which project or projects to start with debugging?

  o Launch order of the projects by clicking on the up and down arrows on the right column. For example, if our web project depends on a service project, and we want the service project to get started first, because we won't want to get run time errors after our web project started.

  On the left-hand side column, by selecting **Configuration Properties** -> **Configuration,** we can set the architecture of the projects in the solution such as Any CPU, x64, x86, Arm, and so on:

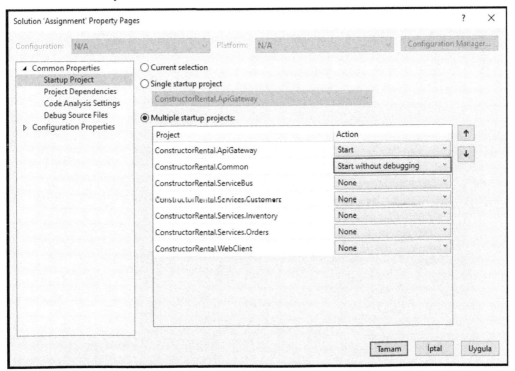

Figure 2.6: *Configuring debugging start-up*

We can set the configuration and platform architectures from **Configuration** as shown in *Figure 2.7*:

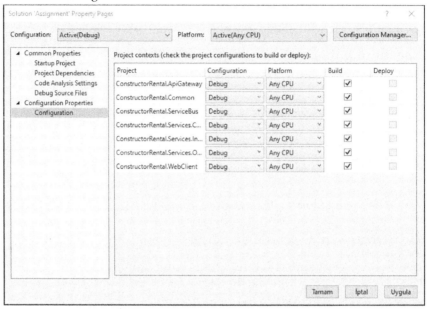

Figure 2.7: *Configuring build architecture*

- **Diagnostic Tools**: We can monitor our applications such as CPU and memory usages and get diagnostic reports. They can be accessible from **Debug** -> **Windows** -> **Show Diagnostic Tools**. The project that needs to be analyzed must be started for debugging before.

It is also possible to benchmark our methods using debug breakpoints together with the Diagnostic tools:

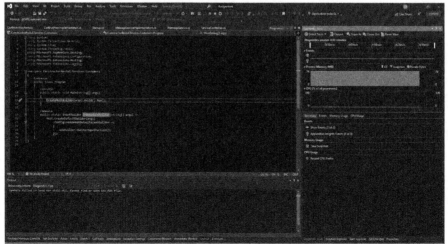

Figure 2.8: *Diagnostic tools*

- **Class Diagrams**: Visual Studio comes with a class diagram tool that we can use for generating diagrams from existing code or generating code by designing class diagrams first.

  Right click on the project you want to add the class diagram file and click on add new item. Select the class diagram and give a name to it.

  We can add classes and interfaces to our diagram by right clicking on an empty place in our diagram and selecting items under the Add context menu. It is automatically added to the project.

  It is also possible to export the diagram as an image:

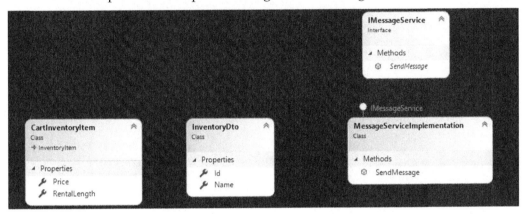

Figure 2.9: Visual studio class diagram tool

- **Test Explorer:** The .NET framework includes the unit testing framework called MS Test. From Visual Studio, we can access Test Explorer from the menu by clicking on **View** -> **Test Explorer**. After building our project, the Test Explorer automatically detects our unit tests and displays them in a hierarchical way. We can run our tests by clicking on buttons on the Test Explorer and get information about their results later.

- **Project Properties**: We can right click on a project file and open the project properties window. It is used to manage the property settings of the projects. In the case of the ASP.NET Core project, the debug properties are as follows:

  o **Launch**: This specifies the local server used to host the application for debugging. For the Windows environment, they can be IIS Express or IIS.

  o **Working Directory**: This is the relative URL address of the start-up page.

  o **Environment Variables**: This is used to set the environment variables whose values are accessed in the project code. The **ASPNETCORE_ ENVIRONMENT** variable is set to the Development by default. We can change it to debug our code for different environments.

○   **App URL**: This specifies the local address and port of the application:

Figure 2.10: *Visual studio test explorer*

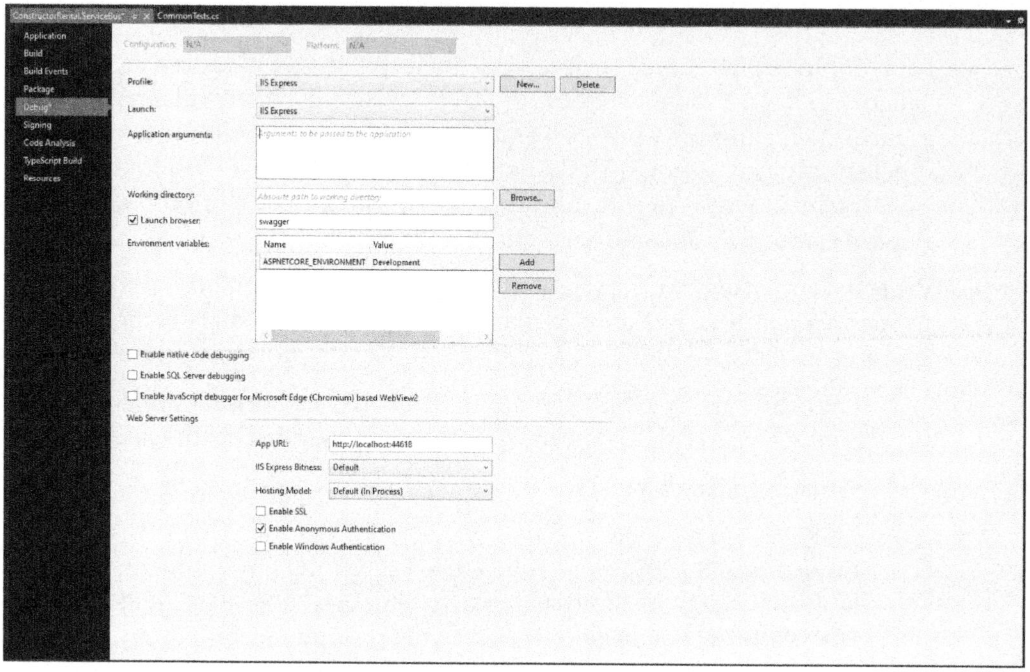

Figure 2.11: *Visual studio project properties*

Introduction to Visual Studio Code

Visual Studio Code is a free open-source code editor. It is based on plugins and actually it is not a fully featured IDE like Visual Studio.

The main differences are:

- It is lightweight, runs faster, and handles a large number of projects in a better way.
- It is based on code files not projects or solutions.
- It does not have a new file or project creation wizards. Usually, new projects are created by the dotnet cli and opened with Visual Studio Code.

> **TIP: If you need to develop the typescript and backend at the same solution, which is common for web projects with Angular. It is better to turn off the typescript compilation in Visual Studio and use Visual Studio Code for typescript development. Having Visual Studio to build C# and typescript at the same time may degrade the total building time. Just use Visual Studio for backend and Vs Code for front-end typescript.**

Let us explain the key points to start developing in Visual Studio Code. There is no solution explorer like Visual Studio in Visual Studio Code, but it has an explorer. We can create projects in a folder with the dotnet cli (assuming we do not have Visual Studio) and then open the folder with Visual Studio Code by clicking on **File** -> **Open folder** in the menu. We can view the source code files and folders with a tree:

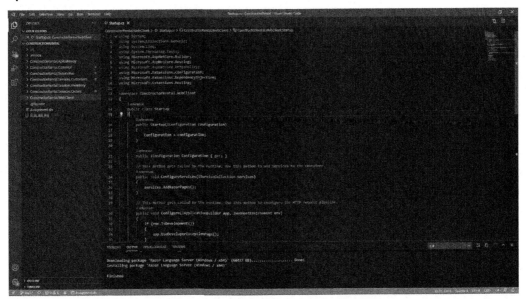

Figure 2.12: Visual studio code explorer and editor

There is no solution file support to configure debugging and launching order. Visual Studio Code uses **launch.json** file. To create it, we need to navigate to the Run and Debug section by clicking on ▷ under the explorer icon. If we do not have the **launch.json** file already, it will ask us to create it. It is placed in the **.vscode** directory in the folder currently opened:

```json
{
    // Use IntelliSense to learn about possible attributes.
    // Hover to view descriptions of existing attributes.
    // For more information, visit: https://go.microsoft.com/
fwlink/?linkid=830387
    "version": "0.2.0",
    "configurations": [
        {
            "name": ".NET Core Launch (web)",
            "type": "coreclr",
            "request": "launch",
            "preLaunchTask": "build",
            "program": "${workspaceFolder}/ConstructorRental.ApiGateway/
bin/Debug/net5.0/ConstructorRental.ApiGateway.dll",
            "args": [],
            "cwd": "${workspaceFolder}/ConstructorRental.ApiGateway",
            "stopAtEntry": false,
            "serverReadyAction": {
                "action": "openExternally",
                "pattern": "\\bNow listening on:\\s+(https?://\\S+)"
            },
            "env": {
                "ASPNETCORE_ENVIRONMENT": "Development"
            },
            "sourceFileMap": {
                "/Views": "${workspaceFolder}/Views"
            }
        },
        {
            "name": ".NET Core Attach",
            "type": "coreclr",
            "request": "attach",
```

```
        "processId": "${command:pickProcess}"
    }
  ]
}
```

We can then choose the program we need to debug by the program field, launch a new browser when debugging was started by the **serverReadyAction** field, and set environment variables in the **env** field. We can duplicate and modify the JSON object in the configurations array for debugging other projects in our folder.

Conclusion

We learned about development environments that .NET supports and saw how to set them up. We also learned different integrated development environments and saw how to use them. We will learn how to debug, deploy, and run our applications in the next chapter.

Questions

1. When should we use the dotnet CLI?

2. Why should we use an IDE or editor for development?

3. What can we do to increase the building performance of the Visual Studio?

4. How do we manage launching the order of projects for debugging in Visual Studio and Visual Studio Code and why should we manage it?

CHAPTER 3
Running, Debugging, and Deploying ASP.NET Core Applications

Introduction

In this chapter, we will explain using reverse proxies, debugging, and deploying of ASP.NET core projects.

Structure

In this chapter, w e will cover the following topics:

- The concept of reverse proxy
- Running ASP.NET core applications
- Debugging ASP.NET core applications
- Deploying ASP.NET core applications

Objectives

After reading this chapter, you should be able to debug and host your ASP.NET core applications on Windows and Linux in a variety of ways.

The concept of reverse proxy

Before we delve into the debugging and deployment of projects, we must explain the meaning and logic of reverse proxy. It is about software architectures, but it is related directly to the deployment and server usage of the projects.

Reverse proxy is a type of proxy server that resides in the outer network, can be accessible from the public network, and directs requests to the appropriate application servers, which are inaccessible from the public network. They provide benefits such as **network load balancing (NLB)**, better serving and caching static content, and handling security before malicious requests arrive at the application servers. The *Figure 3.1* shows a typical monolithic architecture:

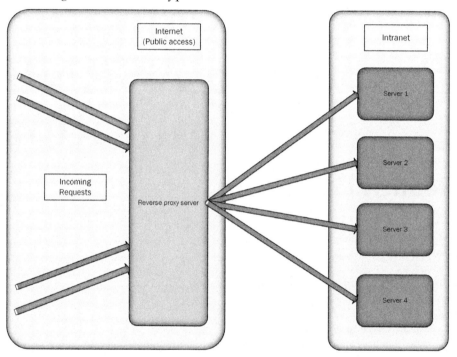

Figure 3.1: *Proxy server in a monolithic architecture*

Now, let us explain the benefits of reverse proxy in detail:

- **Load balancing**: It allows scaling up the system by adding servers to handle more concurrent requests. Usually, the following methods are used for load balancing:
    - **Round robin**: It distributes requests to application servers (the servers in Intranet) sequentially. For example, the first request to Server 1, the second to Server 2, the third to Server 3, the fourth to Server 4, the fifth to Server 5, and so on.

o **Sticky Session**: Reverse proxy assigns a cookie to responses of the requests and tracks the owners of the requests and directs backend servers. For example, when a user sends a request to the application for the first time, reverse proxy directs it to Server 1 and assigns a cookie to the response and keeps it with the directed server info in its storage. When the same user issues a second request, the reverse proxy remembers the user by the cookie and directs it to Server 1 again. The point in sticky session load balancing is allowing application servers to remember the state or information about the users.

- **Security**: It is obvious that we can make our application servers much secure by keeping them behind a reverse proxy's shield. We can enforce whitelist authentication, thus allowing only requests with specific IP addresses to access our application. It includes handling denial of service attacks before requests arrive at our application servers, and so on.

- **Caching and serving static content**: We can configure static content cached and served to the end users' browsers without bothering our application servers and increase their capacity and performance.

In case of ASP.NET Core projects, we may use the following combinations for serving our applications:

OPERATING SYSTEM	REVERSE PROXY	APPLICATION SERVER
Windows	IIS	Kestrel
.	IIS	HTTP.sys
.		IIS
.	NGINX	Kestrel
.	NGINX	HTTP.sys
.	APACHE	Kestrel
.	APACHE	HTTP.sys
Linux	NGINX	Kestrel
.	APACHE	Kestrel

Table 3.1: Reverse proxies with application servers

Running ASP.NET core applications

Running an ASP.NET Core application is relatively simple. With .NET SDK or ASP. NET Core runtime installed, navigate to the folder where your project file is located and type the following command:

```
dotnet {build/publish} {entry point file name}.dll
```

Then, navigate to the output folder of the build or publish the operation and type the following command in your command prompt:

```
dotnet {entry point file name}.dll
```

The application's entry point is the static **Main** method in the **Program.cs** file in your ASP.NET Core project by default. The execution of code starts from when the project is launched for the first time.

We can have multiple entry points. From the Visual Studio, we can change the entry point from the project properties window by right clicking on the project file from our Solution Explorer, selecting properties, and selecting the entry point object from the **Startup object** combo box. Here is a screenshot of the project properties window:

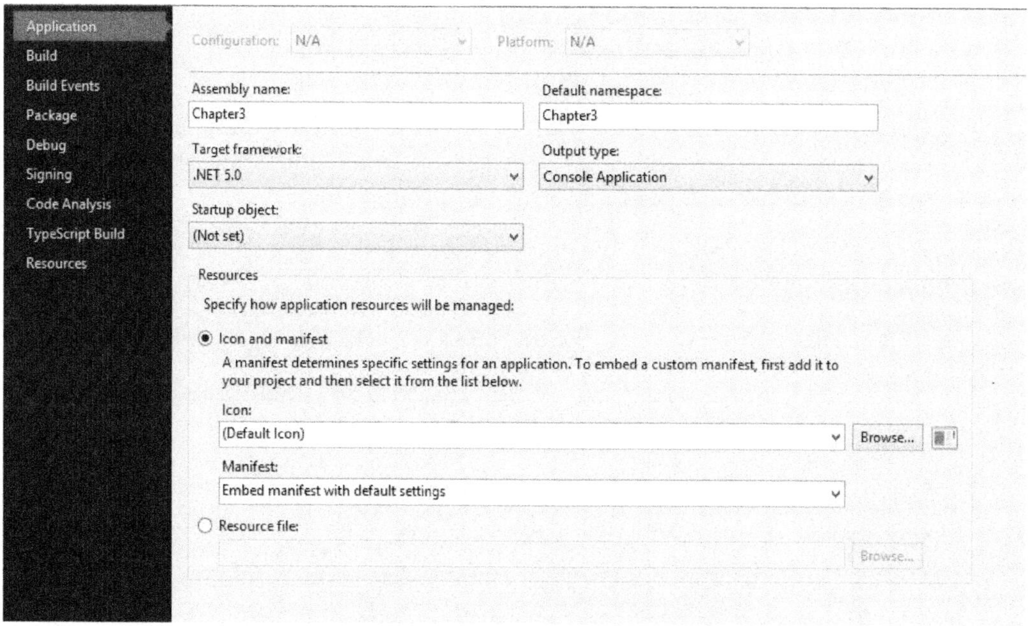

Figure 3.2: Startup object selection from project properties

If we are using the Visual Studio Code or any other editor, changing the entry point can be achieved by opening the project file and specifying **Startup object** with the namespace of its class. The following XML shows a sample configuration in a project file:

```
<Project Sdk="Microsoft.NET.Sdk.Web">
  <PropertyGroup>
    <TargetFramework>net5.0</TargetFramework>
    <StartupObject>Chapter3.Program</StartupObject>
  </PropertyGroup>
</Project>
```

TIP: The project files in .NET are simply XML files ending with csproj or vbproj depending on the programming language of the project. The project files can be modified by right clicking on a project in Solution Explorer and selecting properties, or manually editing by hand. Sometimes, you can get into trouble while editing it with the properties window for various reasons such as corrupted installation or Visual Studio errors; if that is the case, try modifying it by manually to avoid wasting time.

You can also run any .NET application from Visual Studio by clicking on **Debug ->** **Start** without debugging from the menu.

Debugging ASP.NET core applications

Debugging is simply running our application's source code step by step or stopping the execution of code in the location where we want to find errors or verify the code functioning as we want it.

There are some common concepts of debugging. We will explore them before going further. These are usually the same in every framework and programming languages:

- **Breakpoint**: Breakpoints are the locations in our source code that we want the execution of the code to be stopped. This allows us to examine the values of the variables or states of the objects we used in our code. We can add a breakpoint by navigating to the line we want and click on the left mouse button on the left strip of the editor or by pressing F9 key or opening the context menu by right clicking and selecting **Breakpoint -> Insert** **Breakpoint**.

- **Step Over**: When the execution of the code stops at some statement in our code, we can execute the current statement with this command and the execution goes to the next statement in the code. We can use the *F10* key to step over.

- **Step Into**: When the execution of the code is stopped on a statement which may be a method or property evaluation, we can use step into to take the execution of the code into the method or property so we can debug that method or property. Visual Studio opens the code of that method that we are stepping into automatically. We can use the *F11* key to step into.

- **Step Out**: When the execution of the code is stopped inside a property or method, we can use step out to quickly pass the execution of the code until the end of the method and execution reaches outside the location where it is called. We can use the key combination *Shift + F11* to step out.

Debugging with Visual Studio

We can start debugging our ASP.NET core project from Visual Studio by clicking on **Debug** > **Start Debugging** from the menu. If we start debugging from the menu, Visual Studio launches the startup projects specified from the configuration of the solution. We mentioned configuring startup projects in *Chapter 2: Setting up the Development Environment*. Or we can start debugging a single project by right clicking on the project we want to from the Solution Explorer and then clicking on **Debug** > **Start Debugging** from the context menu. Therefore, we can bypass the startup projects configuration of the solution and start debugging any single executable project in our solution.

We can set our project's debugging properties by opening debug properties. It is opened by right clicking on the project in the solution explorer and selecting properties from the context menu and then selecting the **Debug** tab on the dialog box. The properties in this window are ignored when we publish and deploy our application in the Release mode. Here is a screenshot of the debugging settings window:

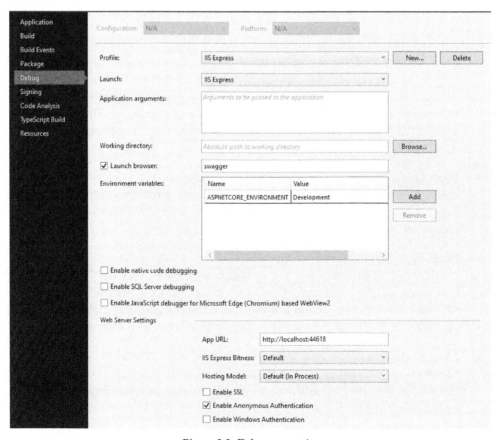

Figure 3.3: Debug properties

Let us explain the properties listed here:

- **Profile**: This specifies the debug profile. Visual Studio uses the **launchSettings.json** file to store the debugging profiles. A simple **launchSettings.json** file is as follows:

```
{
  "iisSettings": {
    "windowsAuthentication": false,
    "anonymousAuthentication": true,
    "iisExpress": {
      "applicationUrl": "http://localhost:26491",
      "sslPort": 0
    }
  },
  "$schema": "http://json.schemastore.org/launchsettings.json",
  "profiles": {
    "IIS Express": {
      "commandName": "IISExpress",
      "environmentVariables": {
        "ASPNETCORE_ENVIRONMENT": "Development"
      }
    },
    "ConstructorRental.ApiGateway": {
      "commandName": "Project",
      "launchBrowser": true,
      "environmentVariables": {
        "ASPNETCORE_ENVIRONMENT": "Development"
      },
      "dotnetRunMessages": "true",
      "applicationUrl": "https://localhost:5001;http://localhost:5000"
    }
  }
}
```

A debug profile is simply a part in the profiles array of this JSON file that stores the values specified in this window. It is located under the Properties node of the project in the solution explorer. We can create new profiles as much as we want to store our different debugging settings. We can debug our application with different ports, different environment variables, and so on.

- **Launch**: We can choose the server to host our project for debugging here. We can choose IIS, IIS Express, Kestrel (denoted as the name of the Project) here.

  IIS Express is a lightweight version of IIS used for debugging. It eases debugging and testing web projects and requires fewer resources because it is launched or terminated based on when we start or stop debugging and supports multiple users independently. It is installed along with Visual Studio.

  If our project is hosted on IIS in the production environment or depends on specific IIS settings, we may choose to debug it from IIS on our computer also. It can be better if our local development environment is like the production environment.

- **Application Arguments**: We can specify command line arguments that are sent to our project here. We can access those arguments from the entry point, which is the Main method of **Program.cs** with the **args** parameter by default. The arguments are separated by the space character. For example, if the arguments are **test=1 adminMode=true**, the args parameter will be a two-dimensional array.

TIP: If you want to access command line arguments in your source code, one of the ways is by calling the UseStartup method overload that allows controlling the creation of the Startup class in the entry point and passing the arguments array to the Startup class constructor. Then, you can create a service and use dependency injection for injecting them to other objects or appending them to configuration.

The following piece of code shows the basic usage of transferring command line arguments to the application:

```
public class Program
{
        public static void Main(string[] args)
        {
//args array are the command line arguments
        CreateHostBuilder(args).Build().Run();
        }


        public static IHostBuilder CreateHostBuilder(string[]
args)
        {
                return Host.CreateDefaultBuilder(args)
```

```
            .ConfigureAppConfiguration((hosting, config) =>
            {
                config.AddJsonFile("ocelot.json", false, true);
            }).ConfigureWebHostDefaults(webBuilder =>
             {
                webBuilder.UseStartup<Startup>(t =>
                {
                    return new Startup(t.Configuration, args);
                });
            });
        }
    }
//startup.cs
    public class Startup
    {
        public Startup(IConfiguration configuration, string[] args)
        {
            //store args here or on  ConfigureServices
        }}
```

- **Working Directory**: This is the directory of the application to debug. It is located in **bin\Debug\{framework version}** by default.

- **Launch Browser**: We can make Visual Studio start a new browser window with the relative or absolute URL here while debugging, or if we are developing a service that that has no web page, we can simply untick the checkbox and prevent Visual Studio to launch a browser.

With this setting, we can avoid launching the browser ourselves and typing the URL of the page we are working for. For example, if we have an action method named Index in the controller **TestController** and we would like to debug it, we can specify the URL address by Test/Index or Test by default and a browser with this address is launched automatically when we start debugging.

We can change the type of the browser to be launched from the debug toolbar on the top by expanding the project name and then selecting a browser under the web browser section:

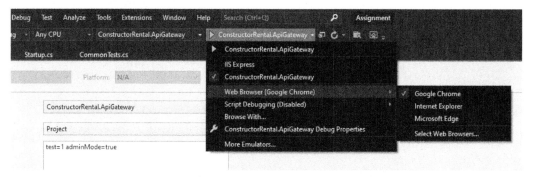

Figure 3.4: Changing the debugging browser

- **Environment variables**: We can specify environment variables here that we can access from our code. The **ASPNETCORE_ENVIRONMENT** variable comes with Development by default, but you can change it to other values (such as test, production, and so on) that you wish to debug if possible.

- **Enable native debugging**: This enables debugging the unmanaged code; for example, if we use a native c++ dll in our code (possible with .net) and would like to debug it, we can check this option.

- **Enable Sql Server Debugging**: This enables the SQL Server stored procedure debugging. This option may be used if there is an SQL Server database project in our solution.

- **Enable JavaScript debugger**: If we have JavaScript files in our web project, we can choose to debug them from Visual Studio along with our ASP.NET Core code. The same controls such as step over, step into, step out, break points, watches, and so on, are also valid in JavaScript debugging.

> TIP: Debugging JavaScript along with ASP.NET code with Visual Studio can degrade the overall debugging performance of Visual Studio. JavaScript debugging is occasionally done with using developer tools from the browser. They have much more debugging information specific to JavaScript.

- **Web Server Settings**: Now, let us explain the Web Server Settings. These are specific to the debugging web server from the preceding Launch field. Here are the debug server options:

    o **IIS Express**:

        ▪ **App URL**: We can set **url** and **port** of our project here. The entered port must be unused and free.

- ▪ **IIS Express Bitness**: If our application has a specific CPU architecture, we can choose to run our debug server with x86 or x64.

- ▪ **Hosting Model**: We can choose the in process or out of process hosting model.

In process hosting model means running the application inside the IIS express process. Out of process hosting means running the application in the Kestrel web server and using IIS Express as a reverse proxy.

NOTE: If your application's architecture is designed to use reverse proxy with specific settings, you may use the out of process model and further configure IIS Express from the applicationhost.config file located in My Documents\IISExpress\config. It is an Xml file with many configurations.

We can notice the difference from the task manager. If we start debugging with the out of process hosting model, you may notice an executable process running along with IIS Express process, which is the process of Kestrel.

This is how in process hosting looks like:

∨ ▷ Microsoft Visual Studio 2019 (32 bit) (17)	%0,1	1.083,3 MB	0 MB/sn	0 Mb/sn
▷ Assignment (Running) - Microsoft Visual Studio	%0,1	358,2 MB	0 MB/sn	0 Mb/sn
IIS Express Sistem Tepsisi	%0	17,8 MB	0 MB/sn	0 Mb/sn
IIS Express Worker Process	%0	5,8 MB	0 MB/sn	0 Mb/sn

Figure 3.5: In process hosting model

And this is how the out of process model looks like:

∨ ▷ Microsoft Visual Studio 2019 (32 bit) (21)	%1,8	1.051,4 MB	0 MB/sn	0 Mb/sn	%0
▷ Assignment (Running) - Microsoft Visual Studio	%0,4	357,1 MB	0 MB/sn	0 Mb/sn	%0
ConstructorRental.ApiGateway	%0	28,9 MB	0 MB/sn	0 Mb/sn	%0
IIS Express Sistem Tepsisi	%0	18,1 MR	0 MB/sn	0 Mb/sn	%0
IIS Express Worker Process	%0	6,7 MB	0 MB/sn	0 Mb/sn	%0

Figure 3.6: Out of process hosting model

- o **Enable SSL**: This allows debugging with SSL. If we choose this option, it assigns a new port to our application accessible from HTTPS.

- o **Enable Anonymous Authentication**: We uncheck this if our application uses built-in authentication of ASP.NET Core. We check this if we are making an application with anonymous access or our project has custom authentication.

- o **Enable Windows Authentication**: We check this if our project uses Active directory authentication such as LDAP and so on.

- **IIS**: This setting allows us to debug our application from the IIS server that comes with Windows installation. Its settings are nearly the same with IIS Express. When we choose this option, it creates a virtual directory in IIS for our application.

- **Project**: This is the option of debugging with the Kestrel server. It only has the App URL option.

Now, let us explain debugging with Visual Studio further. We will explain it with a simple Controller class code, given as follows:

```
using System;
using System.Collections.Generic;
using System.Threading.Tasks;
using ConstructorRental.Common;
using ConstructorRental.Common.Dto;
using ConstructorRental.Common.Dto.System;
using ConstructorRental.Services.Inventory.Classes.Interfaces;
using Microsoft.AspNetCore.Mvc;
namespace ConstructorRental.Services.Inventory.Controllers
{
    [ApiController]
    public class InventoryController : ControllerBase
    {
        IInventoryBusiness inventoryBusiness;

        public InventoryController(InventoryBusiness inventoryBusiness)
        {
            this.inventoryBusiness = inventoryBusiness;
        }

        [HttpGet(«[controller]/[action]»)]
        public async Task<ListObjectResult<InventoryDto>>
        ListAllInventory([FromQuery] String langCode)
        {
            var inventoriesResult =
                await this.inventoryBusiness.ListInventory(langCode);
            DoSomething(inventoriesResult.DataList);
            return inventoriesResult;
```

```
        }

        void DoSomething(List<InventoryDto> inventory)
        {
            //doing something here
        }
    }
}
```

Let us debug the **ListAllInventory** action method. We usually would like to check the parameters of the action method as they were sent from the frontend and check whether the frontend is in the JavaScript or HTML form.

We put a breakpoint here inside the **ListAllInventory** action method. The first line that calls **ListInventory** method should be sufficient for our case, but we may put any line inside the code.

If we need to debug the **DoSomething** method, we simply step over by pressing the ⟳ icon or F10 key until the execution comes over the **DoSomething** method call, and then we can press the **Step Into** icon ↓ from the Debug tool bar or *F11* key to direct the execution into start of the **DoSomething** method. We can then debug the **DoSomething** method with step over or use step into if we are calling methods under **DoSomething** and we would like to debug them. If we need to exit debugging the **DoSomething** method and return to the calling method (**ListAllInventory** action method in our case here), we can press the step out ↑ icon from the debugging toolbar or press *Shift + F11* key to bypass any execution remaining in the DoSomething method and return to the **ListAllInventory** method

When the execution is stopped on the breakpoint, we may hover our mouse over the variables in code and get the values of primitive types, property, or field values of reference types immediately. We can also add watches to view them in detail:

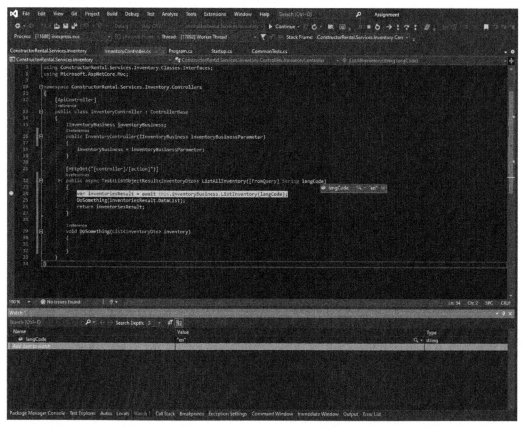

Figure 3.7: Debugging variables and adding watch

TIP: You can distinguish whether the application is running in the debug mode or not by the C# precompile directive DEBUG as shown in the following piece of code. This may come handy if you want to disable some code when your project is published and deployed to a server environment.

```
#If DEBUG
//your debug code here. Only executed in debug configuration
#Endif
```

We can pause execution of the code with the break all ▮▮ button, resume our paused execution with the continue execution button →, restart debugging again by clicking on the ↻ restart button or stop debugging by clicking on the stop debugging button ■. These buttons are located on the debug tool bar.

We can change the value of the variables or their property values while debugging. We hover the mouse over to the variable and click on the value in the small pop-up window that appears and then type the value we would like, or we add a watch for it and then change its value from the watch panel.

There is also a neat feature of .NET named Edit and continue. While debugging, if our execution is paused, we can make changes to our code from the editor and our changes are compiled and integrated automatically without restarting the debugging session.

> **NOTE: You cannot make many changes or some changes like lambda expressions, and so on, with the edit and continue feature. The compiler will warn and force you restart your debugging session.**

Debugging using Visual Studio Code is similar to Visual Studio.

> **NOTE: In olden times (before 2000s) when the integrated development environments were not around, developers debugged their applications with writing logs to std outputs, log files, etc. These old-fashioned ways have not come to pass. If you encounter errors in your applications on the production servers that you do not encounter on your development environment, consider using them.**

Deploying ASP.NET core applications

Debugging comes with a cost. When we build our applications, the compiler generates pdb (program debug database) files which contain debugging symbols, puts debugging instructions in the output files, and disables compiler optimizations. Therefore, when we deploy our projects to real-server environments, first we publish our application which outputs optimized files. To publish an ASP.NET Core application, click on **Build** -> **Publish** from the top menu and open the publish settings dialog.

The Publish settings window contains targets. We can publish Azure, Docker registry, FTP Server, IIS, or File system. We can create separate publishing profiles for different targets and reuse them later. We will explain publishing to the folder only:

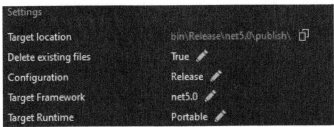

Figure 3.8: Publish settings

Now, let us take a look at the fields in the dialog for publishing to file system:

- **Target Location**: This specifies the output folder of the published files.
- **Delete Existing Files**: This specifies removing files in the target location prior to publish.

> **TIP: Sometimes, Visual Studio may fail silently overwriting files in the target location. You should set this to true to ensure proper publishing.**

- **Configuration**: This specifies the publish configuration. It is release or debug.

> **TIP: You should select release always for deploying to the production server with optimized code. Sometimes, you may need to debug your project while it is running on the server. You can achieve this via remote debugging with using Visual Studio. If that is the case, you can publish your project with the debug configuration.**

- **Target Framework**: This specifies the target framework version. Usually, it is the same with the version in the project file. But if the other framework versions are compatible with our project, we can choose to publish targeting them.
- **Target Runtime**: We can publish an ASP.NET Core project in two ways: framework dependent or self-contained. If we choose the framework dependent deployment, we are required to install ASP.NET Core runtime that has the same target framework version with the published application. We can choose self-contained deployment. As the name implies, framework files are published along with our application files and it consumes more disk space, but we do not have to install runtime.

Now, let us explain deploying our projects to real servers.

Hosting an ASP.NET project on IIS

Microsoft Internet Information Services is the web server software developed by Microsoft and used to host web applications or services. It comes along with Microsoft Windows and Microsoft Windows Server platforms. It comes with a native support for hosting ASP.NET applications and it is built on the following two main concepts:

- **Worker Process (w3wp.exe)**: It is the process that handles requests and responses.
- **Application Pool**: Application pools isolate and contain the worker process. It provides isolation, so they do not affect each other's resources and if one application crashes, it does not bring down the other applications in other pools with itself.

IIS supports many features such as load balancing with web gardens, auto restarting crashed applications with fault tolerance, etc. and configuring it is a large topic by itself and consists of configuring the operating system of the server, which we will not cover in this book.

To open the IIS Management Console, we can type **inetmgr** in the run from the menu in Windows and press enter. It has the connections list pane on the left-hand side and it shows the local IIS server installed by default. The connections pane shows the application pools and hosted web sites in a hierarchical way. When we click on an item on the left connections pane, we get a list of options on the center pane with a categorized view and properties of that item on the actions pane located on the right-hand side:

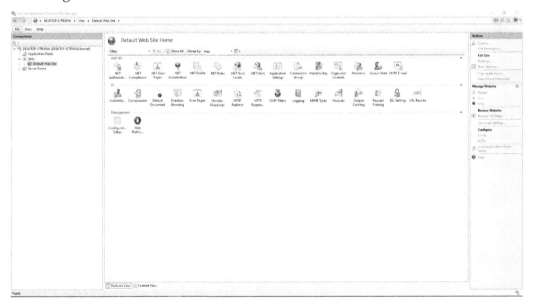

Figure 3.9: *IIS Manager*

As mentioned earlier, if we want to host multiple applications on the same IIS server, we should create separate pools for them to provide isolation. We need to click on **Application Pools** from the connections pane and click on **Add Application Pool** from the actions pane. In the new application pool pop-up dialog, we need to give it a name, select the framework version as **No Managed Code** (other options are for legacy ASP.NET applications), and then select the pipeline mode. We need to select the integrated pipeline which runs ASP.NET applications tightly integrated with the IIS. The classic pipeline is for legacy applications which makes IIS treating the ASP.NET applications running within a separate ISAPI filter and provides no direct integration:

Figure 3.10: Add new application pool dialog

Then, we need to add a web site in the IIS manager (we can host it in the Default Web Site without creating new also) for our application. We right click on the Sites node in the Connections pane and click on **Add Web Site** from the context menu and open the Add New Web Site dialog window:

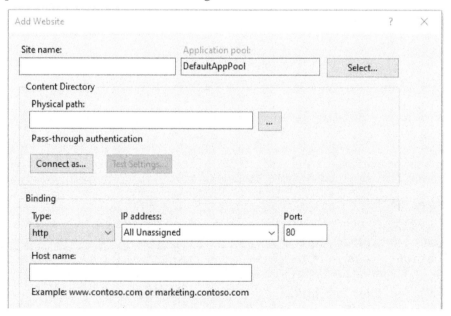

Figure 3.11: Add web site dialog

Let us explain the fields in this dialog box:

- **Site name**: We give the name of the site to display under the Sites node in the connections pane.

- **Application pool**: We select the pool of the application.

- **Physical path**: We set the location of the published files folder.
- **Binding**: We specify the type (http or https), IP address and port of the web site here. We can add multiple bindings for HTTP, HTTPS, or different ports. For HTTPS, an SSL certification must be loaded to the operating system. Usually, the IP address is kept as unassigned, and the application is accessed by the IP address of the server from outside.

After making these settings, we should be able to browse our application by typing `{http or https}://localhost:{port number in the binding}` and by opening a browser on the server.

> **TIP: Sometimes, starting a deployed application on IIS can be a painful exercise. Windows event logs and IIS log files are your best friends.**

Hosting an ASP.NET project on Linux

We will cover deploying our application on Ubuntu with Nginx as a reverse proxy. We will explain it such a way that the reverse proxy and application server are on the same machine for simplicity, but it can be applied to the separate machines in the same way.

First, we will install **nginx**, ASP.NET core runtime for Ubuntu and ensure nginx is running. We navigate to the folder where the project file is located and publish our application with the following command:

`dotnet publish --configuration Release`

Then, we change the directory to the output folder of the published files and copy them to the folder we choose for hosting.

We create a service for our application, so that our application is available when the server reboots and it is restarted automatically in case Kestrel crashes:

`sudo vim /etc/systemd/system/{name of the service}.service`

An example of a service file is as follows:

```
[Unit]
Description=Test application service
[Service]
WorkingDirectory={folder that the published application files are
located}
ExecStart=/usr/bin/dotnet {full path to the file that entry point is
located}
Restart=always
RestartSec=10
KillSignal=SIGINT
```

```
SyslogIdentifier={log identifier}
User={user that is impersonated to run the service}
Environment=ASPNETCORE_ENVIRONMENT=Production
Environment=DOTNET_PRINT_TELEMETRY_MESSAGE=false
[Install]
WantedBy=multi-user.target
```

We can set the **ASPNETCORE_ENVIRONMENT** variable that our application uses and the user that is impersonated running our application. The user must have access to the directory of the deployment.

We enable and start our service with the following command:

```
sudo systemctl enable {name of the service}.service
sudo systemctl start {name of the service}.service
```

We check the status of the service with the following command:

```
sudo systemctl status {name of the service}.service
```

Figure 3.12: A successfully started Kestrel server

If our application fails to start, we can check the logs as follows:

```
sudo journalctl -fu {name of the service}.service
```

We can set up the nginx server by editing the default block (you can use any editor instead of **vim**):

```
sudo vim /etc/nginx/sites-available/default
server {
      listen 82 default_server; #{the port that the reverse proxy is
accessible}
      listen [::]:82 default_server;
      server_name _;
      location / {
            root {location of deployment}
            try_files $uri $uri/ =404;
```

```
proxy_pass              http://localhost:5000; #{the ip address and port of
the Kestrel server}
                proxy_http_version 1.1;
                proxy_set_header    Upgrade $http_upgrade;
                proxy_set_header    Connection keep-alive;
                proxy_set_header    Host $host;
                proxy_cache_bypass $http_upgrade;
                proxy_set_header    X-Forwarded-For $proxy_add_x_
forwarded_for;
                proxy_set_header    X-Forwarded-Proto $scheme;
        }
}
```

We can set the necessary values for the port of the reverse proxy and addresses of the directed kestrel servers. When we type **http://localhost:82,** the nginx directs the request to the Kestrel server which listens with port **5000**.

Conclusion

We covered reverse proxies, debugging, and deploying our ASP.NET Core projects. We will cover Http, CSS, and JavaScript in the next chapter.

Questions

1. Why and when should you use reverse proxies?

2. Is using Kestrel as a production server exposed directly to Internet a good idea?

3. Suppose you are getting errors from your application in the production servers, and you do not encounter them when you debug your code; where it is related to the origin of the error. What should you do?

4. You deployed your application to IIS, but it fails to start. Even the code of the entry point of your application does not run. What should you do?

CHAPTER 4

Introduction to HTTP, HTML, CSS, and JavaScript

Introduction

In this chapter, we will explain the fundamental pillars of web such as HTTP, HTML, CSS, and JavaScript.

Structure

In this chapter, we will learn the following topics:

- Introducing HTTP protocol
- Introducing HTTP requests, Fiddler, and Postman
- Introducing HTML and making web pages with it
- Introducing CSS and using them in web pages
- Introducing Twitter Bootstrap
- Introducing JavaScript, JSON, DOM, and Ajax

Objective

After reading this chapter, you will be able to understand the fundamentals that make a web application, independent of any framework or technology. We assume you do not have any idea about web. If you already know this, please feel free to omit this chapter.

The Hypertext Transfer Protocol

The hypertext transfer protocol is a TCP/IP application layer protocol that is used by World Wide Web. It is a common language between clients and servers and allows clients retrieve resources from the servers. It was developed by Tim Berners-Lee and his team between 1989-1991. Since then, it changed, evolved, and adopted to the modern Internet. It was invented along with HTML and the first browser to visualize HTML files itself. There was only a get method when it was first born, and now there are so many as they are needed.

Network connections are managed by the underlying TCP transport layer and HTTP is not interested in knowing how the connections are managed, but it can control the TCP connections to some degree by the Connections header. HTTP/2 carries making connections further by allowing duplex communication. It allows bidirectional communications such that servers can communicate with clients also.

In case of HTTP/1.1, messages that are sent by the client are requests and messages returned by the server are responses. Let us introduce the basic features of Http:

- **Based on format agreements**: Requests and responses are based on agreements between a client and server. We can create a method on our server that enforces a specific request format such as data in a custom header, a key value pair in the query string, or a field on the request message body. On the contrary, we can determine specific response formats so that we can return a specific object in the message body, a custom response header, or give a meaning to the http status codes returned on the responses. We can set purposes to all those things as we desire and force the clients to obey these formats. This makes Http an extensible protocol.

- **Simple**: Requests and responses are human readable and easy to understand by developers, and so on. But the http/2 packs the Http messages into frames, so the messages are not readable.

- **Stateless**: Either the client or server does not know the state of the other side and the data it contains. The persisting state can be achieved by cookies and some other ways. We will cover them in the upcoming chapters.

Here is a sample request made with a GET method:

```
GET http://localhost:21781/Inventory/ListAllInventory?langCode=en
HTTP/1.1
Host: localhost:21781
Connection: keep-alive
```

```
sec-ch-ua: " Not A;Brand";v="99", "Chromium";v="90", "Google
Chrome";v="90"
sec-ch-ua-mobile: ?0
Upgrade-Insecure-Requests: 1
User-Agent: Mozilla/5.0 (Windows NT 10.0; Win64; x64) AppleWebKit/537.36
(KHTML, like Gecko) Chrome/90.0.4430.85 Safari/537.36
Accept: text/html,application/xhtml+xml,application/xml;q=0.9,image/
avif,image/webp,image/apng,*/*;q=0.8,application/signed-
exchange;v=b3;q=0.9
Sec-Fetch-Site: none
Sec-Fetch-Mode: navigate
Sec-Fetch-User: ?1
Sec-Fetch-Dest: document
Accept-Encoding: gzip, deflate, br
Accept-Language: tr,en-US;q=0.9,en;q=0.8
```

Web requests consist of three parts: the start line, headers, and body.

The start line includes the following:

- **Http Method**: A verb such as get, post, and so on, or a noun like options or head. It describes the method of the action that is performed. There are so many Http methods, but the most used ones are:
    - **Get**: This is used to fetch data.
    - **Post**: This sends an entity or data to the server and causes a change on some data or the state of the server.
    - **Head**: This is like Get but there is no response.
    - **Options**: This is a pre-flight request that determines a different origin that is accessible from the client browser.
    - **Delete**: This deletes data on the server.
- **Request Target**: This is the URL of the resource that is accessed.
- **Protocol Version**: This is the Http version of the request.

The following lines are called request headers. They are key-value pairs. The keys and values are separated by a colon and the keys are case sensitive. There are many standard headers, and they have specific purposes. We can also include our custom headers as key-value pairs; thanks to the extensibility of the Http protocol. In a web application, many standard headers are managed and set by the client browser. Let us explain the most used standard headers:

- **User-Agent**: The user agent string indicates the browser, vendor, and operating system of the client browser that issued the request. We are required to parse it to get the information it contains. It looks like the following statement:

```
User-Agent: Mozilla/5.0 (Windows NT 10.0; Win64; x64) AppleWebKit/537.36
(KHTML, like Gecko) Chrome/90.0.4430.85 Safari/537.36
```

> **TIP:**
>
> You can parse the user agent string on the server side and use it for some useful scenarios which can be as follows:
>
> - You have a desktop and mobile version of your front end. If your desktop web site is accessed from a mobile device, you can detect that and redirect the browser to the mobile version of your front end.
>
> - Let us assume the end users of your application are having issues with your front end. Let it be JavaScript errors or visual abnormalities because of CSS, HTML, and so on. You can determine the browser type and version from the user agent string and that information is sure going to help you come up with a solution to your front-end problem.
>
> You can log the user-agent string of login requests and show them to your end users as the login history. Keep in mind logging the user-agent strings per user can be important for legal issues that may arise depending on the kind of your application.

- **Accept-Language**: From this header, we can determine the language the client may understand. This header contains the locale variant of the client's operating system. We need to parse it to obtain the locale information, which in this case is the preferred order of the locales, may look like the following:

> **NOTE: The q means the q-factor weighting and specifies the order of preference between multiple entries by priority.**

```
Accept-Language: tr,en-US;q=0.9,en;q=0.8
```

- **Accept**: This indicates the content types which are mime types that a client can understand and demands the response in the formats specified here. The Http is quite an extensible protocol and based on agreements between a client and server. The client can use this header and tell the server that it demands the response in specific formats. The server then can take this information and return the response in the specific formats that the client demands by the request. This header can contain more than a value and looks like the following:

```
Accept:text/html,application/xhtml+xml,application/
xml;q=0.9,image/avif,image/webp,image/apng,*/*;q=0.8,application/
```

```
signed-exchange;v=b3;q=0.9
```

Let us explain the mime types mentioned here. It is an important aspect of Http. Multi-purpose Internet mail extension is a standard to describe the nature of the documents, which are simply the content of the requests and responses. They are indicated by the Content-Type header and their format is `type/subtype;parameter=value`. The type is the general type such as a text or video. The subtype indicates the exact data that is represented. The parameter is an optional value and usually provides additional data such as a character set. Some examples of the mime types are as follows:

- ○ **text/plain;charset=UTF-8**: Plain text with UTF-8 encoding
- ○ **text/html;charset=UTF-8**: Html with UTF-8 encoding
- ○ **application/octet-stream**: Generic binary file

TIP: An application mime type is important for downloading files. For example, application/msword is for word files, application/pdf is for pdf files, and application/json is for json files. If the browser supports viewing the downloaded file (especially, if it is a pdf file), you should set Content-Type header of the response to application/pdf other than the application/octet-stream.

- **Content-Type**: This specifies the mime type of the request or response body. The client or server figures out how to handle the content of the body from this header.

- **Content-Length**: This specifies the size of the data in the body in bytes. It is usually used for parsing uploaded files or data.

TIP: You can use this header to validate and constrant the size of uploaded files.

- **Accept-Encoding**: This specifies the compression algorithm of the content. The content of the body in the request or response can be compressed for increasing performance. The client or server figures out the decompression method from this header. It looks like the following:

```
Accept-Encoding: gzip, deflate, br
```

After the start line and headers, the request and responses may or may not contain the message body. A transfer encoding can be applied to the message body and if that is the case, the message body is called the payload body. This part is usually used to send large objects in json or binary format. We will cover how to serialize objects and send within the message body of the request or deserialize and retrieve from the message body of the response when we cover restful services in the *Chapter 6, Developing Restful Services with ASP.NET Core.*

When the client issues a request to a server with HTTP, the client opens one or several TCP connections or reuses existing connections, sends the message, reads the response, and then closes or keeps the connection for further reuse.

Http response is like the requests. They contain headers in key value pairs and may or may not contain the message body. It looks like the following format. The example contains a JSON object in the message body:

```
HTTP/1.1 200 OK
Transfer-Encoding: chunked
Content-Type: application/json; charset=utf-8
Server: Microsoft-IIS/10.0
X-Powered-By: ASP.NET
Date: Fri, 23 Apr 2021 08:30:28 GMT
```

```
e0
{"dataList":[{"id":1,"name":"Caterpillar
bulldozer"},{"id":2,"name":"KamAZ truck"},{"id":3,"name":"Komatsu
crane"},{"id":4,"name":"Volvo steamroller"},{"id":5,"name":"Bosch
jackhammer"}],"hasError":false,"errorMessage":null}
0
```

The first line contains the http version and status code. The status code indicates the result of the request and it tells whether the request is successful or not and if it is not successful, it specifies the reason of failure. Some of the common HTTP status codes are as follows:

- **200 OK**: Server processed the HTTP request, and it is completed successfully.

- **302 Found**: Server indicates requested resource is temporarily located under another URL. The address of the resource is located under the Location header of the response. The browser makes a redirection to the new address in here.

- **301 Permanent Redirect**: It is the same as 302 but indicates redirection is permanent. The client should use the new address.

- **401 Unauthorized**: Server refused to process the request because the user is not authenticated. It is usually used along with session management.

- **403 Forbidden**: Server refused to process the request because the resource is unavailable.

- **404 Not Found**: Server indicates the requested resource is not found. Usually, a custom not found page is shown to the user.

- **500 Internal Server Error**: Server indicates it has encountered an error while processing the request.

HTTP is extensible and is based on negotiations between the client and server. The negotiations are usually called service contracts. We can create services and accept specific data in custom headers, serialized JSON objects in message body, create custom URL patterns for our resources, and the clients of our service use that contract. We will cover service design in *Chapter 6, Developing Restful Services with ASP.NET Core*.

Introducing Fiddler

Fiddler is a web proxy tool to debug, inspect HTTP or HTTPs requests. It captures and lists requests. It shows so much information about the requests and responses. If the web site is behind a proxy, it shows information about it too.

One of the neat features of the Fiddler is the replay feature. You can replay captured requests offline without connecting to the server. It helps debugging or developing clients without real connections being made to the server. The following figure shows fiddler. The left pane lists the request history and the center pane displays detailed info:

Figure 4.1: Fiddler

Introducing Postman

Postman is a useful tool to test and debug web applications. We can use it to test restful services by crafting and firing requests. It evolved in many years and now allows CI/CD integration, service monitoring, etc. It saves the request history in the left pane so we can refire them again, and in the center pane, we can define request URL, body, headers, and fire it to the server:

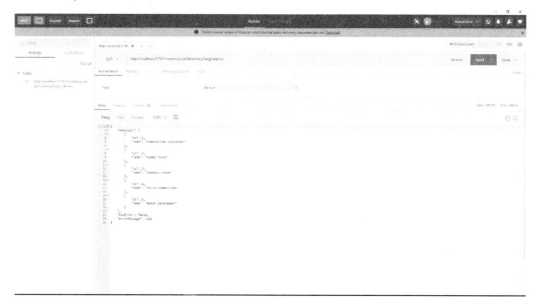

Figure 4.2: Postman

Introduction to HTML

Hypertext markup language is the language of the web. We can create user interfaces for the web sites by writing HTML. The browser downloads the requested web page's Html and renders the user interface with parsing and interpreting it on the screen. It contains many elements, and we use them for UI development. Html was invented along with the Http and evolved in so many years as the new requirements needed. We will cover Html5 in this chapter.

The common structure of html is as follows:

- **Declaration**: Html5 documents begin with a document type declaration. It is usually a `<!DOCTYPE>` or `<!DOCTYPE html>` and it comes from the xml standard. HTML has a similar structure to XML. This does not mean every Html5 document must be a valid XML document. Unlike XML, HTML5 allows closing tags omitted, attributes without values, and so on.

> **NOTE: XHTML (Extensible hypertext markup language) format is a variation of HTML which is well-formed and more XML like version of HTML**

- **Html tag**: After declaration, there are opening and closing HTML tags `<html> </html>`. These tags contain head and body tags.

- **Head tag**: This contains basic information about the web page. One of them is title tag which specifies the page title. The browser displays it on its title bar.

- **Script tag**: This specifies JavaScript codes of the html document. They can be specified as inline which are written scripts directly in the Html document or as URL links that the browser downloads. In either format, the browser runs those along with HTML document.

- **Style tag**: This specifies stylesheets (CSS) of the html document. Unlike the scripts, internal and external style specifications are different. Internal CSS is written between style tags. External CSS files are specified in the link tag.

- **Body tag**: The content of the html document is located between body tags.

We can write comments in html files between <!-- --> tags.

> **TIP: Be advised keeping the size of Html, CSS, and JavaScript as small as possible is important. The browser of your project's users download these resources like downloading any other file from Internet.**

A simple HTML document with internal JavaScript and CSS is as follows:

```
<!DOCTYPE html>
<html>
<head>
    <meta charset="utf-8" />
    <title>A simple page</title>
    <script type="text/javascript">
        document.addEventListener('DOMContentLoaded', (event) => {
            alert('document loaded');
        })
    </script>
    <style>
        .heading{
            border:1px solid black
        }
    </style>
</head>
<body>
    <h3 class="heading">
        Heading
    </h3>
```

```
<p id="summaryParagraph">
    some paragraph here
</p>
</body>
</html>
```

Introduction to CSS

Cascading Style Sheets are used to manage the layout and set the visual properties of the elements in Html such as the form size to color and margins to borders. It may be contained inline, internal, or external within HTML.

> **NOTE: The ID attribute in Html is used to give unique identifiers to elements. This allows accessing them from CSS and JavaScript.**
>
> **You may use it like <{any html tag} id="{any string unique among entire html }">.....</{any html tag}>.**

- **Inline CSS**: Inline CSS is specified via key value pairs in style attributes inside html elements. The keys and values are separated with a colon and pairs are separated with a semicolon. It looks like the following:

  ```
  <p style="background-color: dimgrey ; border: 1px solid
  black">
          A paragraph
  </p>
  ```

- **External CSS**: External CSS is specified in the header part of the HTML document with the link tag's **href** attribute. It can be a relative or an absolute URL. We can reuse the CSS classes in other HTML documents in this way. It looks like the following example:

  ```
  <!DOCTYPE html>
  <html>
  <head>
      <meta charset="utf-8" />
      <title>A simple page</title>
      <link href="StyleSheet.css" rel="stylesheet" />
  </head>
  <body>
      <!-- content here -->
  </body>
  </html>
  ```

- **Internal CSS**: Internal CSS is specified in the header part of the HTML document between the style tags. It looks like the following example:

```
<!DOCTYPE html>
<html>
<head>
    <meta charset="utf-8" />

<title>A simple page</title>
<style>
        #idSelector {
    background-color: aliceblue;
    font-size: 5px;
}

.classSelector {
    margin: 5px;
}

p{
    padding: 10px;
}
    </style>
</head>
<body>
    <!-- content here -->
</body>
</html>
```

Now, let us explain CSS selectors. We use them to give CSS properties to the visual element tags in the HTML document:

- **Tag selector**: They are specified via the name of the tag itself. For example, to set the padding size for all paragraphs in the document, we can write the following:

```
p{
    padding: 10px;
}
```

- **Class selector**: They are specified as names beginning with dots. Here is an example:

```
.classSelector {
    margin: 5px;
}
```

Then, we use this in the class attribute of the HTML elements. We can write multiple CSS classes separated with spaces. Here is an example that sets the margin size of the div element it belongs:

```
<div class="classSelector someSecondSelector; .........">
        <!-- content of the div -->
</div>
```

> **TIP:** You can use CSS classes in the class attributes for labeling and grouping. You can add some class names to the elements of your HTML document that does not have to necessarily exist and you can access them all together from the JavaScript.
>
> For example, you have some headings; let us say h4 tags that you want to change the background color of both of them together. You can give a CSS class name to them; for example, `headingWithBackground` and access all of them from the JavaScript later. The `headingWithBackground` does not have to exist in any CSS definition. This technique is completely valid. The following html code explains this considering there is not a CSS class defined headingWithBackground.

```
<!-- first heading -->
<h4 class="headingWithBackground"> The first heading content</h4>


<!-- somewhere later in html the second heading -->
<h4 class="headingWithBackground"> The second heading content</h4>


<!-- somewhere later in html the third  heading -->
<h4 class="headingWithBackground"> The third heading content</h4>


<script type="text/javascript">
//access all three heading elements with the class selector.
var headings = document.getElementsByClassName("headingWithBackground");
</script>
```

The standards and rules for web including Http, Html, CSS, and JavaScript is governed by World Wide Web Consortium (W3C **https://www.w3.org**). One of its missions is to develop guidelines and standards for web.

Although you may think CSS classes and JavaScript methods work the same way in all browsers because they are standardized by W3C, you are going to be disappointed. There is always a competition between browser vendors, and this causes differences in executing CSS and JavaScript methods.

You can quickly realize your CSS classes do not work as expected in every browser, so we occasionally need special CSS or JavaScript libraries which encapsulates browser features in our projects to ensure our applications are worked and displayed in every browser as expected.

Introduction to Twitter Bootstrap

Twitter Bootstrap (or shortly Bootstrap) is a CSS baseline, component, and tools library for developing the front-end of web applications. It is open-source, and its target audience is usually developers who want to quickly set up layouts and front-end designs quickly. You may visit the GitHub page **https://github.com/twbs/ bootstrap,** and you may read the documentation from the quick start web site **https:// getbootstrap.com/docs/5.0/getting-started/introduction/**. It contains CSS files and JavaScript files you must add to your project.

Bootstrap has many nice visual components, and it has a cool 12 columns grid system at your disposal. We can use the grid system to create responsive table layouts for our applications.

Here is an example of a grid layout with two rows in which the first row has two columns, and the second row has three columns:

```html
<!DOCTYPE html>
<html>
<head>
    <meta charset="utf-8" />
    <link href="css/bootstrap.css" rel="stylesheet" />
    <style>
        .col{
            border: 1px solid black
        }
    </style>
    <title>A simple page</title>
    <script src="js/bootstrap.js"></script>
</head>
<body>
    <div class="container">
```

```
        <div class="row">
            <div class="col">
                Row 1, column 1
            </div>
            <div class="col">
                Row 1, column 2
            </div>
        </div>
        <div class="row">
            <div class="col">
                Row 2, column 1
            </div>
            <div class="col">
                Row 2, column 2
            </div>
            <div class="col">
                Row 2, column 3
            </div>
        </div>
    </div>
</body>
</html>
```

The output obtained for the preceding code is as follows:

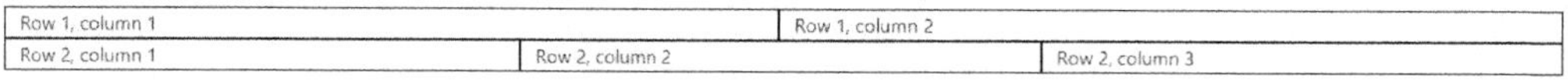

Row 1, column 1		Row 1, column 2	
Row 2, column 1	Row 2, column 2	Row 2, column 3	

Figure 4.3: *Bootstrap grid*

The bootstrap grid can be adapted to six different sized devices. It allows us to create a responsive UI such that our application can be displayed from a desktop computer and mobile cellphone or a tablet.

- **Extra small (xs)**: Width < 576
- **Small (sm)**: Width >= 576
- **Medium (md)**: Width < 768
- **Large (lg)**: Width >= 992
- **Extra large (xl)**: Width ≥1200px
- **Extra extra large (xxl)**: Width ≥1400px

Here is a responsive example (bordered class is just for making them appear):

```html
<!DOCTYPE html>
<html>
<head>
    <meta charset="utf-8" />
    <link href="css/bootstrap.css" rel="stylesheet" />
    <style>
        .bordered {
            border: 1px solid black
        }
    </style>
    <title>A simple page</title>
    <script src="js/bootstrap.js"></script>
</head>
<body>
    <div class="container">
        <div class="row">
            <div class="bordered col-sm-8">Row 1, column 1</div>
            <div class="bordered col-sm-4">Row 1, column 2</div>
        </div>
        <div class="row">
            <div class="bordered col-sm">Row 2, column 1</div>
            <div class="bordered col-sm">Row 2, column 2</div>
            <div class="bordered col-sm">Row 2, column 3</div>
        </div>
    </div>
</body>
</html>
```

The first and second rows indicate when the width of the device is less than 576 pixels break the columns and display them as one row. We can observe this when we reduce the size of our browser:

Figure 4.4: *Responsive grid*

TIP: If you are not good at CSS and you want to quickly develop the front-end of your applications, you really should consider using Bootstrap or another library like it. It is going to save you tons of trouble and ensure browser compatibility of your application to a high degree.

Introduction to JavaScript

JavaScript allows developers to program HTML pages. We can modify the HTML document, create animations, make requests to the server, and do so much more things. Its standards and structures are governed by ECMA International and specified by ECMAScript specification. It is designed and developed for the browser named Navigator of the company Netscape and it is a core technology of web along with Html and CSS.

JavaScript is an event-driven script language. It is an interpreted and not a compiled script language. It has evolved and adopted in so many years. It is also used in Node.js nowadays, a popular framework that allows developing server-side applications with JavaScript.

We can specify the internal JavaScript code between script tags or external JavaScript with a URL in the script tag's **src** attribute in the HTML document. It looks like the following:

```html
<!DOCTYPE html>
<html>
<head>
    <meta charset="utf-8" />
    <title>A simple page</title>
    <script src="js/bootstrap.js"></script>
    <script type="text/javascript">
        // internal javascript
        var x = 10;
    </script>
    <!-- external javascript -->
    <script src="js/JavaScript.js"></script>
</head>
<body>
</body>
</html>
```

We can write single line comments with double slash // or multiline comments between /* and */ . The statements are terminated by a semicolon character.

Now, let us explain data types of JavaScript. JavaScript has eight data types. Variables are specified by the **var** keyword:

- **String**: This type defines the text data:

  Example:
  ```
  var x='some string data';
  ```

- **Number**: This type defines the integer or floating-point number:

  Example:
  ```
  var x= 3.14;
  ```

- **BigInt**: This type defines the integer with an arbitrary precision. It is specified with *n* suffix or **BigInt()** function.

  Example:
  ```
  var x= 45634564564563456456568546n;
  ```

- **Null**: This type specifies an empty value:

  Example:
  ```
  var x=null;
  ```

- Boolean: This type defines the Boolean value **true** or **false**:

  Example:
  ```
  var x= true;
  ```

- **undefined**: This type specifies the variable that is not initialized:

  Example:
  ```
  var x;
  ```

- **Symbol:** This specifies unique and immutable data types.

- **Object**: This specifies an object with key-value pairs.

  Example:
  ```
  var x = {
          a:'test string',
          n:55344
              };
  ```

JavaScript has as many features as any server-side language. It has loops, objects, methods, and so on. It is not a type-safe language; we can declare a number variable and assign it to a string variable. It has prototypal inheritance and does not have class inheritance like object-oriented languages.

NOTE: When you compare JavaScript with object-oriented type-safe languages, you may find JavaScript weird and frustrating. Keep in mind the nature of JavaScript is by design. It is designed to work alongside with HTML and CSS in a browser environment. You can use the latest ECMAScript versions or use superset languages of JavaScript such as TypeScript or DartScript. They have similar features like compiled, type-safe and object-oriented languages.

Document Object Model (DOM)

When an HTML page is downloaded, the browser loads and creates a tree structure. Every node in the tree is a **DOM** object and has common or specific properties. The following HTML document has a DOM as shown in *Figure 4.5*:

```
<!DOCTYPE html>
<html>
<head>
    <meta charset="utf-8" />
    <link href="css/bootstrap.css" rel="stylesheet" />
    <title>A simple page</title>
    <script src="js/bootstrap.js"></script>
</head>
<body>
    <div>
        <h1>Heading</h1>
        <p>
            <span>Test</span>. A sample text
        </p>
    </div>
</body>
</html>
```

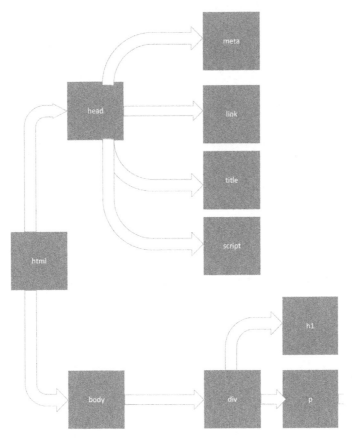

Figure 4.5: *Dom tree*

JavaScript provides DOM query methods for us. We can utilize them to find and alter any html element by different kinds of criteria.

For example, let us suppose we would like to set the content of the **h1** element with **id** equals to the heading in the following HTML document:

```
<!DOCTYPE html>
<html>
<head>
    <meta charset="utf-8" />
    <link href="css/bootstrap.css" rel="stylesheet" />
    <title>A simple page</title>
    <script src="js/bootstrap.js"></script>
    <script type="text/javascript">
        var heading = document.getElementById("heading");
        heading.innerHTML = 'custom heading';
```

```
        </script>
</head>
<body>
    <div>
        <h1 id="heading" class="textData">Heading</h1>
        <p>
            <span class="textData">Test</span>. A sample text
        </p>
    </div>
</body>
</html>
```

We can use the document object's **getElementById** method and give the ID parameter the ID of the element we would like to find. Every DOM query method returns a DOM object or an array of DOM objects. Then, we can use the **innerHtml** property of the html object and set its content. It is reflected to the browser immediately.

But when we run the preceding code, we will get an error, which says "cannot set property **innerHTML** of undefined". Which means the **document.getElementById** returned nothing and we are trying to set inner html of an undefined object. That means there is no element with the ID heading, but there is because it is not loaded into DOM yet and query methods return undefined.

The reason is that the html is not parsed and the DOM tree is not loaded yet. When a web browser loads a web page, it starts to execute scripts lightning fast and loads the DOM at the same time in parallel. We should always wait until the DOM is loaded. We can achieve it by registering to the **DOMContentLoaded** event of the document. It will fire when the DOM is ready:

```
<script type="text/javascript">
    document.addEventListener('DOMContentLoaded',function () {
        var heading = document.getElementById("heading");
        heading.innerHTML = 'custom heading';
    });
</script>
```

> **NOTE: Whether you use plain JavaScript or any JavaScript library, framework, you must wait until the DOM is loaded to access its elements.**

We can use **getElementById**, **getElementsByClassName**, **getElementsByName**, and so on, to query and access DOM objects. This allows us to manipulate the html document such as changing CSS, adding, or removing DOM objects. It is reflected to the browser immediately.

JavaScript Object Notation (JSON)

JSON is a human readable data format. It used for sending and receiving data. It is lightweight and can be easily generated or parsed easily. It is based on key value pairs and can contain strings, numbers, arrays, Boolean, or object data. JSON objects are specified as key value pairs between curly braces. JSON arrays are specified between square brackets and their elements are separated by commas.

The key value pairs are separated by commas and the keys and values are separated by colons. The keys in JSON objects must be unique and specified as strings between double quotes. This makes JSON objects like the hash table data structure.

For example, the following code specifies a JSON object which has a name, age, vehicles object array, and marital status:

```
{
      "name":"John Doe",
      "age": 50,
      "vehicles":[{"type":"Car","model":"mazda"},
{"type":"pickup","model":"mitsubishi"}],
      "married": true
}
```

JSON is used in JavaScript and rest services to transfer data. We may use **JSON.parse** to convert the JSON string to JavaScript objects or convert JavaScript objects to JSON using the **JSON.stringify** methods. Declaring a literal object in JavaScript is done as the same as declaring a JSON object.

Asynchronous JavaScript and XML (Ajax)

Let us explain how to send data to a server from an HTML document:

- **Posting data with the HTML form**: There is an html element called form. It includes fields with name attributes to collect data. Let us assume we have a simple form that the user enters his social security number and name, surname. When the user presses the **Send Data** button, we will send the entered data to the server, and we will display a popup that the operation is successful:

    ```
    <form method="post" action="/sendSsnData">
        <label for="ssn">SSN:</label>
        <input type="text" id="ssn" name="SocialSecurityId" />
        <label for="nameSurname">Name Surname:</label>
        <input type="text" id="nameSurname" name="NameSurname" />
    ```

```
        <input type="submit" value="Send Data"/>
    </form>
```

When we click on the send data submit button, the browser will collect data between the form tags (which is the text values written by input elements in this example) and encode them by the name attributes of the input elements and make a post request to the server.

We can access the form encoded values from the request message body which is like the following in this example:

```
SocialSecurityId=5465&NameSurname=gerger+ergerg
```

As we can see, it is key-value pairs separated by ampersand. Keys and values are separated by an equal sign. The keys are the same with the name attributes of the input elements. We specify the request method in the method attribute of the form element (which can be get or post) and the URL address on the server in the action attribute.

This is one of the ways to send data to the server from HTML. The issue here is when data is submitted, the current Html document will be destroyed after data is sent and it is rendered with the response Html. We can notice that the browser is cleared and then rendered with new Html returned from the server.

This is too much data transferring just for sending some tiny piece of data and displaying only the operation is successful.

This is synchronous communication with the server. The browser is cleared and locked until the operation is completed and the new html is loaded from the response. Wouldn't it be great if we send only the necessary data located in some part of our page and get only the operation result from the server (not full response html) without destroying and rendering the entire page?

- **Sending data with AJAX**: We can use the JavaScript **XMLHttpRequest** object to send data to the server. When we use AJAX, the operation will be done asynchronously, and the web page is not destroyed and loaded again. The usage of it in the plain JavaScript is as follows:

```
<!DOCTYPE html>
<html>
<head>
    <meta charset="utf-8" />
    <link href="css/bootstrap.css" rel="stylesheet" />
    <title>A simple page</title>
    <script src="js/bootstrap.js"></script>
```

```
    <script type="text/javascript">

        function sendData() {

            var xhttp = new XMLHttpRequest();
            xhttp.onreadystatechange = function () {
                if (this.readyState == 4 && this.status == 200) {
                    if (this.responseText == true) {
                        alert('operation is successfull');
                    }
                }
            };
            xhttp.open("POST", "sendSsnData", true);

            var data = {
                SocialSecurityId: document.getElementById('ssn').
value,
                NameSurname: document.
getElementById('nameSurname').value
            };

            xhttp.send(JSON.stringify(data));
        }
    </script>
</head>
<body>
        <label for="ssn">SSN:</label>
        <input type="text" id="ssn" />
        <label for="nameSurname">Name Surname:</label>
        <input type="text" id="nameSurname" />
        <button onclick="sendData()">Send Data</button>
</body>
</html>
```

We will create a new **XMLHttpRequest** object, register to its **onreadystatechange** event to be notified when the operation is completed, collect data from the input elements, and then call the send method of the **XMLHttpRequest** object.

The page will not be wiped out and the operation will happen asynchronously, and other parts of the page will be accessible. When the operation is completed, the **onreadystatechange** event will be fired and we will be able to check the response from there.

The data will be sent in the json format instead of the form encoded values sent in the form post:

```
{"SocialSecurityId":"45345","NameSurname":"ergerg"}
```

> NOTE: We saw how to make AJAX requests with the plain JavaScript only. Usually, a JavaScript framework or library is used in web projects for simplicity.

AJAX has great performance benefits over traditional form posting because the browser does not have to wipe out the page and render it again. Also, the server does not have to return a HTML page in response, only the necessary data is enough.

> TIP: Whether you are using the form post or AJAX, you must always validate your data before you send it to the server.

Conclusion

We covered the preliminary information about the web just enough to get started with ASP.NET Core Razor pages and explained basics of HTTP, HTML, CSS, and JavaScript. Every single one of them is a huge topic which is outside the scope of this book. We will cover ASP.NET Core Razor in the next chapter.

Questions

1. For which purposes, can we use the user-agent header?

2. Assume you are writing a service that downloads a pdf file. How do you automatically open the pdf file in the browser when it is downloaded?

3. Assume you are in a team and you are coding the backend and another developer coding the front-end. You have written a service but its html page user interface is not ready. How can you test and debug your service?

4. You want to collect data from the user and redirect it to another website or page. Which method should be used?

CHAPTER 5
Developing ASP. NET Core Web Applications with Razor

Introduction

We introduced fundamentals of web in the previous chapter. We will cover Razor pages, routing, model classes, data annotations, html helpers, layout pages, partial pages, tag helpers, and MVC in this chapter. These are the tools you must learn to implement server-side web page generation.

Structure

In this chapter, we will discuss the following topics:

- Introduction to Razor
- Introduction to routing
- Developing ASP.NET Core web applications with Razor pages
- Introduction to model binding
- Developing ASP.NET Core web applications with ASP.NET Core MVC

Objectives

After reading this chapter, you should be able to start developing web pages with ASP.NET Core. We will make a simple phonebook application with ASP.NET Core.

We can develop front-end pages with Razor pages and model view controller with views. We will cover Razor pages and MVC in this chapter.

Introduction to Razor pages projects

Razor is a markup language that enables developers to embed the server-side code into HTML web pages. Razor pages are simply server resources which return HTML pages. We can mix and create the server-side code with HTML easily and create our helper methods that encapsulate HTML components. We can create a web application project with Razor pages from **Create New Project | ASP.NET Core Web App** from the starting dialog of Visual Studio. A web application with the Razor pages project is structured like the following:

- **wwwroot**: This directory contains static files. Assets like CSS files, icons, HTML, and JavaScript files are put here in the respective folders.
  - o **css**: This contains the project's Stylesheet files.
  - o **js**: This contains the project's JavaScript files.
  - o **lib**: This contains third-party library files used in the project. They may contain sub directories for their respective CSS and JavaScript files. The Visual Studio 2019 new Razor pages project template mentioned above will include bootstrap and jQuery for us, but we can remove them or change them with other versions if we wish.
  - o **favicon.ico**: This is the project's favicon.
- **Pages**: This directory contains the Razor pages of the project. They have Razor files with extensions **cshtml** and their code files follow the naming convention **{pagename}.cshtml.cs**. Visual Studio shows the Razor page and their code files hierarchically (*Figure 5.1*). We can create sub directories here as we like and group our pages.
  - o **Shared**: This is the directory that contains the common Razor pages of the project.
  - o **_ViewStart.cshtml**: It is the Razor page file that is executed and included before every Razor page is rendered.
- **appsettings.json**: This is the configuration file of the project.
- **Program.cs**: This contains the entry point of the project.
- **Startup.cs**: This contains service and middleware configurations of the project.

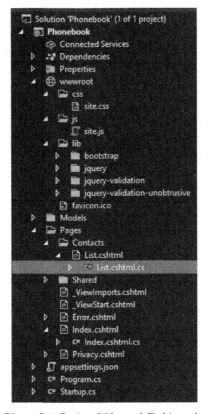

Figure 5.1: *Project folder and file hierarchy*

We can start debugging our project and see the default theme and template is working like in the following figure:

Figure 5.2: *Default ASP.NET Core Razor Pages project template*

Introducing Routing

Routing are rules and conventions specified for matching URL patterns to server resources. Let us add a new Razor page to our project by adding a new folder named Contacts to the Pages folder and a new Razor page named List under it:

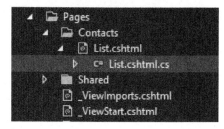

Figure 5.3: New Razor page under a directory

An empty razor page is added to the project with a default code and empty content. Now, let us add a simple heading to the project like the following:

```
@page
@{
}
<h4>Hello world!!</h4>
```

Let us start debugging and try our page. We added our page under the **Contacts** folder with the name **List**. When the main page opened in our browser (which is **Index.cshtml** located right under the **Pages** folder by default) type **{root localhost URL of the application}/Contacts/List** in the address bar and view our page:

Phonebook   Home   Privacy

Hello world!!

Figure 5.4: Default routing for a new Razor page

The default routing in a Razor pages application starts with the content root which is the **Pages** folder by default (can be overridden) and followed by **{folder hierarchy}/{Razor page name}**. But it can be modified by service configuration. Let us suppose we would like to access our page from the URL **/ContactList** along with /Contacts/List. We open our **Startup.cs** file and navigate to the **ConfigureServices** method and then go to the line **AddRazorPages** called (this method call should be generated automatically by the new project template). There is an overload of this method which takes an action delegate which we can specify our custom routes. Let us route the address **/ContactList** to **/Contacts/List** by calling the **AddPageRoute** method as shown in the following code:

```
public void ConfigureServices(IServiceCollection services)
{
services.AddRazorPages((options)=>
        {
    options.Conventions.AddPageRoute("/Contacts/List", "ContactList");
        });
}
```

The **AddPageRoute** method takes two parameters: the first one is the slash separated by the location of the Razor page relative to the **Pages** folder (like the default route), the second parameter is the route string we would like to access the page with. When we run our application and type **/ContactList** instead of the default route **/Contacts/List**, we will see that the same Razor page is viewed without the default route.

Another way of setting custom routes for pages is by using the @page Razor directive indicated on the top of every Razor page. Let us suppose we would like to open our phonebook list page by the address **/Contacts**. We can add this custom route to the @page directive with **@page "/Contacts"**:

```
@page "/Contacts"

@{

}
```

```
<h4>Hello world!!</h4>
```

When we type **/Contacts** on the browser address bar, we can see that the same page is opened again. Notice we can access the same page with specifying **/Contacts** or **/ContactList** at the same time but not with the default route **/Contacts/List** because we have overridden it with the **@page** directive. When we set multiple routing rules to the same Razor page, they are evaluated and fit by most specific rules to fewer specific ones.

> **NOTE: If you are developing an application that requires search engine optimization (SEO), routing is quite important, and ASP.NET Core presents you many opportunities for easily defining routes.**

Now, we explained routing. Let us move on to the models and start building our phonebook application step by step.

Introducing Models

The ASP.NET Core Models are objects that are specific to a business or domain of the project. They can be database entities but on enterprise projects, they are usually the data transfer objects. The data is fetched from databases or remote sources and then tailored and shaped to fit into the user interface data. They can be criteria or similar objects that come from the user interface also. In short, they are programmatic representation of the data that Razor pages require.

Let us suppose we have user information on a database table and contact information on another database table. For example, we may have the following database entities. A **UserInformation** table and **ContactInformation** table and one-to-one relation between them:

```
public class UserInformation
{
    public int Id { get; set; }
    public string Name { get; set; }
    public string Surname { get; set; }
    public DateTime DateOfBirth { get; set; }
}
public class ContactInformation
{
    public int UserId { get; set; }
    public string PhoneNumber { get; set; }
    public string Address { get; set; }
    public String Country { get; set; }
}
```

We assume in our List page, we would like to list the database primary key **Id**, **name**, **surname**, **country** data. Let us call it **ListPageModel**:

```
public class ListPageModel
{
    public int Id { get; set; }
    public string Name { get; set; }
    public string Surname { get; set; }
    public string Country { get; set; }
}
```

And assume we have a search panel in our List page that takes the name, surname, and birth year criteria. Let us call it **ListPageCriteriaModel**:

```
public class ListPageCriteriaModel
{
    public string Name { get; set; }
    public string Surname { get; set; }
    public int BirthYear { get; set; }
}
```

And assume we have a detail page (we will add it to the project after we discuss the List page) that edits the existing user or adds new. We collect and display the name, surname, date of birth, country, phone number, address information. Let us call it **UserContactInfoDetailModel**:

```
public class UserContactInfoDetailModel
{
    public int Id { get; set; }
    public string Name { get; set; }
    public string Surname { get; set; }
    public DateTime DateOfBirth { get; set; }
    public string PhoneNumber { get; set; }
    public string Address { get; set; }
    public String Country { get; set; }
}
```

The model classes are located under the Models folder in the Razor pages application. Let us add **ListPageModel**, **ListPageCriteriaModel**, and **UserContactInfoDetailModel** classes there.

> NOTE: We choose this database design and model for simplicity. In real life, the current scenario is going to be different.

Now, let us open **List.cshtml.cs** located under **List.cshtml**. It is our pages model class and derived from **PageModel**. It looks like this.

> TIP: You may consider a data mapper framework for mapping entities to model objects automatically. Automapper is a mature and popular mapping framework. You may get more information on the web site https://automapper.org/.

```
namespace Phonebook.Pages.PhoneBook
{
    public class ListModel : PageModel
    {
        public void OnGet()
```

```
        {
        }
    }
}
```

We decided that our list page will query and display the contact records by criteria, so we need to add a property of **ListPageCriteriaModel** to our model class. Let us call this property **Criteria**. Our List page also displays a list of contact records, so we need to add a collection property of the **ListPageModel** class. Let us call this property **List**. Our List pages model looks like this:

```
using System.Collections.Generic;

using Microsoft.AspNetCore.Mvc.RazorPages;

using Phonebook.Models;


namespace Phonebook.Pages.PhoneBook

{
    public class ListModel : PageModel

    {
        public ListPageCriteriaModel Criteria { get; set; }

        public List<ListPageModel> List { get; set; }

        public void OnGet()
        {
        }
    }
}
```

We can consider using the **OnGet** method for initialization like the loading event of pages. It is executed when the page is first called by the browser.

> NOTE: The List page in our example will collect criteria data and display a collection of records so our page model class needs to have a criteria model and a collection of records models. Be aware that page model classes in ASP.NET Core are a programmatic representation of the view pages.

Introduction to the Razor syntax and HTML helpers

We have added the **List.cshtml** Razor page. Let us suppose we need to search and list contacts persisted on the system here. We open **List.cshtml** and start modifying it like this:

```
@page "/PhonebookList"
@using Phonebook.Pages.Contacts
@model ListModel
@* this is
    a comment*@
```

If we examine **List.cshtml,** we notice that the first line starts with the @page directive. This means this **cshtml** file is a Razor page and not a MVC view and it needs to be handled differently. The MVC views are written in the same way with Razor pages, but they are structured and run differently. We will cover them later.

The second line is the using directive. Here, we specify the namespaces of the classes we are going to use in the Razor page, and they can be as many as we want. Remember Razor pages are HTML pages mixed with C# codes so we can specify the namespaces of the classes we use in our Razor pages here. Here, we will use **ListModel** as the model of our page, so we include its namespace here.

The third line specifies the model class of the page. Razor pages are compiled a bit differently from the regular C# code and one of the most important things is that they are strongly typed. HTML helpers work with lambda expressions and simplifies coding Razor.

The fourth line is a comment. The comments in Razor are enclosed between @* *@ characters and can be multi line.

We decided that we will include a search criteria panel on the top of the page, and it will allow you to search the phonebook records by the name, surname, and birth date. We will achieve this by using HTML helpers. We assume that twitter bootstrap is included in the project by the create new project wizard, and we will use its grid to make a 2x4 table layout. Our **List.cshml** page looks like this:

```
@page "/PhonebookList"
@using Phonebook.Pages.PhoneBook
@model ListModel

<div class="container-fluid">
    <div class="row m-2">
```

```
        <div class="col-sm-3">
            Name:
        </div>
        <div class="col-sm-3">
            @Html.TextBoxFor(t => t.Criteria.Name)
        </div>
        <div class="col-sm-3">
            Surname:
        </div>
        <div class="col-sm-3">
            @Html.TextBoxFor(t => t.Criteria.Surname)
        </div>
    </div>
    <div class="row m-2">
        <div class="col-sm-3">
            Birth Year:
        </div>
        <div class="col-sm-3">
            @Html.TextBoxFor(t => t.Criteria.BirthYear)
        </div>
        <div class="col-sm-3">
        </div>
        <div class="col-sm-3">
            <input type="submit" value="Search" />
        </div>
    </div>
</div>
</div>
```

Razor codes start with **@** sign. **Html.TextBoxFor** extension method creates HTML input tags for us. Notice that the lambda expression parameter (**t** in the previous code) is of the same type specified on the **@model** directive previously.

We need to send our criteria data to the server, so we can list our data. We can achieve this by using the **Html.BeginForm** extension method:

```
@using (Html.BeginForm(FormMethod.Post))
{
//content here
}
```

The using Razor directive is used for HTML elements with opening and closing tags. We can use it along with **Html.BeginForm** for creating the **<form></form>** tags. The content between the curly braces goes between the **<form> </form>** tags. Our razor page is now as follows:

```
@page "/PhonebookList"
@using Phonebook.Pages.PhoneBook
@model ListModel
```

```
Then, we write the markup for our HTML form:
@using (Html.BeginForm(FormMethod.Post))
{
    <div class="container-fluid">
        <div class="row m-2">
            <div class="col-sm-3">
                Name:
            </div>
            <div class="col-sm-3">
                @Html.TextBoxFor(t => t.Criteria.Name)
            </div>
            <div class="col-sm-3">
                Surname:
            </div>
            <div class="col-sm-3">
                @Html.TextBoxFor(t => t.Criteria.Surname)
            </div>
        </div>
        <div class="row m-2">
            <div class="col-sm-3">
                Birth Year:
            </div>
            <div class="col-sm-3">
                @Html.TextBoxFor(t => t.Criteria.BirthYear)
            </div>
            <div class="col-sm-3">
            </div>
            <div class="col-sm-3">
```

```
                    <input type="submit" value="Search" />
                </div>
            </div>
        </div>
}
```

When we execute this Razor page by navigating **ContactList**, it will render a page like this:

```
<form action="/ContactList" method="post">
    <div class="container-fluid">
        <div class="row m-2">
            <div class="col-sm-3">
                Name:
            </div>
            <div class="col-sm-3">
                <input id="Criteria_Name" name="Criteria.Name"
type="text" value="">
            </div>
            <div class="col-sm-3">
                Surname:
            </div>
            <div class="col-sm-3">
                <input id="Criteria_Surname" name="Criteria.Surname"
type="text" value="">
            </div>
        </div>
        <div class="row m-2">
            <div class="col-sm-3">
                Birth Year:
            </div>
            <div class="col-sm-3">
                <input data-val="true" data-val-required="The BirthYear
field is required." id="Criteria_BirthYear" name="Criteria.BirthYear"
type="text" value="">
            </div>
            <div class="col-sm-3">
            </div>
```

```
        <div class="col-sm-3">
            <input type="submit" value="Search">
        </div>
    </div>
  </div>
</form>
```

Which will be rendered like the following:

| Name: | | Surname: | |
| Birth Year: | | | Search |

Figure 5.5: A sample razor page output

NOTE: Please note the benefits of the Html helpers. They provide strong typing with lambda expressions. This allows separation of concerns and parallel development. For example, front end developer can develop the cshtml razor page and backend developer can develop the page model classes at the same time. This can boost the development speed in teams.

Also note that strongly typed Razor pages with lambda expressions allow us to easily refactor the pages. We can rename a property of a model class and it is automatically reflected to the Razor page lambda expressions using that property by the refactor feature of Visual Studio.

Notice the name properties. They are generated from the lambda expressions in the Razor page.

TIP: Html helpers in Razor pages are executed codes like any .NET code so they consume server resources. If you have performance concerns, you should use static Html without helpers as much as possible. For example, we have the Search submit button in our List page that posts the form, and we do not need to change its properties name, attributes, CSS, etc. from the server side. Therefore, we do not need to use any helper method for it.

We have explained HTML helpers with a simple example. They are frequently used for server-side HTML generation.

TIP: While developing Razor pages, you do not need to stop and restart debugging. You can make any changes in them, save, and refresh your page. The Razor page will be compiled and run automatically. If you have made a compile time error, the ASP.NET Core error page will be displayed.

> You can also debug Razor codes in cshtml files by putting breakpoints on @ directives.

Now, we have developed our criteria page so we must post the criteria data to the server and use the data that comes from the user interface. This is achieved by model binding.

Introducing model binding

Let us start debugging, open our browsers developer tools, and send some criteria data from our contacts page. When we fill the input fields and click on the search button, we observe that our HTML form data is posted to the server like the following form encoded data in the message body. The HTML form values are key value pairs separated with an equal sign as mentioned in the previous *Chapter 4: Introduction to HTTP, HTML, CSS, and JavaScript*:

Criteria.Name=name&Criteria.Surname=surname&Criteria.BirthYear=1995

We have a criteria property with the type **ListPageCriteriaModel** in our model, and we have used HTML helpers with lambda expressions. Remember that Razor pages are strongly typed by the model class specified at the top, so the lambda parameter **t** is the class specified; in this example, the **ListModel** class in the **List.cshtml.cs** file:

```
@Html.TextBoxFor(t => t.Criteria.Name)
```

And this HTML helper has generated an input tag for us with its name attribute equal to the lambda expressions property selector:

```
<input id="Criteria_Surname" name="Criteria.Surname" type="text" value="">
```

To get this data on our page model, we must add the **OnPost** method that returns an **IActionResult** interface and put the **BindProperty** attribute to the model property (**Criteria** property for our example) which looks like this:

```
    public class ListModel : PageModel
    {
        [BindProperty]
        public ListPageCriteriaModel Criteria { get; set; }

        public List<ListPageModel> List { get; set; }

        public void OnGet()
        {
```

```
        }

        public IActionResult OnPost()
        {
            String name = this.Criteria.Name;
    // searching code here
            return Page();

        }

    }
```

We put a breakpoint in the **OnPost** action method, and start debugging our page and stop the execution. At the start of the **OnPost** method, we notice that the **Criteria** property is filled with the form encoded data on the message body, and we can access property values by this reference:

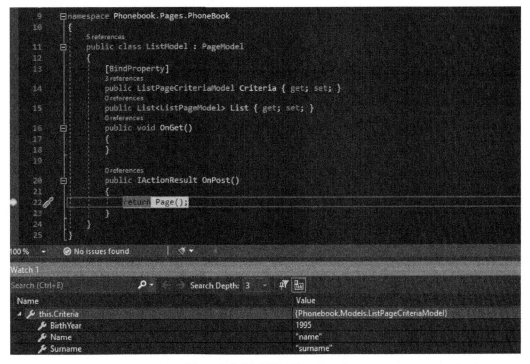

Figure 5.6: Model binding at work

This is a feature of ASP.NET Core called model binding. The post data in the message body is automatically parsed and loaded into the model object. It can work on form encoded data for HTML forms or JSON data on Ajax requests. This feature greatly saves the time of developers. Model object properties are evaluated from parsing the form data keys. The form data keys are model object property hierarchies that are specified by property names separated by dots, and they are created by HTML helpers.

Now, we have received the form data from our HTML user interface and we must validate it. The data that comes from other layers or user interfaces is never to be trusted, and we must protect the server side of our applications.

Introducing model validation

We have decided that our List page takes the name, surname, year of birth, and queries phonebook data. Our birth year field should allow you to enter only four-digit numbers. Let us put a breakpoint at the beginning of **OnPost** method, start debugging, put a string field in the birth year field, and click on the **Search** button:

Figure 5.7: Sending an invalid value in a form

When the execution is stopped at the **OnPost** method, we inspect the **Criteria** property and notice that the **BirthYear** property is zero because we put a string value to it. The model binding encountered an error, and our model state has errors. We can check this from the **ModelState.IsValid** property of the **PageModel** object. We can get faulted properties that the model binder failed to bind from the **ModelState** property on the **PageModel** class. Please notice the red bordered rectangles in *Figure 5.8*.

We should tell the user that the entered birth year is invalid. We can add extra properties to our model class and use them to reflect errors to our Razor page. Let us add a Boolean property named **HasError**, a property with the type **List** of strings named **Errors**. We check the **ModelState.IsValid** property and set these new properties as required. The type of the **ModelState** property of the **PageModel** class is **ModelStateDictionary** and contains key value pairs. The keys are the dot separated property hierarchy strings. The values are objects with type **ModelStateEntry** which contains a **ValidationState** enum that we can use it to check whether binding that property has failed as shown in the following figure from a debugging session:

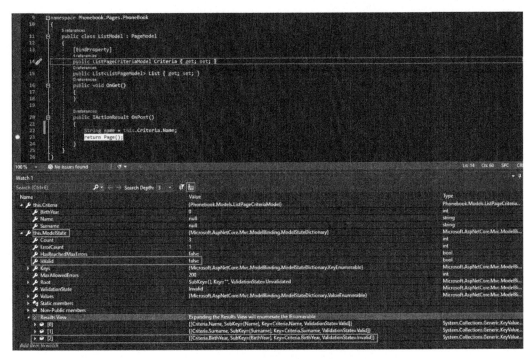

Figure 5.8: *Model binding failure*

The following code shows how to check model validation:

```
using System;
using System.Linq;
using System.Threading.Tasks;
using Microsoft.AspNetCore.Mvc;
using System.Collections.Generic;
using Microsoft.AspNetCore.Mvc.RazorPages;
using Phonebook.Models;
using Microsoft.AspNetCore.Mvc.ModelBinding;

namespace Phonebook.Pages.PhoneBook
{
    public class ListModel : PageModel
    {
        [BindProperty]
        public ListPageCriteriaModel Criteria { get; set; }

        public List<ListPageModel> List { get; set; }
```

```
public bool HasError { get; set; }

public List<String> Errors { get; set; }

public ListModel()
{
    this.Errors = new List<string>();
}

public void OnGet()
{
}


public IActionResult OnPost()
{
    if (!this.ModelState.IsValid)
    {
        this.HasError = true;
        var birthYearModelState = this.ModelState.Where(t =>
t.Key == "Criteria.BirthYear").FirstOrDefault();

        if (birthYearModelState.Value.ValidationState ==
ModelValidationState.Invalid)
        {
            this.HasError = true;
            this.Errors.Add("Please enter a valid birth year
criteria");
        }
    }
    else{
//contact query code here
    }
    return Page();
}
    }
}
```

Please notice the end line of the **OnPost** method. We call the Page method of the **PageModel** class. It returns the **PageResult** object which implements the

IActionResult interface. This executes the current Razor page by the current model class the code executed.

Now, we have added the necessary properties and code for showing errors, we are ready to reflect those on the Razor page. Let us open **List.cshtml** and add the property calls inside a bootstrap alert panel:

```
@if (Model.HasError) {

    <div class="alert alert-danger" role="alert">
        @foreach(var error in Model.Errors)
        {
            <p>@error</p>
        }
    </div>
}
```

We can access our model object and its properties from the Razor page by the **Model** keyword. Since Razor pages are strongly typed, Visual Studio Intellisense will autocomplete them for us.

If we examine the Razor syntax here what we are using is called Razor code blocks. We have a **@if(....)** **{..........}** directive and it allows us to generate the conditional HTML content. In our example, if the HasError property of our model is true, then the code inside it is executed and a bootstrap alert panel is rendered to the page which is simply a **div** tag with **alert** CSS classes (bootstrap alert is just for the example here, there are various error showing methods and they can be used too).

We can also use the code block syntax to write a foreach loop and generate the content by iterating a collection in the pages model. The result looks like the following figure:

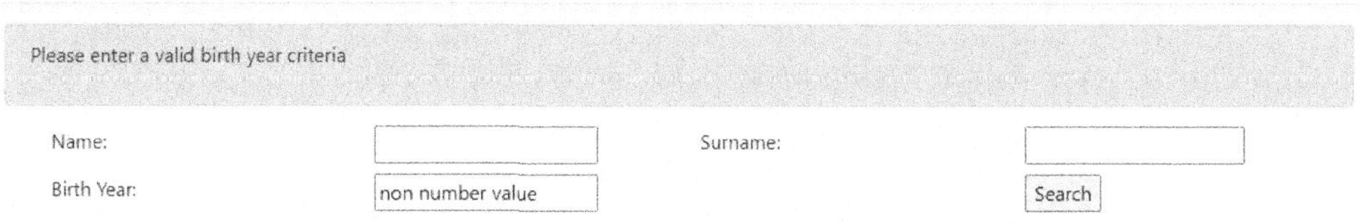

Figure 5.9: Rendering error messages from the model object

We can prevent the end user from entering a string to the **Birth Year** field on our form by generating an input tag with the type attribute equal to number. We can achieve that by using overloaded methods of HTML helpers which takes HTML attributes. We can specify HTML attributes by anonym types of C# like the following and add native HTML or custom attributes:

```
@Html.TextBoxFor(t => t.Criteria.BirthYear, new { type="number" })
```

The Razor code generates the html input tag with **type="number"**:

```
<input name="Criteria.BirthYear" type="number">
```

This does not mean that we can remove the guarding **if** code in the **OnPost** method. The generated HTML and JavaScript code can always be manipulated by the malicious end users.

But do we have to write the if else code for every property in our model? Is there any way to automate and simplify the validation in ASP.NET Core? Here come the data annotations.

Introduction to data annotations

The data annotations framework contains validation attributes that help us to validate properties of model objects during model binding. Let us consider our criteria model and say that our List page will require the **Name** field with character count between 3 and 20. The **Surname** field is not required, but if it is entered, it must be between 3 and 20 characters also. The birth year is not required but if it is entered, it must be a four-digit number and between 1970 and 2020. To implement this validation, we must open the **ListPageCriteriaModel** class and modify it like the following:

```
public class ListPageCriteriaModel
{
        [Required(AllowEmptyStrings = false, ErrorMessage = "Name field
is mandatory")]
        [StringLength(20, ErrorMessage = "Name field must be between 3
and 20 characters long", MinimumLength = 3)]
        public string Name { get; set; }


        [StringLength(20, ErrorMessage = "Surname field must be between 3
and 20 characters long", MinimumLength = 3)]
        public string Surname { get; set; }


        [Range(1970, 2020, ErrorMessage = "Birth year must be between
1970 and 2020")]
        public int? BirthYear { get; set; }
}
```

Then, we modify the **OnPost** method of our List page model like the following.

```
public IActionResult OnPost()
{
```

```
  if (!this.ModelState.IsValid)
  {
this.HasError = true;

var validationErrors = this.ModelState.Values.SelectMany(t => t.Errors).
Select(t => t.ErrorMessage).ToList();

  this.Errors.AddRange(validationErrors);
  }
  else
  {
      // query phonebooks here
  }
  return Page();
}
```

When we try our page, we will see the result as shown in the following figure:

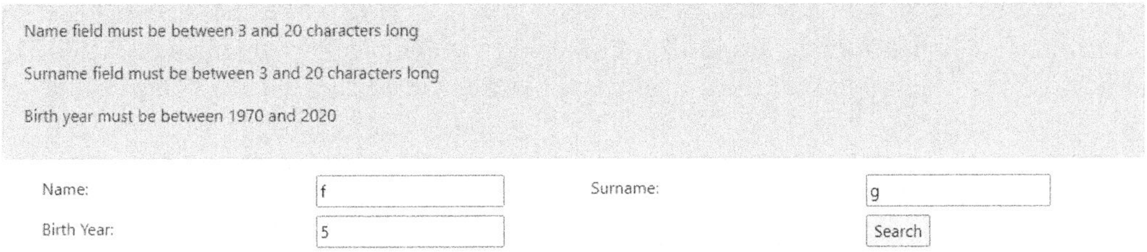

Figure 5.10: *Data annotation validation results*

Besides the required string length and range annotations, there are built in data annotations for validating credit card numbers, comparing two properties, phone numbers, email addresses, and URL strings. There are even annotations for remote validation by making a request to the server from the client side, regular expressions, and we can create custom annotations also.

> **TIP: Sometimes, the data annotations framework can be cumbersome and may not be enough for complex validation scenarios. You can try custom third-party validation frameworks. One of them is the fluent validation framework. It is very dynamic, extensible and allows coding validation by lambda expressions. You can find more information on its website https://fluentvalidation.net/.**

Validating the model from the server-side is essential but not enough. We need to do validation from the client side also so we can stop invalid data before arrived to our servers and save server resources.

Introduction to unobtrusive JavaScript

We can register necessary events and write our custom JavaScript validation, but ASP.NET Core contains unobtrusive JavaScript libraries and can generate JavaScript validation code based on data annotations for us.

The unobtrusive JavaScript is a custom jQuery library. jQuery is a small sized fast library that simplifies JavaScript operations such as DOM querying, DOM manipulation, creating animations, making AJAX requests, and so on. It encapsulates all those things and provide cross-browser development to some degree which can save us from a lot of trouble. Many other JavaScript libraries use jQuery in their code base too. It is a popular library and has a long way back to 2000s.

When we create a new ASP.NET Core project, the jQuery and unobtrusive validation library comes along with bootstrap automatically. It is in a partial page named **_ValidationScriptsPartial** for us. We must include it on our page by the **RenderPartial** helper (we will cover partial pages shortly). The section directive is used to group the content in the Layout Razor pages. We can remove the validation summary we used before and use the **Html.ValidationMessageFor** helper extension. We can also remove the code we have written on the **OnPost** method, **HasError** and **Errors** properties because unobtrusive validation handles it automatically. Protecting the **OnPost** method by checking **ModelState.IsValid** will be enough. Here is the revised form of **List.cshtml** and **List.cshtml.cs**:

```
@* List.cshtml *@

@page "/PhonebookList"
@using Phonebook.Pages.PhoneBook
@model ListModel


@using (Html.BeginForm(FormMethod.Post))
{
    <div class="container-fluid">
        <div class="row m-2">
            <div class="col-sm-2">
                Name:
            </div>
            <div class="col-sm-4">
                @Html.TextBoxFor(t => t.Criteria.Name)<br />
                @Html.ValidationMessageFor(t=>t.Criteria.Name,null, new {
style="color:red" })
            </div>
```

```
                <div class="col-sm-2">
                    Surname:
                </div>
                <div class="col-sm-4">
                    @Html.TextBoxFor(t => t.Criteria.Surname)<br />
                    @Html.ValidationMessageFor(t => t.Criteria.Surname,
null, new { style = "color:red" })
                </div>
            </div>
            <div class="row m-2">
                <div class="col-sm-2">
                    Birth Year:
                </div>
                <div class="col-sm-4">
                    @Html.TextBoxFor(t => t.Criteria.BirthYear, new { type =
"number" })<br />
                    @Html.ValidationMessageFor(t => t.Criteria.BirthYear,
null, new { style = "color:red" })
                </div>
                <div class="col-sm-2">
                </div>
                <div class="col-sm-4">
                    <input type="submit" value="Search" />
                </div>
            </div>
        </div>
}

@section Scripts {
    @{ await Html.RenderPartialAsync("_ValidationScriptsPartial"); }
}

//List.cshtml.cs

namespace Phonebook.Pages.PhoneBook
{
    public class ListModel : PageModel
    {
```

```
[BindProperty]
public ListPageCriteriaModel Criteria { get; set; }

public List<ListPageModel> List { get; set; }

public ListModel()
{
}

public void OnGet()
{
}

public IActionResult OnPost()
{
    if (this.ModelState.IsValid)
    {
        // query phonebooks here
    }
    return Page();
}
    }
}
```

And our validation output looks as shown in the following figure. Validation works right after HTML input elements lose their focus. We can check whether any requests are made to the server until the form is valid by fiddler or developer tools of our browser:

***Figure 5.11**: Unobtrusive client JavaScript in action*

It is nice to have ASP.NET Core provides client-side validation from data annotations for us. Keep in mind we can always write the custom JavaScript validation code.

One of the fundamental principles of making software is developing reusable codes and components. This is also valid for UI components. Now, we will cover how to achieve this in Razor pages.

Introduction to layout Razor pages

Occasionally, software with more than a few user interfaces are developed with reusable UI components and instead of putting common UI components into every page, they are put to a parent page. Those common parts can be menu, banner, breadcrumb, or any common UI element of the application. By using layout pages in Razor, we can code once and manage them in one place instead of every page and focus our attention to the actual content page. The following figure shows a common usage of a layout page. The banner, user preferences menu, and left menu are common and contained in the layout page:

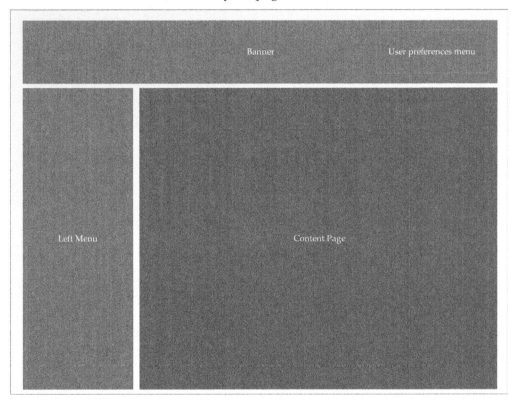

Figure 5.12: A sample layout design

The layout pages are in the Pages/Shared folder. The default layout page is named with **_Layout.cshtml** and it is a Razor page also. When we open it in our phonebook project, we will notice that the common parts of our application are the top header and footer:

```
<body>
    <header>
        <nav class="navbar navbar-expand-sm navbar-toggleable-sm navbar-
```

```
light bg-white border-bottom box-shadow mb-3">
            <div class="container">
    <!-- menu here -->
            </div>
        </nav>
    </header>
    <div class="container">
        <main role="main" class="pb-3">
            @RenderBody()
        </main>
    </div>

    <footer class="border-top footer text-muted">
        <div class="container">
            &copy; 2021 - Phonebook - <a asp-area="" asp-page="/
Privacy">Privacy</a>
        </div>
    </footer>

    <script src="~/lib/jquery/dist/jquery.min.js"></script>
    <script src="~/lib/bootstrap/dist/js/bootstrap.bundle.min.js"></
script>
    <script src="~/js/site.js" asp-append-version="true"></script>
    @await RenderSectionAsync("Scripts", required: false)
</body>
```

This is the common HTML page that carries every other content page. The **RenderBody** method renders the executed Razor page content. At the end of the layout, we include static JavaScript files every page is going to need and **RenderSectionAsync** is called after the static scripts. This is one of the ways to include script files. When we use the **@section** Razor directive in a Razor page, we can render that section on the layout page with this method. Remember we included unobtrusive JavaScript files in our List page as follows:

```
@section Scripts {
    @{ await Html.RenderPartialAsync("_ValidationScriptsPartial"); }
}
```

Then, our **Layout.cshtml** renders the scripts section as the following. We can control the rendered Scripts of the layout page from the content page by calling **RenderSectionAsync** in the following way in layout pages:

```
@await RenderSectionAsync("Scripts", required: false)
```

We can put common JavaScript and CSS files into the Layout page statically with link and script HTML tags. We can control the scripts and stylesheets specific to the content page with section directives. Here in our example, the scripts in the partial **_ValidationScriptsPartial cshtml** file are rendered by the call to the **RenderPartialAsync** method and placed inside **Layout.cshtml** by **RenderSectionAsync**.

The **_ValidationScriptsPartial** is a partial Razor page which contains the unobtrusive JavaScript files. We can render this page wherever we want client-side validation:

```
<script src="~/lib/jquery-validation/dist/jquery.validate.min.js"></
script>
```

```
<script src="~/lib/jquery-validation unobtrusive/jquery.validate.
unobtrusive.min.js"></script>
```

We can have multiple layout pages, and we can specify the layout page of the content page with the **Layout** property:

```
@{
    Layout = "_Layout";
}
```

We do not have to write the full path to the layout. If that is the case, the layout is discovered by the standard discovery in Razor projects. First, the shared folder of the current executed folder that contains view is searched, and if it is not found, the Shared folder in the root View or Pages folder is searched.

Let us assume we would like to include a bread crumb component in our project for navigation. We will need to make a layout page for it so we can include it on the pages if necessary. We will start by adding a breadcrumb model class to the project and a Razor page to the Shared folder. We will generate a bootstrap breadcrumb component and need at least an array of the text and URL couples:

```
public class BreadCrumbModel
{
    public string Text { get; set; }

    public string Url { get; set; }
}
```

Then, we will add the **_BreadCrumbLayout.cshtml** layout page to the Shared folder. Notice that the layout and partial page names usually begin with the underscore character to distinguish them from the content Razor pages:

```
@{
    Layout = "_Layout";
}

@{
    var breadcrumbData = ViewData["BreadCrumbData"] as
List<BreadCrumbModel>;

    if (breadcrumbData == null)
    {
        breadcrumbData = new List<BreadCrumbModel>();
    }
}

<nav aria-label="breadcrumb">
    <ol class="breadcrumb">
        @for (int i = 0; i < breadcrumbData.Count; i++)
        {
            @if (i != breadcrumbData.Count - 1)
            {
                <li class="breadcrumb-item">
                    <a href="@breadcrumbData[i].Url">
                        @breadcrumbData[i].Text
                    </a>
                </li>
            }
            else
            {
                <li class="breadcrumb-item active" aria-current="page">
                    @breadcrumbData[i].Text
                </li>
            }
        }
    </ol>
</nav>
@RenderBody()
```

```
@section Scripts {
    @await RenderSectionAsync("Scripts", false)
}
```

We change the layout of our **List.cshtml** Razor page like the following directive:

```
@{
    Layout = "_BreadCrumbLayout";
}
```

We should transfer the breadcrumb data from the **PageModel** to **_BreadCrumbLayout** page. We can achieve this by making a custom page model derived from **PageModel** and set our breadcrumb data. We have already shown transferring data by using strongly typed models in the Razor pages, but we will show you other weakly typed ways of transferring data to Razor pages:

```
//ListModel.cshtml.cs
public void OnGet()
{
    //get the breadcrumb data here
List<BreadCrumbModel> breadCrumbData = new List<BreadCrumbModel>();
    breadCrumbData.Add(new BreadCrumbModel()
    {
Text = "Main Page",
        Url = "/"
    });
    breadCrumbData.Add(new BreadCrumbModel()
    {
Text = "Phonebook List",
        Url = "/PhonebookList"
    });
this.ViewData["BreadCrumbData"] = breadCrumbData;
}
```

> **NOTE: There are various ways to implement a breadcrumb component in ASP. NET Core, and we will omit them for the sake of simplicity.**

The base **PageModel** class contains some dictionary structures such as **ViewData**, **ViewBag**, **TempData** for transferring data to the Razor pages. Let us explain them:

- **ViewData**: The **ViewData** is a dictionary used for transferring data to the Razor page from the page model. We must use typecasting in our Razor (as in our preceding example) to access the value contained. The data inside it survives until the current request ends. If a redirection occurs, its contents are wiped out. We can use it from the page model as follows:

```
this.ViewData["BreadCrumbData"] = breadCrumbData;
```

And access its data from the Razor page similarly by accessing data from a C# dictionary:

```
var breadcrumbData = ViewData["BreadCrumbData"] as @* the type of
the data*@
```

- **ViewBag**: It is like **ViewData,** but it uses the dynamic run time resolution feature of C#. We do not have to use typecasting to get the data we want. They are available only to ASP.NET Core controllers and not Razor page models. We can set and retrieve our data without the dictionary indexer:

```
// from controller
this.ViewBag.BreadCrumbData = //some breadcrumb data


// from view
var breadcrumbdata = ViewBag.BreadCrumbData;


String somePropertyValue = breadcrumbdata.SomeProperty
```

Since there is no indexer, type and properties are resolved dynamically at runtime and not in compile time. We must use **ViewBag** with caution. For the preceding example, if the object **BreadCrumbData** does not have **SomeProperty** or its property type is not a string, we will encounter an error. Like **ViewData,** the contents of **ViewBag** is wiped out when the request ends.

- **TempData**: The **TempData** is a dictionary and can be used like **ViewData** in the Razor Pages, but the data in it can survive between consecutive requests. We will discuss it at *Chapter 9: State Management in ASP.NET Core.*

Observe that we first create the breadcrumb data when our page is first loaded in the **OnGet** method and then we put it into the **ViewData** dictionary, and we can access the **ViewData** dictionary in the content page (**List.cshtml**) or its layout page (**_BreadCrumbLayout**) to the parent layout page (**_Layout.cshtml**) and all the way back to the root Layout page.

Here is our Razor page hierarchy for our List page:

- _Layout.cshtml
  - o _BreadCrumbLayout.cshtml
    - ▪ List.cshtml

The final look of our List page with the layout is as shown in the following screenshot:

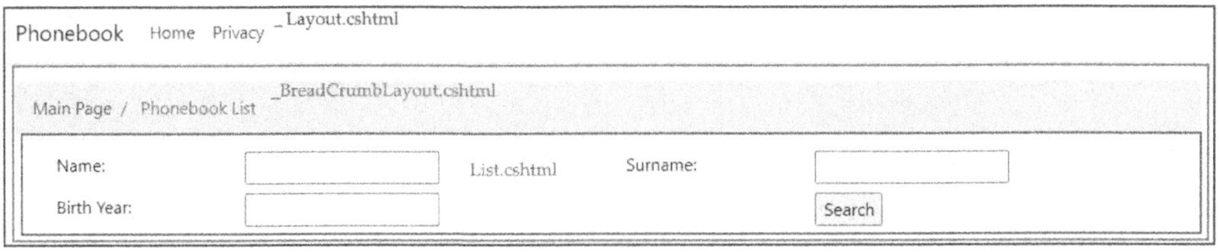

Figure 5.13: Nested layout pages

Now, let us consider a scenario in which we must show the list of queried contact records in the List page and the last entered ten contact records on the main page of the application in a table. We will list the contacts with the name, surname, phone number, and country columns both in our main and list pages, and we will include an action column named edit in the list page and use it to redirect the browser to our detail page. So, the only difference of tables between our list and main page is we will include an extra column in list page. We will create a reusable UI component with a partial page and use it to render our data both in list and main pages.

Introduction to partial Razor pages

Partial pages allow us to create re-usable HTML or Razor markup. They can be strongly typed and bound to model objects or can receive data from **ViewBag**, **ViewData**, and **TempData** dictionaries. Let us create a partial page in the Shared directory named **_ContactListPartial.cshtml** and render our contact data as a HTML table there:

```
@*_ContactListPartial.cshtml*@

@using Phonebook.Models;
@model List<ListPageModel>

@if (Model != null && Model.Count > 0)
{
    <table style="width:100%">
        <thead>
            <tr style="border-bottom: 1px solid gray">
                <td>
                    NAME
                </td>
                <td>
                    SURNAME
```

```
                    </td>
                    <td>
                        Phone Number
                    </td>
                    @if (ViewBag.RenderActionColumn)
                    {
                        <td>
                        </td>
                    }
                </tr>
            </thead>
            <tbody>
                @foreach (var contactData in Model)
                {
                    <tr style="border-bottom: 1px solid red">
                        <td>
                            @contactData.Name
                        </td>
                        <td>
                            @contactData.Surname
                        </td>
                        <td>
                            @contactData.Country
                        </td>
                        @if (ViewBag.RenderActionColumn)
                        {
                            <td>
                                <a href="/Detail/@(contactData.Id)">Edit
Contact</a>
                            </td>
                        }
                    </tr>
                }
            </tbody>
        </table>
}
```

Observe that we use a List of the **ListPageModel** as a model of the page (model classes may be collections if necessary). We render a HTML table if the list has data by using a **foreach** loop. We decided to display an action column in our list page for redirecting to the Detail page and we decided to omit this column on the main page. We can control this condition by adding a Boolean field to the **ViewData** on the respective page model:

```
//List.cshtml.cs
    public class ListModel : PageModel
    {
        [BindProperty]
        public ListPageCriteriaModel Criteria { get; set; }

        public List<ListPageModel> List { get; set; }

        public ListModel()
        {
        }

        public void OnGet()
        {
            SetInitialData();
        }

        void SetInitialData()
        {

            this.ViewData["RenderActionColumn"] = true;
            //get the breadcrumb data here
            List<BreadCrumbModel> breadCrumbData = new
List<BreadCrumbModel>();
            breadCrumbData.Add(new BreadCrumbModel()
            {
                Text = "Main Page",
                Url = "/"
            });
            breadCrumbData.Add(new BreadCrumbModel()
            {
```

```csharp
                Text = "Phonebook List",
                Url = "/PhonebookList"
            });

        this.ViewData["BreadCrumbData"] = breadCrumbData;
    }


    public IActionResult OnPost()
    {
        SetInitialData();
        if (this.ModelState.IsValid)
        {
            // query phonebooks here

            this.List = new List<ListPageModel>()
            {
                new ListPageModel()
                {
                    Id=5,
                    Country="India",
                    Name="Queried Contact Name 1",
                    Surname="Queried Contact Surname 1"
                },
                new ListPageModel()
                {
                    Id=6,
                    Country="Russia",
                    Name="Queried Contact Name 2",
                    Surname="Queried Contact Surname 2"
                }
            };

        }
        return Page();
    }
}
```

Remember the **OnGet** and **OnPost** methods. The **OnGet** method runs when the page is first run. The **OnPost** method runs when a form is posted. We have made a private method **SetInitialData** to initialize the **ViewData** dictionary variable for our extra column and breadcrumb data.

> NOTE: When the page is first loaded, we must initialize the breadcrumb and extra column data for our table. We must do the same on the OnPost method because Http is stateless the server renders html, sends it to the client as a response, and forgets about the rest. The page rendered on the OnGet method is destroyed and must be rendered again. If not, our breadcrumb component will be rendered empty.

We also set the **RenderActionColumn** key to true in our list page, so the last column is rendered on the Razor page.

> TIP: Like the implementation in our example, we can set ViewData dictionary from our page model (we must because ASP.NET Core will not let us set ViewBag on the page model):
>
> this.ViewData["RenderActionColumn"] = true;
>
> And use the same key in our Razor page to access it from ViewBag:
>
> @if (ViewBag.RenderActionColumn)
>
> The reason for this is that the ViewBag looks up the ViewData dictionary internally, but the return type is dynamically resolved at run time, so we are not required to type cast the result value.

We put the **RenderPartial** method to our List page after the criteria panel just like we did to include the unobtrusive JavaScript:

```
@{ await Html.RenderPartialAsync("_ContactListPartial",Model.List); }
```

This extension method renders a partial Razor page. The first parameter is its name and the second parameter is its model. Here, the **List** property of the list page model becomes the model of the **_ContactListPartial** partial page.

We then modify the **OnGet** method of **Index.cshtml** (our main page) in the same manner. We set the **RenderActionColumn** parameter to false because we do not want to render the last action column in the table of our main page:

```
//index.cshtml.cs
        public List<ListPageModel> LastContactsList { get; set; }


        public void OnGet()
        {
            this.ViewData["RenderActionColumn"] = false;
```

```
    // load last contact records.
        this.LastContactsList = new List<ListPageModel>()
        {
            new ListPageModel()
            {
                Id=1,
                Country="India",
                Name="Last Contact Name 1",
                Surname="Last Contact Surname 1"
            },
            new ListPageModel()
            {
                Id=2,
                Country="Russia",
                Name="Last Contact Name 2",
                Surname="Last Contact Surname 2"
            },
            new ListPageModel()
            {
                Id=3,
                Country="Sweden",
                Name="Last Contact Name 3",
                Surname="Last Contact Surname 3"
            },
            new ListPageModel()
            {
                Id=4,
                Country="Germany",
                Name="Last Contact Name 4",
                Surname="Last Contact Surname 4"
            }
        };
    }

@* Index.cshtml *@
@page
```

```
@model IndexModel
@{
    ViewData["Title"] = "Home page";
}

<p>
    Latest contact information
</p>
@{ await Html.RenderPartialAsync("_ContactListPartial", Model.
LastContactsList); }
```

We call the **RenderPartial** method in a similar manner. Here is the output of our main page.

Latest contact information

NAME	SURNAME	Phone Number
Last Contact Name 1	Last Contact Surname 1	4896415365
Last Contact Name 2	Last Contact Surname 2	1645685643
Last Contact Name 3	Last Contact Surname 3	7981656532
Last Contact Name 4	Last Contact Surname 4	1231685445

Figure 5.14: Partial Razor in the main page

And here is the output of our list page:

Main Page / Contact List

Name:	test		Surname:	test	
Birth Year:				Search	

NAME	SURNAME	Phone Number	
Queried Contact Name 1	Queried Contact Surname 1	789478942	Edit Contact
Queried Contact Name 2	Queried Contact Surname 2	456565165	Edit Contact

Figure 5.15: Partial Razor in the list page

Partial pages help us developing common UI components for our applications in one place and improve productivity of front-end development greatly.

Controlling responses in Razor pages

We mentioned HTTP is a communication protocol between clients and servers; clients make requests and servers return responses. ASP.NET Core allows us to control the status code and content type of the response by the return type of the action methods of controllers or page model methods.

The Razor page models use convention over the configuration paradigm (the same with ASP.NET Core MVC) to save us from coding a lot of configuration. If we want to write the code to respond to specific Http methods, we must add a method with the naming convention `On{method name}Async`. The last Async part is optional. For example, to respond to post requests, we add the `OnPost` method, put requests `OnPut`, delete requests `OnDelete`, and so on.

Apart from `OnGet`, the other methods should return an implementation of the `IActionResult` interface. The `OnGet` returns nothing because it is executed when the page is first requested by the browser.

There are many methods we can use from the `PageModel` class to control response status codes and the type of response content (which is Content-Type header of the response). Some of them look like the following:

- **Page**: This returns a `PageResult` object. The Razor page associated with the page model is rendered and its HTML is returned.

- **File**: This takes a byte array and a string as the content type header as parameters. This returns a `FileContentResult` object. It allows downloading files.

- **Redirect**: This takes a URL as a parameter and returns a redirect result (sets one of **302**, **301**, **308** or **307** Http status codes).

These are the most common action results with the code Http 200. ASP.NET Core also has other result objects for status codes different than 200. Please refer to the methods section of the documentation located at **https://docs.microsoft.com/en-us/dotnet/api/microsoft.aspnetcore.mvc.razorpages.pagebase?view=aspnetcore-5.0** .

Now, we covered controlling responses. We will now explain ASP.NET Core tag helpers along with route parameters.

ASP.NET Core tag helpers, route parameters

Tag helpers are like helper extension methods and used for creating HTML markup in Razor files. The main difference between a tag helper and a HTML helper is that the tag helper looks like HTML markup by itself. For example, if we want to create a label and input HTML for a **title** field in our model, we can use the tag helper asp-for like the following:

```
<label asp-for="Title">Title Field</label>
<input asp-for="Title"/>
```

We can achieve the same thing with helper methods like the following:

```
@Html.LabelFor(t=> t.Title,"Title Field")
@Html.TextBoxFor(t=> t.Title)
```

> **NOTE:** The first thing comes to your mind may be tag helpers are markup strings, not method calls like HTML extensions, so we lose strongly typing. That is wrong. Tag helpers are compiled, error checked and Visual Studio Intellisense autocompletes our expressions like it does while using the HTML helper methods.

Tag helpers provide HTML-like front-end development experience. If you have front-end developers that do not know C#, you may consider using Tag helpers because extension methods require some C# coding knowledge.

Now, let us add a Detail page to our project for adding new contacts or editing existing contacts and see tag helpers in action along with route parameters.

Let us assume our detail page works in two ways. If the URL of the page is **/Contacts/Detail/{id of the contact}**, then our page is going to load the contact by its database id and render it on the screen. If the URL of the page is **/Contacts/Detail,** then we will open the page for saving new contact records.

We will add a route parameter named id for that. As described, it will be an optional parameter. We can define the route parameters on the **Startup** class inside the **ConfigureServices** method like we did to the contact lists:

```
public void ConfigureServices(IServiceCollection services)
{
    services.AddRazorPages((options) =>
    {
     options.Conventions.AddPageRoute("/Contacts/List", "ContactList");
        options.Conventions.AddPageRoute("/Contacts/Detail", "/Contacts/
Detail/{id:int?}");
    });
}
```

Or, on the Razor page itself with the **@page** directive:

```
@page "{id:int?}"
```

We can define the route parameter with its name between curly braces. We can also define its type after a colon character, and we can specify whether it is optional or not with the question mark parameter at the end.

We can define constraints such as range like the following:

```
"/Contacts/Detail/{id:range(10,50)}"
```

When we issue a request against the defined route constraints, ASP.NET Core returns a 404 not found response for us automatically.

Here is the Page model class of our detail page:

```csharp
//DetailModel.cshtml.cs
public class DetailModel : PageModel
{
 [BindProperty]
        public UserContactInfoDetailModel Detail { get; set; }

        [BindProperty(Name = "id", SupportsGet = true)]
        public int? Id { get; set; }

        public string Message { get; set; }

        public void OnGet()
        {
            SetBreadcrumbData();
            this.ViewData["RenderMessage"] = false;
            if (this.Id != null)
            {
                /*open the page in edit contact mode
                 load the contact record with id and assign it to the
Detail property
                 */
                this.Detail = new UserContactInfoDetailModel()
                {
                    Id = this.Id.Value
                };
            }
            else
            {
                /* open the page in new contact mode
                 */
            }
        }

public IActionResult OnPost()
{
SetBreadcrumbData();
```

```
      this.ViewData["RenderMessage"] = true;


      try
      {
            if (this.Id != null)
            {
                //contact already exists, update the contact
            }
            else
            {
                //contact is new, insert the contact
            }
         this.Message = "Contact is saved";
      }
      catch(Exception)
      {
//log error here
      Guid errorCode = Guid.NewGuid();
this.Message = $"An error occured in the application with code
{errorCode}. Please contact support";
}
      return Page();
}


void SetBreadcrumbData()
{
 //set breadcrumb data here
this.ViewData["BreadCrumbData"] = breadCrumbData;
}
}
```

We will need to define the **UserContactInfoDetailModel** class earlier for model binding, so we define a property named **Detail** with that type. We must also put the **BindProperty** attribute on it so we can get the posted detail data.

We also need to get the Id route parameter from the URL. Model binding can do that for us too. Remember it is an optional integer parameter, so we define a nullable integer parameter Id and put the **BindProperty** attribute on it. Model binding is case sensitive by default so we need to specify the route parameter with the **Name** property (because our properties' name is **Id** and our route parameters' name is **id**) and we must set the **SupportsGet** property true because we need the model binding bind route parameter upon opening page for the first time.

Let us explain the OnGet method next. We initialize the breadcrumb data because we use _BreadCrumbLayout as we use on the List page. Before this method is run, model binding has already bound necessary properties and we have access to them. We check whether there is an Id parameter in the route or not. If there is, then we load it by this Id property and set the Detail property with the loaded data; if there is no route parameter, then we render the page with default values.

We will also explain how to render JavaScript from Razor. We display messages by the alert JavaScript function and control it by the **RenderMessage** Boolean parameter inside the **ViewData** dictionary.

Next, we define the **OnPost** method because we want to get contact data from the UI via the form post. We would like to render a JavaScript alert function with the **Message** property. We use try catch and set the message appropriately. We check here if the route parameter Id is not null, then we update the contact; if it is null, we add a new contact. Now, we have explained using route parameters; let us show the Razor markup of the Detail page:

```
@page "{id:int?}"
@model Phonebook.Pages.Contacts.DetailModel
@{
    Layout = "_BreadCrumbLayout";
}
@if (ViewBag.RenderMessage)
{
    <script type="text/javascript">
        alert('@Model.Message');
    </script>
}


<form method="post">
    <input type="hidden" asp-for="Detail.Id" />
    <div class="container-fluid">
        <div class="row m-2">
            <div class="col-sm-2">
                Name:
            </div>
```

```
        <div class="col-sm-4">
            <input class="form-control" asp-for="Detail.Name" />
        </div>
        <div class="col-sm-2">
            Surname:
        </div>
        <div class="col-sm-4">
            <input class="form-control" asp-for="Detail.Surname" />
        </div>
    </div>
    <div class="row m-2">
        <div class="col-sm-2">
            Birth Date:
        </div>
        <div class="col-sm-4">
            <input class="form-control" asp-for="Detail.DateOfBirth"
/>
        </div>
        <div class="col-sm-2">
            Phone Number:
        </div>
        <div class="col-sm-4">
            <input class="form-control" asp-for="Detail.PhoneNumber"
/>
        </div>
    </div>
    <div class="row m-2">
        <div class="col-sm-2">
            Adress:
        </div>
        <div class="col-sm-10">
            <textarea class="form-control" asp-for="Detail.Address">
            </textarea>
        </div>
    </div>
    <div class="row m-2">
        <div class="col-sm-2">
```

```
            Country:
        </div>
        <div class="col-sm-4">
            <input class="form-control" asp-for="Detail.Country" />
        </div>
        <div class="col-sm-2">
        </div>
        <div class="col-sm-4">
            <input type="submit" value="Save" />
        </div>
    </div>
</div>
</form>
```

We define the route parameter ID on the @page directive, set the model, layout, and we render the alert JavaScript with our message property conditionally. We then use asp-for tag helpers for generating model bindings (which are generating the name HTML attributes like HTML helpers do). We put a hidden input field for binding the Id property of the **UserContactInfoDetailModel** object because we do not want to show it to the end user.

There are many tag helpers as much as html helper methods. They provide simpler front-end development compared to HTML helpers which are coded using the C#. For more information, please refer to the documentation located at **https://docs.microsoft.com/en-us/aspnet/core/mvc/views/tag-helpers/built-in/?view=aspnetcore-5.0**.

Introduction ASP.NET Core MVC

ASP.NET Core presents another framework named model view controller for developing web applications. The same framework was presented in ASP.NET in mid 2000s after ASP.NET web forms.

The user interfaces in MVC are written in the same way with Razor pages. We may use HTML helpers along with Razor markup or tag helpers. Before we delve into ASP.NET Core MVC, we will introduce the model view controller design pattern.

The model view controller is a design pattern and used for separating user interfaces with business logic. It accomplishes this by using three loose coupled components: Models, views, and controllers:

- **Model**: The object that carries data that is rendered on the view. View takes model objects and renders them. They are independent and unaware of the controller and view. In case of ASP.NET Core, model objects are C# classes that carry data. They can be commonly used **data transfer objects (DTO)** also.

- **View**: They are visual representations of data in model objects. They receive data from model objects and render user interfaces from them. They are aware of model objects, but they do not know about controllers. In case of ASP.NET Core, they are **cshtml** Razor views.

- **Controller**: It is the managing object and does the following in order:

    o   Receives input via web request.

    o   Processes input and prepares the model object.

    o   Passes the model object to the View.

    o   Returns rendered HTML via the view as a response.

If we compare Razor pages and MVC, Razor pages are simpler than MVC. There is only a page, its model, and data binding mechanism work between them. We can even add the @functions block to Razor pages and omit the page model class. Figuring the location of items in MVC can be hard but MVC is much more organized and structured. If your project has too many user interfaces and dynamic navigations between them, you should consider using MVC instead of Razor pages:

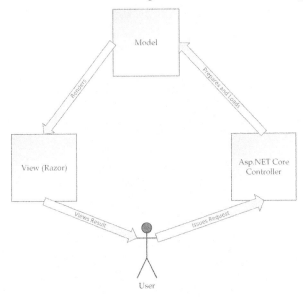

Figure 5.16: *MVC design pattern*

Let us add a new project from **Create New Project** | **ASP.NET Core Web App (Model-View-Control)** and explore the folder structure:

- **wwwroot**: This contains static assets like CSS, JavaScript, and custom library files.

- **Controllers**: This contains controller classes.

- **Models**: This contains model classes.

- **Views**: This contains subfolders for every controller and every subfolder contains respective Razor views that belong to their controllers. The `Index.cshtml` is the default view for every controller. Also, it contains the shared folder for common partial views and layout pages.

The default routing in ASP.NET Core MVC is `/{controller name}/{action method name}/{route parameters}`. Every controller follows the same naming convention {name}Controller and derived from a base class named `Controller`. Action methods are the actual methods in controllers that do the job. They are executed by issued requests and they return responses.

Let us try to create the same application as we did with Razor pages for MVC. We add a controller class named `ListController` under the `Controllers` folder and derive it from the `Controller` class, and then we add a folder named `List` under the `Views` folder, add a Razor page `Index.cshtml` inside of it and add a model class named `ListModel` in the `Models` folder:

Figure 5.17: ASP.NET Core MVC folder structure

Please note we use the same model classes and views from the previous Razor pages project:

```
// ListModel class
public class ListModel
{
    public List<ListPageModel> List { get; set; }

    public ListPageCriteriaModel Criteria { get; set; }
}


// ListController class
public class ListController : Controller
{
public IActionResult Index()
        {
            SetInitialData();
            ListModel model = new ListModel();
            return View(model);
        }


        [HttpPost]
    public IActionResult PostFormData([FromForm] ListPageCriteriaModel
criteria)
        {
            SetInitialData();
            ListModel model = null;
            if (this.ModelState.IsValid)
            {
                // query phonebooks here
                model = new ListModel()
                {
                    List = new List<ListPageModel>()
                    {
                        new ListPageModel()
                        {
                            Id=5,
```

```
                        PhoneNumber="789478942",
                        Name="Queried Contact Name 1",
                        Surname="Queried Contact Surname 1"
                    },
                    new ListPageModel()
                    {
                        Id=6,
                        PhoneNumber="456565165",
                        Name="Queried Contact Name 2",
                        Surname="Queried Contact Surname 2"
                    }
                }
            };
        }
        return View("Index",model);
    }
}
```

We use the same Razor page as a view with its model changed to **ListModel,** and we will omit Views in this part of the chapter. MVC views are developed by the same Razor markup, layout and partial views work the same way as they do in Razor pages.

Let us examine controllers. They are the manager objects that handle requests, prepare, and send the model to the appropriate views. They run this process with the methods called action methods. The **Index** method is the default action method of controllers; they are executed when the controller is first issued from the browser. When we type **/List** or **/List/Index,** the **Index** action method of the **ListController** is executed. Notice the action methods return an object that implements the **IActionResult** interface. When we examine the **Index** method of **ListController,** we will notice that it prepares the default model and returns a **ViewResult** by executing the View method and passing the model to it.

This is how a controller controls response types like page model classes in Razor Pages. The action methods return result objects by using methods from the base Controller class. The **View** method returns **ViewResult** by passing the model and executing the associated View. In the case of **ListController,** it returns **ViewResult** by rendering the **Index.cshtml** located in **Views/List/Index.cshtml** along with passing an instance of **ListPageModel**.

Then, we create an action method named **PostFormData** (can be anything you like) for receiving the criteria data from the HTML form and rendering it on the page. We can control routing with attributes in the MVC framework. Some of them are **Route**, **HttpGet**, **HttpPost**, and so on. We put the **HttpPost** attribute here for restricting this action method to Post requests only.

Model binding works nearly the same way as Razor pages. We add a parameter to our method **PostFormData** with type **ListPageCriteriaModel** to load our criteria data from the request. We must specify the source of data for model binding to work. Notice that we put a **FromForm** attribute to the criteria parameter and this instructs the model binder to bind the form encoded data from the request message body. We can instruct the model binder to bind objects from the query string with **FromQuery**, JSON objects with **FromBody,** or route parameters from route with **FromRoute**.

Notice that we return a **ViewResult** by executing an overload of the View method. It takes the name of the view and model. We give the view name Index because if we do not, it will look for a view that is named the same with the action method name (which is **PostFormData** in this example) by default.

Conclusion

We covered how to create web applications with Razor pages and the MVC framework. We will cover how to develop Restful services with ASP.NET Core in the next chapter.

Questions

1. Suppose you are developing a web page and you coded the necessary validation by JavaScript. Is this enough? If not, explain reasons.

2. Suppose you are developing a web page and you coded the necessary validation in the backend server side. Is this enough? If not, explain reasons.

3. Let us assume you are developing a web application with many pages. Some of the pages require a menu on the top and some of the pages require menu on the left. How do you handle this without rendering the menu on every page?

4. Let us assume you redirect your user to another page in your application, but you want to carry a small amount of data. How can you achieve it in a simple way?

5. You are asked to create a web application with four or five UI pages. Should you use MVC or Razor pages?

CHAPTER 6
Developing Restful Services with ASP. NET Core

Introduction

We covered razor pages and MVC in the previous chapter. We will cover web services, REST, and creating web API applications with ASP.NET Core. We will show how easy developing Restful services or web services with ASP.NET Core.

Structure

In this chapter, we will discuss the following topics:

- Introducing web services, web APIs, and REST
- Developing ASP.NET Core web API applications
- Using configuration in ASP.NET Core applications

Objectives

After reading this chapter, you will be able to understand web APIs and start developing web API applications with ASP.NET Core.

Introducing web services, web API, and REST

We connect to Internet, open our browsers, type an URL, and navigate through World Wide Web every day. We manipulate or query data and get what we need for. The same thing is also relevant for software programs. Sometimes, they need to query or manipulate data on other software programs. But they do not use browsers or mobile apps like we do. They use web services.

The web services are programmatic interfaces that allow a software program to manipulate or query data of other software programs. It is like a human accessing a web site with a browser. Web services are programmatic interfaces for software applications like user interfaces for humans.

The web services brought new advantages for software development. A new paradigm, **service-oriented architecture (SOA)** is invented.

SOA is a software architecture that allows us to divide the software into loosely coupled, cohesive web service applications. We get a better separation of concerns, and we maintain and scale the certain parts of software without affecting other parts.

It is like the class design. When a module or component of a software is developed, its classes are designed by applying SOLID principles, loose coupling, cohesion, and so on. Designing the software with SOA is someway the macro level of class design. We divide the software into small service applications and encapsulate them into loosely coupled, independent, cohesive web services.

With the advance of cloud computing and cloud native, SOA evolved into microservices, which is popular nowadays.

The web services allow integration between software applications, and they are independent of the platform and programming language. For example, a web service developed in Java can be consumed by a .NET application or vice versa. Since it uses HTTP for transportation, the server platform becomes irrelevant also. A web service hosted in Windows can access another web service hosted in Linux. Common protocols and standards were developed for this requirement.

Simple Object Access Protocol (SOAP) was a protocol developed for exchanging messages over http for web services. It is an xml-based intermediate language that can invoke resources on the servers. Nearly, every programming language can understand and use XML. A soap message XML has a special structure and must satisfy the soap xml schema. It contains an envelope, and the envelope contains header block and body block (these are XML tags).

Microsoft has **Windows Communication Foundation (WCF)** for developing web services. WCF supports multiple protocols such as `http`, `udp`, `named pipe`.

The term **Application Programming Interface (API)** is a communication agreement with conventions based on data used by software programs for communicating and integrating them. The web services and web APIs are overlapping terms and they are confused with each other.

Both are remote procedure activation calls but web services are resources that fulfill a specific task. APIs allow us to create applications that depend on other application data. All web services are APIs but not every API is a web service. Web services can use different protocols, but they must use the SOAP convention. APIs are not tied to any protocol or format, and they are based on negotiations determined by the designers of the API.

One of the common patterns for web APIs is **Representational State Transfer (REST)**. It uses http protocols and http methods like get, post, and so on.

A restful service is a web API that is defined by:

- A base URL such as {http}://{some IP or DNS name}/ or {http}://{some IP or DNS name}/{api or whatever we want}. Then, the operations are appended as suffixes to this base URL. For example, if our base service is **https://someservice.com/api,** then we define our service operations by **https://someservice.com/api/getitems,** **https://someservice.com/api/insertitems**, and so on.

- Its operations are defined by http methods. The common ones are as follows:
    - GET: This fetches data from the web API.
    - POST: This creates a new item in the web API.
    - PUT: This updates an item in the web API.
    - PATCH: This updates an item in the web API by defining a   set of instructions.
    - DELETE: This deletes an item on the web API.

- A content type for serialization, deserialization of data. May be an XML but occasionally JSON is used.

There are certain benefits of using RESTful services compared to traditional web services. They can use HTTPS by default. JSON serialization, deserialization is much faster than SOAP XML messages and JSON data occupy less space. We also have the ASP.NET Core features such as model binding, routing, URL rewriting at our disposal.

Let us consider a scenario where we create a web API for our phonebook project that enables listing, inserting, or deleting phonebook data. The other programs will be able to use this service for the specified operations and integrate into our phonebook application. We will open the MVC project we created in *Chapter 5, Developing ASP.NET Core Web Applications with Razor* and add a controller named

ContactController and then add an action method named **QueryContacts** as in the following code:

```
public class ContactController : Controller
{
 [HttpPost]
 public IActionResult QueryContacts([FromBody] ListPageCriteriaModel
criteria)
 {
    var list = new List<ListPageModel>()
    //query contacts here
    return Json(list);
 }
}
```

We make it to work with post requests and accept our criteria model class discussed earlier. When we send the following request, we will see that the model binding works and our action method is triggered and works correctly:

```
POST /Contact/QueryContacts HTTP/1.1
Host: localhost:26972
Content-Type: application/json
Cache-Control: no-cache
Postman-Token: 57000a1d-ab53-037a-49a7-41733df2e7c5

{
"Name":"abc",
      "Surname":"def"
}
```

Notice that we use the Json method of the **Controller** class that we derived from and return a list of contacts:

```
[
    {
        "id": 5,
        "name": "Queried Contact Name 1",
        "surname": "Queried Contact Surname 1",
        "phoneNumber": "789478942"
```

```
    },
    {
        "id": 6,
        "name": "Queried Contact Name 2",
        "surname": "Queried Contact Surname 2",
        "phoneNumber": "456565165"
    }
]
```

Our action method returns a **JsonResult** object and serializes our list of contacts to json and returns it as a response. This is one way of creating a web API in ASP.NET Core. This method can be useful if you are developing a web site with user interfaces making a few Ajax requests, and you want a few other software applications integrate to your application by using a limited number of endpoints.

But if you plan to develop:

- A service project with no user interfaces.

- An enterprise application that has many different front ends for the same backend. For example, an application with web user interfaces consists of HTML pages, mobile applications, desktop clients, other software applications and all these connect to your backend as shown in *Figure 6.1*.

You should consider using the ASP.NET Core web API project with API controllers for your backend instead of ASP.NET Core MVC. Unlike MVC controllers that render Razor, API controllers are optimized for return of data in various formats (JSON, XML, and so on).

Consider using the ASP.NET Core MVC project with a monolithic architecture as shown in the following figure. You have many different front-end clients, including web and third-party applications that integrate your backend application:

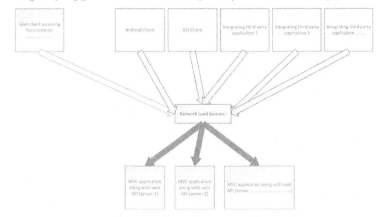

Figure 6.1: *Monolithic architecture with MVC application*

The problem in this architecture, the API that mobile clients and integrating applications use the same application with html renderers (Razor). The concurrent load comes from mobile applications together with integrating third-party applications and the browsers that render user interfaces (Razor pages) are in the same server application and affecting each other. For example, in a period of a month we can have more load coming from web clients (browsers) and in some other period, we can have more load coming from mobile clients and integrating applications for using our API. We also must deploy the same API just for deploying changes made to the razor pages which complicates maintenance.

For these types of scenarios such as enterprise applications that have many different front ends or many integrating applications, it is much better to separate front-end operations and data operations like in the following figure:

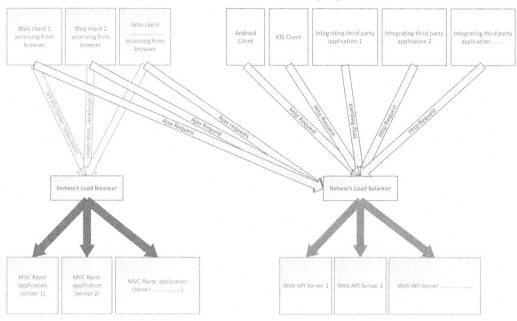

Figure 6.2: *A monolithic architecture with separated UI and API layers*

> **NOTE: There are more different types of monolithic architectures; we will omit the rest for the sake of simplicity. You can also omit ASP.NET Core MVC for front-end and develop the front end with one of the popular front-end frameworks such as Angular, React, and so on.**

The advantage of separating UI rendering and API for backend operations is, we can scale the API and web user interface rendering independent of each other. We may require more processing power for the applications to integrate into our services and add another web API server behind the network load balancer, if we require more processing power for server-side HTML rendering (usually this is not required, and the API part of the applications are scaled most) we can add another server for the front-end MVC application.

> NOTE: If your project contains many different parts of domains and it is not certain how many concurrent request handling for every part you require, then you should consider the Microservices architecture.

Developing ASP.NET Core Web API applications

Let us explore ASP.NET by adding a new project named **Phonebook.API** from **Create New Project | ASP.NET Core Web API** and transfer our model classes we developed for our MVC project earlier.

> TIP: We are copy pasting model classes for the sake of simplicity. You should put these classes in the library projects to avoid code duplication and consider using the layered architecture.

Since API controllers are optimized for returning data, there are only controllers in ASP.NET Core API projects. Let us add a new controller named **ContactsController** to our project.

We also need to return error messages and error status to the consumer of our service. Remember, **http** is an extensible protocol, and it is based on negotiation. We can do it in different ways; one of them is creating a base structure to carry common data (error status of the service operation, messages, and other common data). Let us add a service result class to return data from our services:

```
public class ServiceResult
{
    public bool HasError { get; private set; } = false;

    public String Message { get; private set; }

    public ServiceResult(String errorMessage)
    {
        this.HasError = true;
        this.Message = errorMessage;
    }

    public ServiceResult()
    {
```

```
        }
    }
```

If an error happened during service operation, we need to inform the consumers of the service that an error occurred with an error message at response as a bare minimum requirement. We can add an Enum for the type of errors, separate business logic errors or validation errors, and so on, and fill this class with extra information as we want.

We can use the preceding **ServiceResult** class for running operations that do not need to return an object such as adding, updating, or deleting. For the service operations that return an object or a collection of objects, we can create classes that can be derived from **ServiceResult**:

```
public class ServiceObjectResult<T> : ServiceResult
{
    public T Data { get; private set; }

    public ServiceObjectResult(string errorMessage) : base(errorMessage)
    {

    }

    public ServiceObjectResult(T data)
    {
        this.Data = data;
    }
}
```

We can return single objects as a response in this class. We can take the advantage of C# generics for type independence. For returning a collection of objects, we can use the following **ServiceListResult** class:

```
public class ServiceListResult<T> : ServiceResult
{
    public List<T> Data { get; private set; }

    public ServiceListResult(List<T> data)
    {
        this.Data = data;
    }
```

```
    public ServiceListResult() : base()
    {

    }

    public ServiceListResult(String errorMessage) : base(errorMessage)
    {

    }
}
```

> **TIP: Always plan your service projects contract at the design phase. It is essential how common or varying data is placed at responses or requests. Http is an extensible protocol and consistency is the key here. You can get a negative reaction from the consumers of your service if you decide to change your services contract after consumers start using your service.**

As mentioned here, we will always include the error status and message whether we return an object, collection of objects or not. The consumers of the service can create similar classes like this and use deserialization:

```
[ApiController]
public class ContactsController : ControllerBase
{
    [HttpGet("api/[controller]/[action]")]
    public ActionResult<ServiceListResult<ListPageModel>> GetAll()
    {
        ActionResult<ServiceListResult<ListPageModel>> result = null;
        ServiceListResult<ListPageModel> serviceListingResult = null;
        try
        {
            List<ListPageModel> list = null;
            //get all contacts and prepare list
            serviceListingResult = new
ServiceListResult<ListPageModel>(list);
            result = new ActionResult<ServiceListResult<ListPageModel>>(
            serviceListingResult
            );
        }
```

```
        catch (Exception ex)
        {
            //log error and return a meaningfull message
            serviceListingResult = new
ServiceListResult<ListPageModel>("error code .... please consult system
administrator");
        }
        return result;
    }


    [HttpGet("api/[controller]/[action]/{id}")]
    public ActionResult<ServiceObjectResult<UserContactInfoDetailModel>>
GetById(
    [FromRoute] int id)
    {
        ActionResult<ServiceObjectResult<UserContactInfoDetailModel>>
result = null;
        ServiceObjectResult<UserContactInfoDetailModel>
contactOperationResult = null;
        try
        {
            //get contact by id
            UserContactInfoDetailModel contact = null;
            if (contact == null)
            {
                return NotFound();
            }
            contactOperationResult = new
ServiceObjectResult<UserContactInfoDetailModel>          (contact);
        }
        catch (Exception e)
        {
            //log error and return a meaningfull message
            contactOperationResult = new
ServiceObjectResult<UserContactInfoDetailModel>("error code .... please
consult system administrator");
        }
        result = new
```

```
ActionResult<ServiceObjectResult<UserContactInfoDetailModel>>(
        contactOperationResult);
        return result;
    }
}
```

After we define our data fetching operations by the get request, we define manipulating action methods by **post, put,** and **delete**:

```
bool HasAuthorization()
{
    //implement authorization check
}


[HttpPost("api/[controller]/[action]")]
public ActionResult<ServiceResult> Insert([FromBody]
UserContactInfoDetailModel model)
{
    ActionResult<ServiceResult> result = null;
    ServiceResult serviceInsertOperationResult = null;
    try
    {
        if (!HasAuthorization())
        {
            return Unauthorized();
        }
        //insert new contact
        serviceInsertOperationResult = new ServiceResult();
    }
    catch (Exception e)
    {
        //log error and return a meaningfull message
        serviceInsertOperationResult = new ServiceResult("An error
occured with code....please consult system administrator");
    }
    result = new
ActionResult<ServiceResult>(serviceInsertOperationResult);
    return result;
}
```

```
[HttpPut("api/[controller]/[action]/{id}")]
public ActionResult<ServiceResult> Update([FromRoute] int id, [FromBody]
UserContactInfoDetailModel model)
{
    ActionResult<ServiceResult> result = null;
    ServiceResult serviceUpdateOperationResult = null;
    try
    {
        if (!HasAuthorization())
        {
            return Unauthorized();
        }
        //update existing contact
        serviceUpdateOperationResult = new ServiceResult();
    }
    catch (Exception e)
    {
        //log error and return a meaningfull message
        serviceUpdateOperationResult = new ServiceResult("An error
occured with code....please consult system administrator");
    }
    result = new
ActionResult<ServiceResult>(serviceUpdateOperationResult);
    return result;
}


[HttpDelete("api/[controller]/[action]/{id}")]
public ActionResult<ServiceResult> Delete([FromRoute] int id)
{
    ActionResult<ServiceResult> result = null;
    ServiceResult serviceDeleteOperationResult = null;
    try
    {
        if (!HasAuthorization())
        {
            return Unauthorized();
```

```
        }
        //delete contact
        serviceDeleteOperationResult = new ServiceResult();
    }
    catch (Exception e)
    {
        //log error and return a meaningfull message
        serviceDeleteOperationResult = new ServiceResult("An error
occured with code....please consult system administrator");
    }
    result = new
ActionResult<ServiceResult>(serviceDeleteOperationResult);
    return result;
}
```

> **NOTE: We show one of the many ways to return and receive data in service contracts. You may choose various other ways. For example, adding or asking custom http headers, using query strings, and so on. There are surely more sophisticated ways to handle authorization and error handling; we will omit them for simplicity.**

ASP.NET Core API controllers are derived from **ControllerBase** and have the **ApiController** attributes. As mentioned earlier, these enable optimizations specific to API controllers.

We return **ActionResult< >** as a response and the generic parameter changes to:

- **ServiceObjectResult<>** if we return a single object such as getting object by ID.

- **ServiceListResult<>** if we return a collection of objects such as listing.

- **ServiceResult** if we return only the status of the service operation.

We also utilize model binding by **FromRoute** and **FromBody** attributes on our method parameters and use routing by **HttpGet**, **HttpPost**, **HttpPut**, **HttpDelete** attributes above our methods. The route patterns in these routing attributes such as **api/[controller]/[action]/{id}** are like the route patterns we explained in the previous chapter, but we have tokens at our disposal this time such as [controller] and [action]. The route pattern **api/[controller]/[action]/{id}** means the request URL must contain controller class name and action method name and an **id** parameter. Therefore we can specify the URL like **api/{controller class name without controller suffix }/{action method name}/{id}**. This provides simplified route specification.

We can also use the methods in **ControllerBase** to change the response status code other than 200. We set the status code to 404 not found if the **GetById** method fails to find the contact by the ID, or we set the code to 401 if the user is unauthorized.

> **NOTE: We return ActionResult<> if everything goes smoothly in every method and NotFoundResult for trying to fetch contacts that do not exist and UnauthorizedResult if the user is not authorized. If we go to the definition of these classes, we find that they are derived from the ActionResult interface (ActionResult<> is not derived but converted to ActionResult by C# operators). If you plan to employ http headers in response, then it is good to use ActionResult<> for simplicity. But if you do not need to employ http status codes and use another way to tell the clients about the status of the service operation, you may just return your types from action methods.**

Also note how we handle errors; all our objects we return are derived from **ServiceResult** and we set the **HasError** property and error message in the catch fields of our code.

This is enough for web API development; just remember you need to decide for a reasonable and consistent service contract and stick to it while developing its methods.

Using configuration in ASP.NET Core applications

We will explain loading and using configuration data in ASP.NET Core. It is not just specific to ASP.NET Core but common in all .NET Core projects. .NET Core can build configuration data from many different sources such as the **appsettings.json** file in the project, environment variables, command line arguments, and so on.

We explained entry point of the ASP.NET Core projects located in the static Main method of the Program class. When we examine, a method named **CreateHostBuilder** is created automatically:

```
public static IHostBuilder CreateHostBuilder(string[] args) =>
    Host.CreateDefaultBuilder(args)
        .ConfigureWebHostDefaults(webBuilder =>
        {
            webBuilder.UseStartup<Startup>();
        });
```

There is a fluent syntax and a call to **CreateDefaultBuilder** method. It loads and prepares the configuration by the default configuration builder and prepares configuration by the **appsettings.json** file in the project, environment variables, and command line arguments.

> **NOTE: The appsettings files must be included in the output directory of the published application if you want to load the configuration from it. Do not forget to include them by right clicking on them and setting the Copy To Output Directory value to Copy Always or Copy If Newer in the properties window.**

If we want to include configuration just from environment variables or command line arguments, we can use the **ConfigureAppConfiguration** method and set them in the action method parameter:

```
ConfigureAppConfiguration(builder =>
        {
                builder.AddEnvironmentVariables("VariablePrefx");
                builder.AddCommandLine(args);
        })
```

We can have different configurations for our different runtime environments. We can set configuration variables and have different **appsettings.json** files for each of them. We put common and immutable variables in every runtime environment to the **appsettings.{environment name}.json** file. For example, if we would like to enable our logging in development, test, production environments. We can give it a name **EnableLogging** and set it **true** in the **appsettings.json** file. .NET Core takes the **appsettings.json** and **appsettings.{ASPNETCORE_ENVIRONMENT environment variable value}.json** files and merges their values while loading the configuration data. We can include as many **appsettings.json** files as we would like to such as **appsettings.Development.json**, **appsettings.Test.json**, **appsettings.Production.json**, **appsettings.Staging.json**, and so on. The values **appsettings.{env name}.json** file with the environment name overrides the same values in **appsettings.json** file. For example if we have EnableLogging key with value equals to 0 in **appsettings.json** and we have the same key has the value 1 in **appsettings.Test.json** file and our environment name is **Test** then we will get EnableLogging configuration value to 1 in our code.

Now, we have explained loading the configuration data; let us explain using it. We simply inject the **IConfiguration** interface in a controller or a class registered by dependency injection. We can access key value pair config data by C# index notation ["{key name}"]. Let us assume we have the following **appsettings.json** file and injected **IConfiguration** interface by the variable named configuration:

```
{
  "Logging": {
    "LogLevel": {
```

```
      "Default": "Information",
      "Microsoft": "Warning",
      "Microsoft.Hosting.Lifetime": "Information"
    }
  },
  "FileUploadConfiguration": [
    {
      "Extension": "pdf",
      "AllowedSize": "10",
      "CanPreview": true,
      "MimeType": "application/pdf"
    },
    {
      "Extension": "JPG",
      "AllowedSize": "5",
      "CanPreview": true,
      "MimeType": "image/jpeg"
    },
    {
      "Extension": "zip",
      "AllowedSize": "10",
      "CanPreview": false
    }
  ],
  "StoragePath": "C:\\Storage"
}
```

We can get the value of the **StoragePath** configuration variable by getting the return value of **configuration["StoragePath"]**. We can also use the generic get<> method of the **IConfiguration** interface for number and Boolean variables.

We can also use binding to bind object and arrays to our classes. Let us assume we have an array of configuration with the key **FileUploadConfiguration**. We can create a class with properties having the same name with JSON keys in appsettings file:

```
public class FileUploadConfig
{
public string Extension { get; set; }
```

```
//the size in megabytes
public int AllowedSize { get; set; }

public bool CanPreview { get; set; }

public String MimeType { get; set; }
}
```

Then, we can use the **getsection** method of **IConfiguration** to get the partial section of the **appsettings.json** file and then use the generic get method to bind configuration data to our list of objects:

```
var arrayOfConfig= configuration.GetSection("FileUploadConfig").
Get<List<FileUploadConfig>>();
```

Conclusion

We learned the web APIs, its importance, and usage fields of ASP.NET Core Web API projects and how to manage the configuration. We will learn middleware and async await pattern in the next chapter.

Questions

1. Assume you start a new project that has a web client, Android client, IOS client and many potential third-party applications that would like to integrate to your application. Should you separate your UI rendering part and API part? Why?

2. You have common configuration variables that are the same for every runtime environment. Where do you include them? Why?

CHAPTER 7

The Async/Await Pattern and Middleware in ASP. NET Core

Introduction

We covered web and restful services in the previous chapter. We will cover asynchronous programming with the async/await pattern and middleware in ASP. NET Core.

Structure

In this chapter, we will discuss the following topics:

- Introducing the asynchronous programming model in .NET
- Using the async/await pattern and its importance
- Configuring the ASP.NET Core pipeline with middlewares

Objectives

After reading this chapter, you will be able to understand asynchronous code in ASP. NET Core with the async/await pattern and learn how to program the ASP.NET Core pipeline with middlewares.

Introduction to the asynchronous programming model

Asynchronous programming allows us to write non-blocking responsive applications or applications that can take advantage of more CPU cores. We can avoid performance loss, make our UI responsive, and most importantly utilize more CPU cores of the application server. This enables us to scale our application by moving it to a server with more CPU cores (or with more threading capability) without changing our code and improve its performance. It is essential to make the user interface responsive and applications that render a user interface runs with a message loop.

The message loop is simply a loop just like while or similar loops that runs endlessly until the application is terminated. At every loop cycle, the framework checks whether there is any user input, executes events based on that input, and renders the UI. The UI thread is simply the main thread of the program that runs this loop:

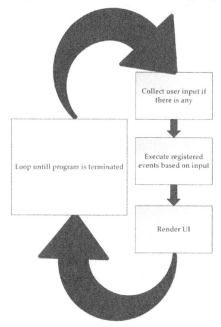

Figure 7.1: *A simple message loop in a UI thread*

> **TIP:** Earlier, the message loop was exposed directly to the developers such as in **Win32 C++ programming, but now it is hidden from the developer and the UI development is based on event driven programming or MVVM.**

Now, let us assume we have a long running job in a button or mouse click event. The message loop is blocked until that job is finished and UI rendering is stopped. We can prove that by checking whether the UI is locked and no other button or UI elements are working until that blocking code is finished and the loop continues to run and render the UI. With the help of asynchronous programming, we can avoid blocking the UI thread.

> **NOTE: Browsers are also UI rendering programs, and they have a message loop too. We explained AJAX requests to avoid blocking the UI thread which is working with the same principles.**

We can create a new thread in the event handlers of UI elements and run our time-consuming tasks inside them. The message loop is not blocked, and our UI becomes responsive because the time-consuming task code is run in parallel with the message loop. We can set and arrange necessary variables in the message loop from the code, run in the thread, and control UI rendering by them from our separate thread:

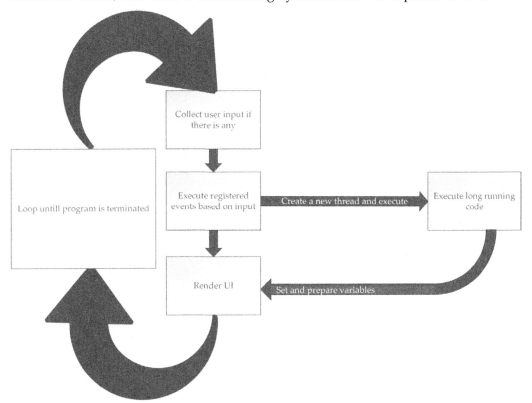

Figure 7.2: Non-blocking asynchronous code outside of UI thread

We have mentioned about not blocking the UI thread as subsidiary information. ASP. NET Core works on the server side and of course, does not have an UI thread, but server applications need to utilize CPU cores as much as they do. If your application is CPU sensitive, adding another server behind the network load balancer simply will not be enough. You should move and deploy your application to stronger servers with more CPU cores. If you do not employ asynchronous programming in your code, you will not benefit from the servers with more cores to their full potential.

Asynchronous programming was hard, uncomfortable to write, and error prone. The async/await pattern simplifies it greatly. Earlier, we would write the async code like the following in a sketchy event-driven manner:

```
var someAsyncTask1=new …..
someAsyncTask1.Start();
    someAsyncTask1.Completed += ()=>{
    var someAsyncTask2 = new …..
    someAsyncTask2.Start();
    someAsyncTask2.Completed += ()=>{
        ………goes on
    }
}
```

We have sequential tasks that start one after another, and we start the next asynchronous task in the completed events and the preceding code can become a spaghetti and hard to understand.

The async/await pattern saves us from events and eases our asynchronous development experience greatly. Let us assume we have a method named **DoSomethingAsync** like the following:

```
public async Task<string> DoSomethingAsync()
{
    Task<string> timeConsumingTask= Do_SomethingTimeConsuming_Async();
    DoSomethingIndependent();

    …

    …

    …

    …

    string resultString = await timeConsumingTask;
    return resultString;
}
```

The preceding code runs **Do_SomethingTimeConsuming_Async** asynchronously and the execution of the code is not stopped because it is an asynchronous method and a separate thread is created to run it. To use the async/await pattern, every asynchronous method must return **Task<{return type}>** and their return type must be in the generic parameter. For async methods with void return type, the return type must be **Task**.

> **NOTE:** If you have both synchronous and asynchronous versions of the same method (you easily notice .NET Core framework built in methods have), you would like to follow the same convention with .NET for synchronous {method name} and asynchronous {method name}Async versions.

After starting **DoSomethingTimeConsumingAsync** on another thread, we can run another synchronous method **DoSomethingIndependent** independent from the job being done in the previously started **DoSomethingTimeConsumingAsync** method. We then wait until **DoSomethingTimeConsumingAsync** finishes. The Await keyword blocks the execution until the asynchronous method is completed and automatically assigns the generic parameter of the Task type as a return value. The execution of the preceding code ends in two possible orders:

- The **DoSomethingTimeConsumingAsync** method finishes before the completion of **DoSomethingIndependent**.

- The **DoSomethingIndependent** method finishes before **DoSomethingTimeConsumingAsync** is completed.

In either way, we managed to run two methods at the same time without blocking one by another. We can also use the **WhenAll** method (also returns a Task object) of the **Task** class to wait until multiple asynchronous tasks are completed as shown in the following code:

```
public async Task DoSomethingAsync()
{
    Task task1=StartTask1Async();
    Task task2=StartTask2Async();
    Task task3=StartTask3Async();


    DoSomethingIndependent();
    …

    …

    …

    …
    List<Task> tasks=new List<Task>(){task1,task2,task3};
    await Task.WhenAll(tasks);
}
```

The **await** keyword in the preceding code blocks all the tasks until they are completed. This way we can parallelize independent tasks run together.

> TIP: You may parallelize independent tasks easily, but if they are interdependent on each other to some extent, you must use synchronization constructs such as locks, mutexes, or concurrent data structures and fine tune them carefully. If you do not, you may not get advantage of asynchronous programming as you expect, or your code may produce a dead lock.

If we want to cancel an async task, the .NET framework provides the cancellation token, and we can use it to cancel our async tasks. We must create a **CancellationTokenSource** object and pass its **Token** property to the **async** method:

```
CancellationTokenSource cts = new CancellationTokenSource();
.
.
.
.
var task = System.IO.File.AppendAllLinesAsync("some path to a file",
null, cts.Token);
.
.
.
//cancel in case of something happens
cts.Cancel();
```

Then, we can call the **Cancel** method of the cancellation token to cancel the async task. We can apply this to the action methods of ASP.NET Core Controllers too:

```
public async ActionResult<Task> GetSomethingAsync(CancellationToken
token)
{
...
.
}
```

We can include **CancellationToken** as a method parameter in the action method, and it is passed to the method automatically by the model binding. Then, we pass this token to the async methods called inside the action method. When the browser that is making the request is refreshed or stopped by the command button in the address bar, the async method currently running inside the action method is automatically cancelled by ASP.NET Core. We can use this to save server resources to some extent if we do not need the request to be completed whether it is stopped or if the browser is refreshed.

The point is making things execute parallel as much as possible. For example, if you have a database layer and a business layer calling methods from database layers, do not await at the database layer. Make them async methods and return the **Task<>** objects and await at the business layer. This way you can parallelize independent database operations.

Introducing Middlewares and ASP.NET Core pipeline

ASP.NET Core has a very flexible request pipeline. Before introducing it, we will explain the chain of responsibility design pattern.

The chain of responsibility pattern decouples the sender of a request and multiple receivers and allows multiple handlers to handle the request. It abstracts the processing of elements as a pipeline and the sender sends a request to the beginning of the pipeline and the request passes from handler to handler until some handler is found and handles it:

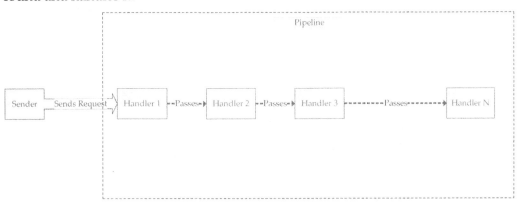

Figure 7.3: A pipeline by chain of responsibility

The sender sends a request to the pipeline and each handler checks whether it is suitable to handle, and if it is not, then it passes to the next handler until it is handled or is not.

Design patterns are proven practices that are used to solve a specific problem. They are used by developers and contained in some parts of the frameworks. The Middleware pipeline of ASP.NET Core is a different example of the chain of responsibility pattern. Requests can be handled more than one handler (middleware) and responses are handled by more than a handler too before they are returned to the sender (client). The pipeline is configured in the **Configure** method of the Startup class. We call the Run, Map, Use extension methods of the **IApplicationBuilder** interface passed to the Startup class:

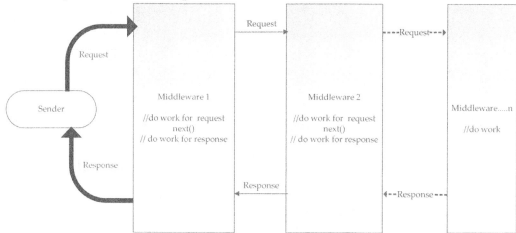

Figure 7.4: *ASP.NET Core middleware pipeline*

The order of middlewares is important and many of them are built in middleware in the pipeline of ASP.NET Core. The built in middlewares handle exceptions, cors, hsts, redirection, static files, routing, authorization, authentication, and many more. The order and configuration of them are different in API, MVC, and Razor pages.

The **use** method is used for both request and response handling. It has the following structure:

```
app.Use(async (context, next) =>
{
    //analyze request and do work
    //context.Request;
    await next.Invoke();
    //analyze response and do work
    //context.Response;
});
```

The delegate of the first middleware is executed when a request arrives at the server, and we can check whether our middleware is interested in that request such as by checking the URL or a request header. Then, we can write something to response, short circuit and terminate the request or pass the execution to the next middleware by calling the **Invoke** method of the **next** parameter. Then, the next middleware is executed the same way and after all of their completion, the action method is executed and a response written (assuming no middleware is short circuited until here), the middleware delegates are executed in reverse order for the response and execution comes to the next statement after the **Invoke** method call of the **next** parameter. We can check the response data such as headers, body, and so on. If we are interested, we can do some work by using them or modify the response. The **next** parameter is a type of Task and a handle to the next middleware. We can intercept requests before calling **Invoke** of the **next** and intercept responses after **Invoke** of the **next** is called.

> NOTE: You may not always be able to write a response. The headers may be already sent to the sender and manipulating the response throws an exception after invoking next. You can check the HasStarted property of the response before.

If we do not call invoke of the next parameter, the pipeline is short circuited, and it will not execute the next middleware and any data written in the response is returned to the sender. The short-circuiting middleware is called the terminal middleware.

The **Run** extension method is like the **Use** method. The only difference is that it cannot call the next handler because its delegate does not have any next parameter. It is used for creating terminal middlewares:

```
app.Run(async context =>
{
 // final middleware in the pipeline
});
```

The **Map** extension method is used for branching the pipeline. It does by checking the request path:

```
app.Map("/Test",async (context) =>
{

});
app.Map("/Test2",async (context) =>
{

});
...
.

.

remaining middlewares
```

According to the preceding code, when the request does not start with **/Test** or **/Test2** the remaining middlewares are executed and the middlewares in the map are passed without execution. When a request URL starts with /Test, then the first middleware is executed and the others will not be, and the second middleware is executed for requests with the URL **/Test2**.

NOTE: Since Map is used for branching the pipeline if their tests are successful, the remaining middlewares will not be executed.

There is an overload of **Map**, taking a predicate. It is used for checking a condition without the URL segment:

```
app.MapWhen(context => /*predicate checks a condition*/, async context =>
{
//middleware code
});
```

We can also use nesting in **Map** to check for sub path segments:

```
app.Map("/test", test => {
    test.Map("/subTest1", subTest1 => {
        // process for "/test/subTest1"
    });
    test.Map("/subTest2", subTest2 => {
        // process for "/test/subTest2"
    });
});
```

Since the calling order of middlewares is important, we can use extension methods to group and encapsulate them in one method:

```
public void ACustomMiddleware(this IApplicationBuilder app,/*possible extra parameters*/)
{
    //first middleware
    app.Run(async (context) =>
    {
        //do some work
    });

    //second middleware
    app.Run(async (context) =>
    {
        //do some work
    });
    .

    .
```

```
        app.AnotherCustomMiddleware();
}
.
.
.
//startup.cs
public void Configure(IApplicationBuilder app, IHostingEnvironment env)
{
    ...
    app.ACustomMiddleware(/*possible extra parameters*/);
    ...
}
```

This way we can group and order our middlewares into one and register them in the pipeline together as we desire.

> **NOTE: Try to perform operations that bring less overhead to the server in your middlewares. Or the requests can start to take longer time and hinder end user experience.**

URL rewriting

URL rewriting is an important feature in ASP.NET Core. IIS web server also has a similar functionality on the server side. We will explain this feature in ASP.NET Core.

Sometimes, we need to redirect a request to a different resource. We can return a http redirect response, but it is costly for the client, and we cannot transfer every parameter of a request to a redirect response. We can use the URL rewrite feature in the ASP.NET Core pipeline. We can check the request for certain conditions and set the URL of the incoming request:

```
app.Use(async (context,next) =>
{
    if (/*check for a condition*/)
    {
        // rewrite the url
        context.Request.Path = /*A valid route string in the project*/;
    }
    await next();
});
```

This way we redirect the same request without a full http redirect response. The path string must be a valid and working route in the project that points to an action.

Built-in Middlewares in the ASP.NET Core pipeline

There are many built-in middlewares at your disposal to perform common tasks. They are ready-to-use extension methods and called in the **Configure** method. Keep in mind that they must be registered by the appropriate order among the other middlewares. Let us explain some of them:

- **Health Check**: Health check is important for cloud computing and many cloud providers or cloud native systems require to check the health of the services or applications. Health check here means the container orchestrator makes a request to the service or application, and if that request fails, it tears down the container hosting the service and recreates it. To do the health check, the container orchestrator requires an endpoint on the hosted service to be invoked. This is called **health probe**.

  We usually make a quick check for a working database connection or we have access to an external service. If the application uses disk storage, we can check whether the application can access storage. The health check procedure should not take long by its nature because the container orchestrator or a monitoring application can call it frequently. For example, it is not wise to do a huge database operation just to control the database access is working.

  ASP.NET Core provides us an easy way to implement health check. First, we must add the NuGet package **Microsoft.AspNetCore.Diagnostics. HealthChecks** to our project.

  We must then create a health checker; a class implements the **IHealthCheck** interface:

```
using Microsoft.Extensions.Diagnostics.HealthChecks;

using System.Threading;

using System.Threading.Tasks;


namespace Phonebook.WebApi

{

    public class SomeHealthChecker : IHealthCheck

    {

        public Task<HealthCheckResult>
CheckHealthAsync(HealthCheckContext context,
```

```
            CancellationToken = default)
    {
        if (/*health condition*/)
        {
            return Task.FromResult(
                HealthCheckResult.Healthy("System is
healthy")
                );
        }
        else
        {
            return Task.FromResult(
                HealthCheckResult.Degraded("System degraded
")
                );
        }
    }
}
}
```

The **IHealthCheck** interface contains a method **CheckHealthAsync**. We can check the health of our system and return a **HealthCheckResult.Healthy**, **HealthCheckResult.Degraded** or **HealthCheckResult.Unhealthy** result with a message.

We then register health checker as a service on the **Startup** class:

```
public void ConfigureServices(IServiceCollection services)
{
    services.AddHealthChecks()
    .AddCheck<SomeHealthChecker>("some_health_checker",
     HealthStatus.Degraded);

    services.AddControllers();
}
```

We register our health checker type as a generic parameter in our **AddCheck** method call and give it an alias.

Then, we need to register the health check middleware to the pipeline. It will be wise to place it after the exception handler middleware in the second place of the pipeline, so the health check is done earlier and quickly but it is up to you:

```
public void Configure(IApplicationBuilder app, IWebHostEnvironment env)
{
    if (env.IsDevelopment())
    {
            app.UseDeveloperExceptionPage();
    }
    app.UseHealthChecks("/checkhealth");
}
```

When we make a get request to **{our application url}/checkhealth**, we see that our **SomeHealthChecker** is going to run.

Health probes are separated into two kinds: Readiness probes and liveness probes. Readiness probes check whether the system is ready for access for the first time. Liveness probes checks whether the system has access to its basic elements. ASP.NET Core provides ways for creating liveness and readiness probes. Some platforms also support startup probes to determine if the container has started successfully or not.

Let us describe the usage of these probes from Kubernetes to explain the difference of probes. Kubernetes uses health, liveness, and startup probes to manage pods.

> **NOTE: Kubernetes (K8s) is an open-source container management system developed by Google and used for automatic scaling and deployment. You can check it out at https://kubernetes.io/. Pods are fundamental execution units for K8s, and they can contain one or more application containers.**

It supports the types of probes in the following ways:

- o **Liveness probe**: K8s uses the liveness probe to check whether an application container in a pod has crashed. It will stop and start a new pod if a liveness probe fails.

- o **Readiness probe**: K8s uses the readiness probe to check whether an application container in a pod is ready to handle requests. If a readiness probe fails, it will keep the pod running, but it will not forward any request.

- o **Startup probe**: K8s uses the startup probe to check whether an application container in a pod has started. If it has started successfully, K8s starts pinging the application by liveness and readiness probes.

TIP: ASP.NET Core applications may need some time to start for the first time and become ready to receive requests. This depends on the number of library files they require and environment hardware such as CPU and memory. You may need to use different timeout settings for the probes, depending on the environment and application. You can also benefit from configuration management at this point.

- **CORS**: Cross origin resource sharing is a security rule exception that allows a web application to access another resource hosted on the other than its host. Let us assume you have a web application hosted on **https://www.somedomain.com** and you make AJAX requests to the same domain, but you also want to make an AJAX request to some other domain with a different DNS; let us call it **http://www.someforeigndomain.com**. When we try it, the browser immediately logs an error to the console and tells us that a request with a different origin is issued and blocked by the browser (*Figure 7.5*).

This is a security protocol named the same origin policy that browsers must comply by the w3wc standards. An attacker can find a way to inject a script that makes a web request to a malicious site.

But sometimes, we need to make exceptions so we can access another site via JavaScript. The CORS allows us to relax this security rule and add exceptions. First, a request with option method is made to the foreign resource and the foreign resource checks whether the request from the origin is allowed and authorizes it by setting specific response headers. These response headers start with Access-Control-Allow… Then, the browser knows it can make a request to the foreign resource without being blocked as shown in *Figure 7.6*.

NOTE: Geographical Information Systems (GIS) applications are nice examples of CORS. Many applications allow providers to download maps based on the zoom level and of course, they are hosted on different domains.

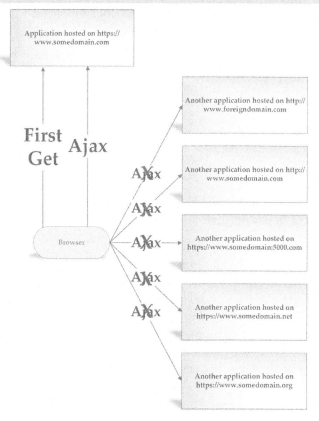

Figure 7.5: Same origin policy

NOTE: As seen in *Figure 7.5*, the same origin policy implies that the origin changes whether the scheme, port, or top-level domain changes. https://somedomain.com, http://somedomain.com, https://somedomain.com:5000, and https://somedomain. net are all different domains and accessing from one another by Ajax requests are blocked by browsers.

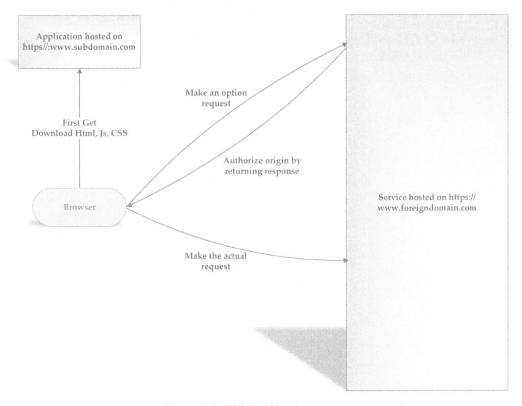

Figure 7.6: CORS with options request

NOTE: It is obvious that the request count is doubled by using CORS. It is better to control it earlier on the request pipeline and return the result of the option request.

Figure 7.7 shows pre-flight option requests (204) made to the server:

customer-types	204	preflight
customer-types	200	xhr
clients?page=0&pageSize=6&filters=%5B%5D	204	preflight
clients?page=0&pageSize=6&filters=%5B%5D	200	xhr
clients?page=0&pageSize=6&filters=%5B%5D	204	preflight
clients?page=0&pageSize=6&filters=%5B%5D	200	xhr

Figure 7.7: Pre-flight options requests

NOTE: Allowing CORS is a widely used practice for separating the UI rendering application and API service. We explained it in *Chapter 6, Developing Restful Services with ASP.NET Core,* as shown in *Figure 6.2*.

ASP.NET Core provides an easy way to configure CORS for us. We just add CORS services in the **ConfigureServices** method. We use the origins method to define the allowed domains by CORS:

```
services.AddCors(options =>
{
        options.AddDefaultPolicy(
        builder =>
        {
                builder.WithOrigins("url of the allowd origin
here");
        });
});
```

We then add the CORS middlewares by calling **UseCors**:

```
public void Configure(IApplicationBuilder app, IWebHostEnvironment
env)
{
        app.UseCors();
}
```

There are more method overloads and parameters to configure CORS in ASP. NET Core. We omit them for simplicity.

• **Handling Global Errors**: ASP.NET Core provides a set of middlewares to handle errors and ease getting information of errors that occur during the development:

```
public void Configure(IApplicationBuilder app, IWebHostEnvironment
env)
{
    if (env.IsDevelopment())
    {
        app.UseDeveloperExceptionPage();
    }
    else
    {
        app.UseExceptionHandler("/ErrorPage");
        app.UseHsts();
    }
}
```

As the usage implies, in the development mode, we register the developer exception page middleware. It is the default middleware that shows the exception and the stack trace. Since it is dangerous to show this information to the end user in the production environment, we redirect them to an error page. This middleware should be the first one registered on the pipeline so it can catch all unhandled exceptions that happen in the next middlewares, action filters, action methods, and many more.

NOTE: You may have registered an exception filter for catching unhandled exceptions that happen in action methods, but you must also register a global handler for catching unhandled exceptions in other places and that should be the first middleware in the pipeline by logic.

If we would like to access the exception, we can use the middleware provided by the **UseExceptionHandler** extension method:

```
app.UseExceptionHandler(error =>
{
    error.Run(async context =>
    {
    context.Response.StatusCode = (int)HttpStatusCode.
InternalServerError;

    var exceptionHandlerPathFeature = context.Features.
Get<IExceptionHandlerPathFeature>();

        await context.Response.WriteAsync("Some error occured");
    });
});
```

- **Https Redirection**: If we serve our application with an SSL certificate and would like our users to be redirected to the address with the https scheme automatically when they navigate to with the one having http, we can use this middleware. It checks whether the request is issued with an URL with http and redirects it to https one if so.

NOTE: You can achieve the same functionality if your application is behind a reverse proxy. In that case, you do not need this middleware.

It is registered by the **UseHttpsRedirection** extension method:

```
public void Configure(IApplicationBuilder app, IWebHostEnvironment
env)
{
```

```
        app.UseHttpsRedirection();
}
```

- **Serving static files**: By default, ASP.NET Core expects the static files placed in **wwwroot** folder in the projects directory by default. We can serve our JavaScript, CSS, and image files there. The static files middleware resolves the static files relative to the **wwwroot** folder:

```
<img src="~/images/logo.png" />
```

ASP.NET Core resolves the preceding tag by **wwwroot/images/logo.png**. Static files middleware is registered by the **UseStaticFiles** extension method:

```
public void Configure(IApplicationBuilder app, IWebHostEnvironment env)
{
        app. UseStaticFiles();
}
```

We can also use the lambda in the overloaded method to change the root folder other than **wwwroot** in the project folder structure:

```
app.UseStaticFiles(new StaticFileOptions
{
    FileProvider = new PhysicalFileProvider("C:\\ProjectAssets"),
    RequestPath = "/Assets"
});
```

The preceding code resolves the URL **/Assets/CSS/Styles.css** as **C:\ProjectAssets\CSS\Styles.css** and serves the file from there.

Conclusion

We learned about asynchronous programming in ASP.NET Core and programming the middleware pipeline. We will cover action filters and dependency injection in the next chapter. They are automatically added by the default new project template.

Questions

1. Assume you have an action method that takes a long time. You decided to move your application to another server that has the same clock speed of the previous server's CPUs but more CPU cores. Your action method still takes a long time. What is it that you miss?

2. Assume you need to log certain types of responses for application level. What should you do?

3. Assume you have some middlewares and you need developers to execute them in the order of you want. What should you do?

4. Assume you need to check the request by a specific header value and redirect it to a different action method. What should you do?

CHAPTER 8
Dependency Injection and Action Filters in ASP.NET Core

Introduction

We covered the async/await pattern and programming the middleware pipeline in ASP.NET Core in the previous chapter. We will cover dependency injection and action filters in this chapter. Dependency injection is a variant of the Inversion of Control pattern and plays an important role in enterprise-level ASP.NET Core projects.

Structure

In this chapter, we will discuss the following topics:

- Introduction to the inversion of control principle
- Implementing dependency injection in ASP.NET Core
- Introduction to lifetimes of instances and the singleton design pattern in dependency injection
- Introduction to action filters in ASP.NET Core

Objectives

After reading this chapter, you will be able to understand and implement dependency injection in ASP.NET Core and implement action filters for your projects.

Introduction to the inversion of the control (IoC) principle

C# is an object-oriented language, and we write code by creating classes. As a result some classes depend on others naturally. We try to apply principles such as SOLID to create cohesive, loose coupled classes, or modules. Some classes do the actual low-level work, and some use many of them to do a high-level work. Therefore, we create a dependency between high-level and low-level classes. We should not create that dependency directly because we may need to change their implementations later.

For example, we can create a logger class that logs messages as we desire and use it in other methods of objects. If we create the logger object inside of high-level objects directly, we will have difficulties for switching the logging implementation. We may wish to log to different targets such as the database, file system, a remote service, and so on. These are all different logger implementations with a common interface. To easily switch to other implementations, we need a class design that high-level classes depend on low-level classes by interfaces or abstractions. The IoC principle helps us to achieve that.

The inversion of control is a principle that describes how to transfer the execution and control the lifetime of object instances by a container of objects. To implement IoC, a framework is needed, and we program that framework with the abstraction of our classes and their implementations which are doing the tasks. We add interfaces or abstract classes as contracts and program the container framework with the behaviours as we see fit for them.

IoC gives us advantages in the following fields:

- Execution of a task is decoupled from its implementation. We define contracts which contain the necessary methods with parameters for doing a task or multiple tasks and the result of those tasks. We then implement the contracts elsewhere. When we want to execute a task, we ask the container framework for its implementation, and it gives us the instance of the contract of it. We achieve encapsulation and loose coupling that the consumer of the contracts has no idea how it is implemented, and we can change its implementation without consumers needing to modify their code.

- We can group the related methods in contracts together and can make a contract depend on another contract. IoC provides modularity and cohesion if used correctly. For example, we can create a contract and its implementation for accessing a database and another contract and its implementation that takes the data access contract (dependency injection) and uses it to do a business task by executing methods. IoC helps us to achieve SOLID principles.

- Most importantly, IoC encourages us to practise unit testing. We can create mock, fake, stub implementations of a contract as we see fit and use them to write unit tests of the contracts that depend on them.

The IoC principle can be implemented by the service locator design pattern, strategy and factory design patterns, and dependency injection. We will explain dependency injection because ASP.NET Core provides a built-in framework for it and relies on it heavily.

Dependency injection allows low-level object instances to be injected into high-level object instances by their interfaces. The injection can be done at construction by injecting the instance into a property or into a parameter at the constructor.

Let us assume we have a logger interface like the following:

```
public interface ILogger
{
    void Log(string label, string message);
}
```

We can have as many different implementations of the logger as we desire, and let us assume we have some high-level objects that must use the logger. We create a parameter with the **ILogger** type at the constructor and assign it to a variable like the following:

```
public class SomeHighLevelObject
{
    private ILogger _logger;

    public SomeHighLevelObject(ILogger logger)
    {
        this._logger = logger;
    }
}
```

Now, we have a dependency between **SomeHighLevelObject** and the implementation of **ILogger** object. When we ask a new instance of **SomeHighLevelObject** to be created, an instance of **ILogger** is injected into the constructor automatically. But how and what implementation of **ILogger** is injected? We may wish to inject the database implementation or the file system implementation of **ILogger**. This is where the IoC container comes in. We configure it to inject implementations of interfaces as we desire, and it handles the rest for us.

Implementation of the dependency injection in ASP.NET Core

Let us consider a scenario regarding our phonebook application and assume we have a user interface (MVC view or Razor page) that displays the selected contact, updates, or deletes the selected contact, or adds a new contact (Create Read Update Destroy, CRUD in short term). We use Microsoft SQL Server for our database. The technical requirements tell us that the projects database may be changed later. The validation of our contact information is certain from the beginning but can be changed after a milestone is achieved in the project plan or any time later.

> NOTE: Never forget that requirements can always change in a software project any time. You are obliged to design it as change proof so the impact of the change is as minimal as possible. IoC is one of the many ways to achieve this.

We know the project starts using the SQL Server as a database and can be changed later. We can create a contract for our database operations like the following:

```
public interface IDatabaseOperations
{
 DbConnection OpenConnection();
 DbTransaction StartTransaction();
 IDataReader Select(Criteria criteria);
 void Insert(object entity);
 void Update(object entity);
 void Delete(int entityId);
}
```

We put methods for opening the database connection, starting a database transaction, and methods for selecting, inserting, updating, or deleting an item in the database. We then create an SQL server implementation because we know that the project will use the SQL Server:

```
public class SqlServerDatabaseOperations : IDatabaseOperations
{
 private  string connectionString;

 public SqlServerDatabaseOperations(IConfiguration configuration)
 {
   connectionString= configuration[/* key of connection string */];
 }
```

```
public DbConnection OpenConnection()
{
//Sql server implementation of opening connection.
}


public DbTransaction StartTransaction()
{
//Sql server implementation of starting transaction.
}


public IDataReader Select(Criteria criteria)
{
 //Sql server implementation of querying database
}


public void Insert(object entity)
{
//Sql server implementation of inserting an item in database
}


public void Update(object entity)
{
//Sql server implementation of updating an item in database
}


public void Delete(int entityId)
{
//Sql server implementation of deleting an item in database
 }
}
```

Notice that we pass the **IConfiguration** interface to the constructor. This is the injection by a constructor. Remember it is used to read configuration values from various sources like environment variables, **appsettings.json** files, command line arguments, and so on. Usually, connection strings to the databases are stored in one of these configuration sources so we need to inject it to our implementation of **IDatabaseOperations** which is **SqlServerDatabaseOperations** in this case.

Then, we come to know that there is a validation of a contact that can be changed in the future also. So, we must encapsulate it to a contract and add an implementation also:

```
public interface IContactValidator
{
    ValidationResult Validate(Contact contact);
}
```

Also, we add an implementation; let us name it as the default implementation. It checks the contact for the name, surname, and so on:

```
public class DefaultContactValidator: IContactValidator
{
    public ValidationResult Validate(Contact contact){
    //default validation of contact
    }
}
```

Then, we need a business class which does the actual job. Let us name it **ContactBusiness**:

```
public class ContactBusiness
{
    private IContactValidator contactValidator;
    private IDatabaseOperations databaseOperations;

    public ContactBusiness(IContactValidator contactValidator,
    IDatabaseOperations databaseOperations){
        this.contactValidator = contactValidator;
        this.databaseOperations = databaseOperations;
    }

    public Contact SelectContact(int contactId)
    {
        Contact contact=new Contact();
        Criteria criteria="";
        //prepare criteria for selecting contact by id

        //open connection
        this.databaseOperations.OpenConnection();
        IDataReader dataReader=this.databaseOperations.Select(criteria);
```

```
      //Fill the contact from the information of dataReader
      return contact;
   }

   public Result Insert(Contact contact)
   {
      var validationResult = this.contactValidator.Validate(contact);
      if(validationResult.Success)
      {
         this.databaseOperations.Insert(contact);
      }
      else
      {
         //return validation failure
      }
   }

   public Result Update(Contact contact)
   {
      var validationResult = this.contactValidator.Validate(contact)
      if(validationResult.Success)
      {
         this.databaseOperations.Update(contact);
      }
      else
      {
         //return validation failure
      }
   }

   public Result Delete(int contactId)
   {
      this.databaseOperations.Delete(contactId);
      //return successful
   }

}
```

Our business object **ContactBusiness** selects contacts, inserts, deletes, and updates the contact to the database by the requirements. Also, it validates contacts before insert or update. So, we need to inject our contact validator and database operations implementations as interface contracts. We can also choose to define a business class with a contract for its implementation can be changed in the future, but we will leave it for now.

Then, we need to create a controller with a view so these business operations can be visually represented:

```
public class ContactController : ControllerBase
{

    ContactBusiness contactBusiness;

        public ContactController(ContactBusiness contactBusiness){
            this.contactBusiness = contactBusiness;
    }

    [HttpGet]
        public ActionResult SelectContact(int contactId)
    {
        Contact contact = null;
        contact = contactBusiness.SelectContact(contactId);
return View(contact);
    }

    [HttpPost]
        public ActionResult Insert(Contact contact)
    {
            Result result = contactBusiness.Insert(contact);
            return View("Insert",result);
    }

    [HttpPost]
        public ActionResult Update(Contact contact)
    {
            Result result = contactBusiness.Update(contact);
            return View("Update",result);
```

```
        }


        [HttpPost]
            public ActionResult Delete(int contactId)
        {

                Result result = contactBusiness.Delete(contactId);
                return View("Delete",result);

        }


}
```

We need to inject our **ContactBusiness** object to the constructor of the controller and create necessary action methods by using it. Observe that we do not inject database operations or, contract validator, just **ContactBusiness**.

This is called the dependency chain or dependency graph. The controller depends on **ContactBusiness**, **ContactBusiness** depends on **IContactValidator,** and **IDatabaseOperations** and **SqlServerDatabaseOperations** depend on **IConfiguration**. We register these contracts and their implementations in the dependency injection container and the container resolves them and injects their implementation. We will explain how to configure the **dependency injection (DI)** container shortly.

Now, let us consider we need to migrate our project to the PostgreSQL Server. We just need to create another implementation of **IDatabaseOperations**:

```
public class PostgreSQLDatabaseOperations : IDatabaseOperations
{
    private  string connectionString;

        public PostgreSQLDatabaseOperations(IConfiguration configuration)
        {
            connectionString= configuration[/* key of connection string
*/];
        }

        public DbConnection OpenConnection()
        {
        //PostgreSql implementation of opening connection.
        }


        public DbTransaction StartTransaction()
```

```
    {
    //PostgreSql implementation of starting transaction.
    }

    public IDataReader Select(Criteria criteria)
    {
    //PostgreSql implementation of querying database
    }

    public void Insert(object entity)
    {
    //PostgreSql implementation of inserting an item in database
    }

    public void Update(object entity)
    {
    //PostgreSql implementation of updating an item in database
    }

    public void Delete(int entityId)
    {
    //PostgreSql implementation of deleting an item in database
    }
}
```

Now, we register it in the DI container instead of the SQL server implementation. That would be all. We do not need to change any more code because the **ContactBusiness** class is injected with the PostgreSQL implementation, and it does not need to know how the implementation is working or database operations are implemented. It only knows the contract **IDatabaseOperations**. Please notice how dependency injection helps making a software project change proof.

Then, let us assume we need to validate the contact by the entered social security number by sending it to a service owned by a government organization. But we also need to keep the default validation intact. We can make the **Validate** method of **DefaultContactValidator** virtual:

```
public class DefaultContactValidator : IContactValidator
{
 public virtual ValidationResult Validate(Contact contact){
  //default validation of contact
```

```
    }
}
```

Then we can create a class derived from it. Let us say it has a name with **SsnValidator**. We override the **Validate** method of the base class, call the service inside and then call the **Validate** method of the base class:

```
public class SsnValidator : DefaultContactValidator
{
      public override ValidationResult Validate(Contact contact){

      string ssn = contact.Ssn;
      bool isValidSsn = webService.IsSsnValid(ssn);

      if(isValidSsn)
      {
      return base.Validate(contact);
      }
      else
      {
      //return failed validation result
      }
    }
}
```

We consume the service and check whether the contact has a valid SSN and if that is right, then we call the base class **(DefaultContactValidator) Validate** method and run the default validation code. This way we added extra functionality (**ssn check**) without repeating the same default validation code.

> **NOTE: This entire scenario is just for explaining how DI works and there are more sophisticated ways for implementing it in the real world.**

Note how we add extra functionality or change implementations without changing the code that uses them. The following figure shows the dependency graph:

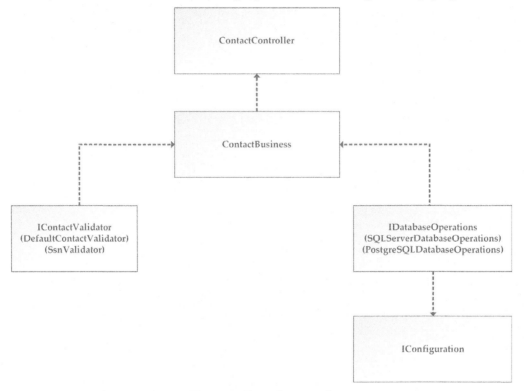

Figure 8.1: Dependency graph

Configuration of the dependency injection container in ASP.NET Core

It is time to explain how to configure the DI container. We need to register contracts and their implementations in the DI container so it can resolve implementations for us. We can achieve this in the **ConfigureServices** method of the **Startup** class:

```
public void ConfigureServices(IServiceCollection services)
{
    .
    .
    .
}
```

The parameter of type **IServiceCollection** is passed to this method automatically by the framework. We use this parameter's methods to configure the DI container and register contracts and implementations.

NOTE: If you ever need any of them, you can inject IWebHostEnvironment, IHostEnvironment, and IConfiguration instances to the Startup class and add some dynamism to your DI configuration.

The DI container creates an instance of the contract to be injected for the specified lifetime and does the same for its dependencies. For example, when we inject an **IDatabaseOperations** instance, the DI container also looks for registration of the **IConfiguration** instance and injects it while creating the instance of **IDatabaseOperations**. This is called resolving dependencies.

NOTE: We can also resolve dependencies by the GetRequiredService method of the IServiceProvider instance. It is supplied by the HttpContext objects RequestServices method. For example, to get the instance of IConfiguration, we can write

IConfiguration config = context.RequestServices. GetRequiredService<IConfiguration>();

This usage method can be used in middleware methods also.

Other than implementations, we can also configure the lifetime of objects. Before we explain them, be aware that we can inject instances to the controllers, action filters, and middleware. There are three types of lifetime configurations, which are as follows:

1. **Transient objects**: The transient object lifetime means the instance of a dependency is always different whether it is injected to a middleware first, then a controller, and then a business class, etc.

   Let us assume we have a service that has a property called `DataId`, and we have a middleware that sets it (please also note how we inject a service contract to the middleware also):

```
app.Use(async (context, next) =>
{
ISomeService service = context.RequestServices.
GetRequiredService<ISomeService>();

        //Set DataId to some number
        service.DataId=5;

        //continue running the pipeline
        await next.Invoke();
});
```

   And a controller that reads it from the same service later:

```
public class SomeController
```

```
{
        public SomeController(ISomeService someService){
                int dataId = someService.DataId;
        }
}
```

We see that **dataId** is not 5 here because a new instance is always created for the transient lifetime. We configure the transient instance by **AddTransient** of the **IServiceCollection** instance in the **ConfigureServices** method. The second generic parameter must implement the first interface type.

Stateless and easy-to-create services are nice candidates for transient services:

```
public void ConfigureServices(IServiceCollection services)
{
        services.AddTransient<IContract,IContractImplementation>();
}
```

2. **Scoped objects**: The scoped object lifetime means the instance of a dependency is the same as in all injections from the start of the request until the end of the request. In the case of the preceding example, we get the same value in the controller that was set in the middleware before. A scoped object registered the same way but using the **AddScoped** method:

```
public void ConfigureServices(IServiceCollection services)
{
        services.AddScoped<IContract,IContractImplementation>();
}
```

Objects that are not thread safe are usually registered as scoped. For example, an entity framework database context is a nice example for a scoped service. It is not thread safe and different requests should not share the same instances. To ensure the same instance of the database context is injected into the instances of classes in the same web request, it should not be registered as a transient service:

3. **Singleton objects**: The singleton object lifetime means the instance of a dependency is the same in all injections across the application lifetime. The instance is first created on the first injection and the same instance is resolved in later injections until the application is shutdown. It is done by the **AddSingleton** method:

```
public void ConfigureServices(IServiceCollection services)
{
        services.AddSingleton<IContract,IContractImplementation>();
```

}

The singleton is a design pattern, and it allows us to have only one instance of an object from the first time it is used to the end of the application. The singleton pattern is used for storing data that takes too much time to load. It can be used for caching purposes primarily.

We can choose whatever lifespan as we see fit for our services and use them for our scenarios. But beware of injecting transient or scoped services into a singleton service. If you try to inject a transient or a scoped service into a singleton service, your service instance may not be garbage collected and stay forever inside the singleton since it is always alive and has only one instance in the application. This is called captive dependency and can lead to memory and concurrency issues.

If you really need to inject a scoped service into a singleton service, you can still achieve this by creating a scope and request the scoped service instance from it. This is done by injecting an **IServiceProvider** instance into the singleton and calling the **CreateScope** method. But ensure the scope is cleaned up and disposed when you are done with it.

NOTE: You may think why bother with dependency injection and let's put everything in action methods and connect to the database directly. Well, you may be right with small projects that contain a few user interfaces and very simple functionality but for large enterprise projects, you really should layer your code across multiple services and separate the concerns. It may be a nightmare to maintain a project full of complicated codes in controllers.

Introduction to action filters in ASP.NET Core

Action filters in ASP.NET Core enables us to run the code before or after the execution of an action method. There are built-in filters and we can write custom filters. We can log information on responses, handle errors, authorize users before an action method is run, and many more. Filters are useful for reusing the common code in those kinds of scenarios.

Action filters are used as attributes. They are put on top of controllers and applied to all the action methods they contain, or they can be put to the specific action methods as we want to apply them to.

The action filters are run after ASP.NET Core determines the action method to run based on the routes. They can contain the code to run before or after the execution of the action method, like middleware requests and responses. There are different types of action filters which run in the following order:

1. **Authorization filters**: They are the first kind of filters run and used for checking whether the user is authorized to execute an action method. It can short circuit and prevent the action method to run in case a user is not authorized. By nature, it cannot intercept method return values. The action filters are run in order and authorization filters are the first to run. It is a best practice not to throw exception in authorization filters because if you also have a filter for handling exceptions, they are run after authorization filters, and they will not catch the exception. Although you may catch unhandled exceptions at application level by middleware, it is a technical decision.

There are mainly two ways of implementing authorization in ASP.NET Core: Role–base or policy-based. We can use the authorized attribute as the following for the entire controller:

```
[Authorize]
public class SomeController : Controller
{
….
}
```

This makes all action methods to require authorization in the controller. We can make an exception of any action method in the controller by the **AllowAnonymous** attribute like the following:

```
[Authorize()]
public class SomeController : Controller
{
        [AllowAnonymous]
        public ActionResult SomeMethod(){
        ….
        }
}
```

Or we can put it on top of action methods like the following. Notice that we can authorize for multiple roles too:

```
public class SomeController : Controller
{
        [Authorize("Accountant","Administrator")]
        public ActionResult SomeMethod(){
        ….
        }
}
```

The role of the user is resolved in the claims principle by default, and we will cover it in the next chapter about *Chapter 9: State Management in ASP. NET Core.*

The concept of authorization in the software world is quite varying and it is either developed specifically for the project's needs or a full-featured authorization module is developed once and used for every project in a company. They are usually put into the companies' frameworks or code bases.

The role-based authorization can be enough for projects that have very less different roles and without role hierarchy. For large enterprise projects, we usually need to make hierarchies of roles, and it may be a nightmare to manage the authorization by the roles. Imagine if you need to authorize an action method for a system administrator, president, vice president, department director, specialist in a department, and so on. We also need to change the permissions of the role or remove a role from the system. Since they are hardcoded in the authorize attribute, this can bring quite complicated maintenance operations.

The policy-based authorization introduces policy requirements to be met for the authorization of a resource. Some criteria specified in the policy must be met by the data from the claims of the user; for example, the location of the user must be in certain countries, the type of the user must be specific, etc. We can define these custom policies and authorize users by these policies. It requires some more coding than the role-based policy.

Let us assume we only want users in India to be authorized for a controller. We must define a class to carry the necessary requirement data that implements **IAuthorizationRequirement**:

```
public class LocationRequirement: IAuthorizationRequirement
{
    public LocationRequirement(string location)
    {
    Location = location;
    }


    public string Location { get; set; }
}
```

Then, we must implement authorization in a handler derived from **AuthorizationHandler**. The handler simply gathers the necessary user data from the claims and applies the rule of the policy:

```
public class AuthorizationByLocationHandler :
```

```
AuthorizationHandler<LocationRequirement>
{
    protected override Task
HandleRequirementAsync(AuthorizationHandlerContext context,
    LocationRequirement requirement)
    {
        if (!context.User.HasClaim(c => c.Type == ClaimTypes.
Country &&
        c.Issuer == "http://projectwebsite.com"))
        {
            context.Fail();
        }

        Claim locationClaim = null;

        locationClaim = context.User.FindFirst(c => c.Type ==
ClaimTypes.Country &&
        c.Issuer == "http://projectwebsite.com");

        if (locationClaim == null)
        {
            context.Fail();
        }

        string location = locationClaim.Value;
        if (String.IsNullOrWhiteSpace(location) || location !=
requirement.Location)
        {
            context.Fail();
        }
        context.Succeed(requirement);
        return Task.FromResult(0);
    }
}
```

We override the **HandleRequirementAsync** method of **AuthorizationHandler**. We check whether the necessary country claim has a value, and if it has, then we get the value from it. If it has an empty value or the location claim is null, then we call the fail method of the context. If it has a value, we compare the location value from the **LocationRequirement** object with it and if they are not equal, we call fail of the context method again. If all checks are passed, then we call the **Succeed** method of the context parameter and that ensures the requirement is fulfilled and authorizes the user.

Then, we must register that policy in the services section of the **Startup** class. We give it a unique alias such as **MustBeInIndia** and register our policy by the **AddAuthorization** extension method:

```
public void ConfigureServices(IServiceCollection services)
{
services.AddAuthorization(options =>
{
      options.AddPolicy("MustBeInIndia", policy => policy.
Requirements.Add
      (new LocationRequirement("India")));
}
});
```

Then, we can use it by specifying alias in the policy parameter of the authorize attribute like the following:

```
[Authorize(Policy="MustBeInIndia")]
public class SomeController : Controller
{

}
```

If we implement **IAuthorizationHandler** in our handler, we can do multiple requirement checks at once. We get the requirements by the property called **PendingRequirements** of a context and then check each one of them by their implementation type:

```
public class AuthorizationByLocationHandler :
IAuthorizationHandler
{
public Task HandleAsync(AuthorizationHandlerContext context)
{
      IEnumerable<IAuthorizationRequirement> pendingRequirements
= null;         pendingRequirements = context.
PendingRequirements.ToList();

      if (requirement is /*type of implementation*/)
      {
```

```
        }
   }
   }
```

We can also mix role-based and policy-based authorization too if necessary.

2. **Resource filters**: The next type of filters that run after authorization filters are resource filters. Resource filters are run before model binding; they can short circuit the pipeline if necessary, before the action method is executed and prevent model binding to perform. They are ideal candidates for setting the result from the cache, preventing the action method to run by short circuiting, and modifying the model data. Every filter type can be developed as synchronous or asynchronous manner and we will give asynchronous example this time.

   Synchronous action filters usually contain two methods; they end with names **Executing** and **Executed**. We can intercept the request in executing and intercept the return value of the action method in **Executed**. Asynchronous action filters have a next delegate, and the same functionality can be achieved by intercepting the request before calling the **Invoke** method of the next delegate, and we can modify the result after the call of the **Invoke** method just like it is implemented in a middleware. We can create an asynchronous resource filter by implementing the interface **IAsyncResourceFilter**:

```
public class SomeResourceFilterAttribute : Attribute,
IAsyncResourceFilter
{

public async Task
OnResourceExecutionAsync(ResourceExecutingContext context,
ResourceExecutionDelegate next)
{
// intercept the request. Model binding is not done yet
await next.Invoke();
// intercept the result.

}

}
```

   We can implement the caching functionality by checking certain conditions from the data in the request and set the result property of the context parameter accordingly. This will short circuit the pipeline and the next filters and the action method will not run:

```
public class SomeResourceFilterAttribute : Attribute,
IAsyncResourceFilter
{

    public async Task
OnResourceExecutionAsync(ResourceExecutingContext context,
    ResourceExecutionDelegate next)
    {
        // intercept the request and check for result is stored in
a cache if so
        //set Result property of context and short circuit the
pipeline
        context.Result = new ContentResult()
        {
            Content = "Some data from the cache"
        };
        await next.Invoke();
    }


}
```

Let us assume we have an action method for adding a new contact to our database, and we need to set the title property based on the gender that comes in the request body. We can modify the model before model binding occurs. The following code shows that we read the request body, deserialize the json, and modify the property as necessary. We then serialize it again and call Invoke of the next:

```
public class SomeResourceFilterAttribute : Attribute,
IAsyncResourceFilter
{

    public async Task
OnResourceExecutionAsync(ResourceExecutingContext context,
    ResourceExecutionDelegate next)
    {
        var request = context.HttpContext.Request;
        using (var reader = new StreamReader(request.Body))
        {
            String json = await reader.ReadToEndAsync();
            Contact contact = null;
```

```
            contact = JsonSerializer.Deserialize<Contact>(json);
            contact.Title = contact.Gender == "Male" ? "Mr" :
"Ms.";

            String serialized = JsonSerializer.
Serialize<Contact>(contact);
            byte[] bytes = Encoding.ASCII.GetBytes(serialized);
            request.Body = new MemoryStream(bytes);
        }
        await next.Invoke();

    }

}
```

When the action method is executed after the filter, we can see the **Title** property is set accordingly:

```
[HttpPost]
[SomeResourceFilter]
public IActionResult Post([FromBody]Contact contact)
{
        return Ok(); ;
}
```

3. **Action filters**: After resource filters are executed, the action filters are the next type of filters. These are the final type of filters that run before action methods. We can intercept the request, change action arguments passed to an action method, and change the result returned from the action method. Action filters are supported in API and MVC projects but not supported in Razor pages.

At this stage of the pipeline, model binding is already run and parameters are ready to be passed to the action methods:

```
public class CustomFilterAttribute : Attribute,
IAsyncActionFilter
{
public async Task OnActionExecutionAsync(ActionExecutingContext
context,
 ActionExecutionDelegate next)
        {
                //before next filter or action method is executed
```

```
                        await next.Invoke();
                        //after action method or next action filter is
executed
        }
}
```

Throwing an exception here is going to short circuit the filter pipeline. We can also do the same by setting the **Result** property of the context parameter having a type **ActionResult** (we must return and not call **next.Invoke**, if we don't, a runtime error will be thrown; this is by design and nature of the action filters):

```
public class CustomFilterAttribute : Attribute,
IAsyncActionFilter
{
public async Task OnActionExecutionAsync(ActionExecutingContext
context,
 ActionExecutionDelegate next)
{
        if (/*some condition*/)
    {
        context.Result = new OkResult();
            return;
        }
        else
                await next.Invoke();
        }
}
```

We can also modify action parameters before **next.Invoke()**. We can access model parameters by the **ActionArguments** property of **ActionExecutingContext**. It is a dictionary and the model values are stored as method parameter names. We can access and modify them like the following:

```
public class CustomFilterAttribute : Attribute,
IAsyncActionFilter
{
public async Task OnActionExecutionAsync(ActionExecutingContext
context,
 ActionExecutionDelegate next)
        {
```

```
                    Contact c = null;
                        c=context.ActionArguments["contact"] as Contact;
                    w.Title = "Mr";
                    await next.Invoke();
                }
            }
```

We can see the effects of the modified property value in the following action method:

```
[HttpPost]
[CustomFilter]
public IActionResult Post([FromBody] Contact contact)
{
        return Ok();
}
```

4. **Exception filters**: The next type of the filters that run after action filters are exception filters. They are used to capture if an unhandled exception happens in the action methods, filters, and controllers. They are only executed for unhandled exceptions and response is written.

We can greatly improve our code and handle the security for error messages using exception filters. Let us assume we have an action method that throws an exception for example purposes:

```
[HttpPost]
[SomeExceptionFilter]
public IActionResult Post([FromBody]WeatherForecast forecast)
{
throw new Exception("some exception here");
return Ok();
}
```

We can write an exception filter to hide the actual error message and return an error code to the user:

```
public class SomeExceptionFilter : Attribute,
IAsyncExceptionFilter
{
    public async Task OnExceptionAsync(ExceptionContext context)
    {
        String errorCode = Guid.NewGuid().ToString();
```

```
        //log the  exception here with code
        Result result = new Result()
        {
         HasError = true,
         ErrorMessage = $"An error occured with code {errorCode}.
    Contact support"
        };
        context.Result = new JsonResult(result);
    }
}


public class Result
{
    public bool HasError { get; set; }

    public string ErrorMessage { get; set; }
}
```

Conclusion

We covered dependency injection and action filters. They are powerful tools at your disposal if used correctly. In the next chapter, we will cover session management in ASP.NET Core.

Questions

1. Assume you have a non-changing static data that can be very hard to load, and it is accessed across your project frequently. What is one of the strategies you can do in a pure ASP.NET Core solution?

2. You need to modify the request body for certain routes that receives post requests in your project. Is writing a middleware for this a good choice?

3. You want to register an interface and its implementation in the DI container, and you want it to be a new instance every time it is injected. Which lifetime should you choose?

CHAPTER 9
State Management in ASP.NET Core

Introduction

We covered dependency injection and action filters in ASP.NET Core in the previous chapter. We will cover state and identity management in this chapter. State management is an important feature in any web application that requires authentication and authorization.

Structure

In this chapter, we will discuss the following topics:

- State management in HTTP
- ASP.NET Core state and session management techniques
  - Cookies
  - Query strings
  - Hidden fields
  - ASP.NET Core Session
- Façade pattern
- ASP.NET Core authentication and identity management

Objectives

After reading this chapter, you will be able to understand and implement session and state management in ASP.NET Core and see how it simplifies those concepts for the developers in different ways.

State management in HTTP

In *Chapter 4, Introduction to HTTP, HTML, CSS, and JavaScript*, we learned that HTTP is a stateless protocol by default. Clients communicate with servers by sending request messages, receive responses, and neither side store any state or data by default. ASP.NET Core offers various ways to handle the state in many ways. Let's explain them as follows:

- **Cookies**: Cookies are strings containing data that come and go between the client's browser and server. Because of this reason, they should be small sized as much as possible. They are specific to domain, browsers guarantee that they are isolated, and no other application can access cookies in another domain. They can have an expiration date, can be accessed and set from JavaScript. They are ideal for storing personalized data and can be used for authenticating users.

  We can create a cookie at the server side by using cookies collection of the response. It is a dictionary and cookies are added by key value pairs. The following code adds a semicolon separated data by the key **SomeCookie**:

```
public IActionResult Index()
{
    SetInitialData();
    ListModel model = new ListModel();

    Response.Cookies
    .Append("SomeCookie",
"FavoriteSearchItem=1;PreferredGridLayout=2,3,4");

    return View(model);
}
```

  We can observe that the cookie arrived at the browser with the response and is stored in it by the developer tools of the browser (URL encoded) as shown in the following screenshot:

Figure 9.1: Cookie in developer tools of Chrome

We can access it from JavaScript by calling **document.cookie**. It returns a string which every cookie is stored for the domain with key value pairs and we are required to parse the string to get the cookie with the key we look for. The following figure shows how it is accessed from the JavaScript console of Chrome.

> **TIP: JQuery has nice plugins for manipulating and parsing cookies. You can have them to parse the cookie string and give you the cookie value for you by its key. You can have more information of jQuery cookie plugin from the following code: https://github.com/carhartl/jquery-cookie/blob/master/src/jquery.cookie.js**

Figure 9.2: Cookie accessed from the document object in JavaScript

The cookies are sent and received in the Cookie header by the browser as shown in the following screenshot:

Figure 9.3: Cookie header in a request

Cookies can be tampered and changed from the JavaScript. If we would like to store sensitive information and prevent the client side to change it, then we can use the **HttpOnly** cookies. The **HttpOnly** cookies can only be created and modified from the server side. We can use the overloaded version of the **Append** method to pass a **CookieOptions** object as a parameter. We can set the **HttpOnly** property to true and control many other properties of cookies by **CookieOptions**, such as expiration date, allow subdomains to access cookie, and so on:

```
public IActionResult Index()
{
    SetInitialData();
    ListModel model = new ListModel();

    CookieOptions options = new CookieOptions()
    {
        Expires = DateTimeOffset.Now.AddDays(30),
        HttpOnly = true
    };

    Response.Cookies.Append("SomeCookie",
"FavoriteSearchItem=1;PreferredGridLayout=2,3,4", options);

    return View(model);
}
```

Note that http-only cookies are inaccessible from JavaScript and calling **document.cookies** will return the empty string for this example. We can observe them from the developer tools of the browser we are using as shown in the following screenshot:

Figure 9.4: *HTTP only cookie with expire date on Chrome developer tools*

NOTE: The user can wipe out cookies any time as he or she wants. You should not rely on data from the cookie. You must also encrypt it if you decide to store security sensitive data.

- **Query strings**: Key value paired data can be transferred with the query string in the URL. The query string in an URL starts by a question mark and key value pairs are separated by the ampersand character; keys and values are separated by the equal character as follows:

http://www.somedomain.com?key1=value1&key2=value2

We can access the query string data in action methods by providing the key to the dictionary in the **Query** property of **Request** as follows:

```
[HttpGet]
public IActionResult Index()
{
    if (Request.Query.ContainsKey("key"))
```

```
    {
        String value = Request.Query["key"];
    }
}
```

We can also use the **FromQuery** attribute to bind the query string parameters model as follows:

```
[HttpGet]
public IActionResult Index([FromQuery] string key)
{

}
```

Query strings are limited to several characters and prone to some security vulnerabilities for stealing and tampering because they are human readable by default. These must be taken into consideration if they are decided to be used. We can also store the state of data in a query string by employing some encryption. This will provide some security to a degree.

- **Hidden Fields**: We can also render hidden input fields with HTML helper methods and make model binding do the work for us.

Let's say we have a model class as follows:

```
public class UserInformationModel
{
    public int Id { get; set; }
    public string UserName { get; set; }
    public string Email { get; set; }
    public string Address { get; set; }
}
```

And we do not want the **Id** field visible to the user, but we need it to make updates and modification to data, and we would like to have it model bound in our action method which works with the http post. We can render a hidden input field and access it from the action method as follows:

```
@model UserInformationModel

<div>
    <div>
        @Html.HiddenFor(t => t.Id)
    </div>
    <div>
```

```
        UserName:
        <div>
            @Html.TextBoxFor(t=> t.UserName)
        </div>
    </div>
    <div>
        Email:
        <div>
            @Html.TextBoxFor(t => t.Email)
        </div>
    </div>
</div>
```

- **Session State**: ASP.NET Core uses a temporary cache to store user specific data on the server. A session ID is created on the server, put in a cookie, and transferred between the client and the server. It is used to access user specific data in the session store. This cookie is specific to the browser session; a new session is created if expired and the user data in it is wiped out. It also must store some data in it; if it is empty, a new session cookie is generated for every request.

ASP.NET Core session management is under the package named **Microsoft. AspNetCore.Session**. We need to configure the necessary service by the **AddSession** method. We can also set the session cookie properties by the **Cookie** property of the lambda expression parameter **SessionOptions** as shown here:

```
        public void ConfigureServices(IServiceCollection services)
        {
            services.AddSession(options =>
            {
                options.IdleTimeout = TimeSpan.FromMinutes(20);
                options.Cookie.HttpOnly = true;
                options.Cookie.IsEssential = true;
            });

            services.AddControllersWithViews();
        }
```

Then, we must register the session middleware. It will read the cookie and load the session from the store. **HttpContext.Session** will be available after this middleware is executed. It is important to put it before the endpoints middleware so session will be ready on action methods as shown here:

```
public void Configure(IApplicationBuilder app, IWebHostEnvironment env)
{
  if (env.IsDevelopment())
  {
      app.UseDeveloperExceptionPage();
  }
  else
  {
      app.UseExceptionHandler("/Home/Error");
  }
  app.UseStaticFiles();
  app.UseRouting();
  app.UseAuthorization();

  app.UseSession();
  app.UseEndpoints(endpoints =>
  {
      endpoints.MapControllerRoute(
      name: "default",
      pattern: "{controller=Home}/{action=Index}/{id?}");
  });
}
```

Now, let's assume we have a view for login as shown in following code:

```
@model UserIdentityModel

@using (Html.BeginForm("Login", "User"))
{
<div>
    <div>
        UserName:
        <div>
            @Html.TextBoxFor(t => t.UserName)
        </div>
```

```
        </div>
        <div>
            Password:
            <div>
                @Html.PasswordFor(t => t.Password)
            </div>
        </div>
        <div>
            <button type="submit">Login</button>
        </div>
    </div>
}
```

The output of a simple login form is shown here:

Figure 9.5: *A simple login form*

We post our form to the action method named login and check whether the information is correct as shown here.

```
[HttpPost]
public IActionResult Login([FromForm] UserIdentityModel model)
{
    int userId = 10;
    //load user information and user id into userId
    HttpContext.Session.SetInt32("UserId", userId);
    return Redirect("/Home");
}
```

Then, we can access our code from the **GetString** or **GetInt32** method of the **ISession** interface:

```
public IActionResult Index()
{
    int? userId = HttpContext.Session.GetInt32("UserId");
    return View();
}
```

We can observe the session cookie with the developer tools from the browser as shown in the following screenshot:

Name	Value	Domain
.AspNetCore.Session	CfDJ8LNepjLX3uVBu1MRciJIHk%2Fg7cxLLJZ%2BZ2rmK5%2FHpA2RjYQ3CW82LMFOceGBK356iGKGfUJEEuCqntej5Cef4gLEh2ORc7mfLKXrbQJa...	localhost
.AspNetCore.Antiforgery.THpmytVNXoU	CfDJ8LNepjLX3uVBu1MRciJIHk_IAw_fh9Y-4Os_JIBSLQacq7jeCKJQ7Q2ytNAKYKM0jgvtftBjWqxQzbkRvxPH2IOGVCsLScLH2ytcxL0QZJFgFESmel...	localhost

Figure 9.6: Session cookie

> **NOTE: Do not forget to clear the session by calling the Clear method of the ISession interface when users log out your application. This will avoid security issues and save system resources.**

We must give a constant key to the store and receive the session data by type conversion. This forces us to remember the type and key of the data always and sometimes, we need convert the string to the type we want. This can be prone to errors and there is a best practice for this.

Façade Design Pattern

Façade is the side of a building looking to the street. It is the visible part of a structure to the outer world. As the description implies, it abstracts and makes an interface simpler to use. There are some ways to implement it, but we can employ the easiest way for getting and setting session variables as shown here:

```
public class SessionHelper
{
 HttpContext _context;

 public SessionHelper(HttpContext context)
 {
    this._context = context;
 }

 public int UserId
 {
   get
   {
     int? userId = _context.Session.GetInt32("UserId");
     if(userId!=null)
     {
        return userId.Value;
     }
```

```
            return 0;
        }
    set
    {
        _context.Session.SetInt32("UserId", value);
    }
}


public string Email
{
    get
    {
        return _context.Session.GetString("UserEmail");
    }
    set
    {
        _context.Session.SetString("UserEmail", value);
    }
}
```

We can also store objects by serializing them into JSON as shown in the following code:

```
public UserIdentityModel Identity
{
    get
    {
        String json= _context.Session.GetString("UserIdentity");
        if (!String.IsNullOrWhiteSpace(json))
        {
            return JsonSerializer.Deserialize<UserIdentityModel>(json);
        }
        else
        {
            return null;
        }
    }
    set
```

```
{

    String json = JsonSerializer.Serialize(value);

    _context.Session.SetString("UserIdentity", json);

}


}
}
```

We can use a helper like this and write the session storage access and mutate code in one place. Session façade saves us from remembering key strings and types.

> **NOTE: If you put too many things into the session façade, it can end up with a huge class. Try to group the primitive values needed into objects and store them in the session.**

Managing distributed session

If we decide to put our application behind a load balancer, we will need to store the session in a common cache; if we do not, the session variables of users may be absent because the balancer distributes requests to deployed machines in order and the data may be absent on the next server as shown in *Figure 9.7*:

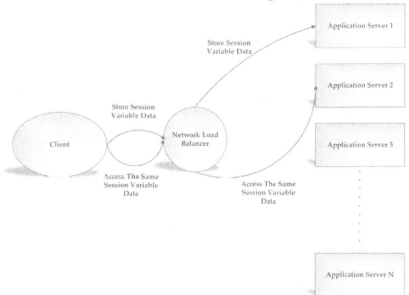

Figure 9.7: Accessing session behind a load balancer

Session storage in ASP.NET Core uses cache mechanism to store the session data. The framework supports in-memory cache or distributed cache. Let us discuss the pros and cons:

- **In-memory cache**: It stores the data in the memory of the server that the application is working on. This is the default caching mechanism in ASP. NET Core.

  It has a faster access since the data resides in the same server with the application itself and it does not add extra complexity for the deployment of the solution.

  But if we decide to scale our application behind a proxy, then we must configure the in-memory session provider and proxy to use sticky scheduling and allow the proxy to distribute requests by user IP addresses.

- **Distributed Cache**: Distributed caching allows you to store session data on a separate server inside the deployment environment. This allows applications with multiple servers behind the proxy to share the session storage along with cache data. ASP.NET Core offers distributed cache by SQL Server, Redis, and NCache.

  The distributed cache can be accessed in the same way across multiple servers. It survives deployments and restarts. Since it does not use the local memory as the default in-memory cache, it may not work as fast as it is and can add extra complexity for the deployment and maintenance of the solution.

  The SQL Server can be chosen as a distributed cache but do not expect it to be as fast as Redis. It can be considered if your application does not rely on so much data in cache along with the session, and you have a ready SQL Server at hand and do not want to install or maintain Redis.

  Cache may come in handy if you need to check some data in every request. If this data is required to be fetched from a database or from a remote server, this can lead to a serious performance penalty. For example, you can store some hard to load authorization data in the cache and make some checks to it at every request quickly.

  The following figure shows how we can centralize and manage the session from a common service by using distributed caching:

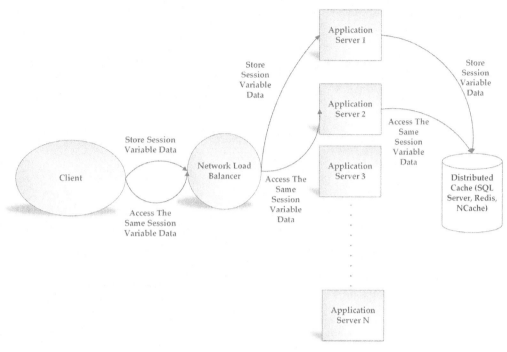

Figure 9.8: *Using distributed session*

NOTE: If the session provider fails to persist the session to the store, the request will continue to execute without any error. It may be possible sometimes that putting something in store may fail. The CommitAsync method of ISession interface can be used to check errors and it is going to throw an exception if something is wrong with the session store.

- Temp data dictionary allows us to store data in a cache until it is read on the next request. It can be used from both razor pages and controllers. We can control the lifetime of the variables and retain them further by the Keep and Peek methods as shown in following code:

```
public class UserController : Controller
{
        public IActionResult Index()
        {
            if (TempData.ContainsKey("SelectedDataId"))
            {
                int selectedDataId = Convert.
ToInt32(TempData["SelectedDataId"]);
            }
            return View();
```

```
        }
}
```

The preceding code tries to access the data with the **SelectedDataId** key. If it exists, it will be wiped out at the end of the request. The **Keep** method will preserve data in temp data marked for deletion as shown here:

```
public class UserController : Controller
{
        public IActionResult Index()
        {
            if (TempData.ContainsKey("SelectedDataId"))
            {
                int selectedDataId = Convert.
ToInt32(TempData["SelectedDataId"]);
                //Data with key SelectedDataId is marked for
deletion.
                TempData.Keep("SelectedDataId ");
                //retain data with key SelectedDataId for another
request
            }
            return View();
        }
}
```

We can also use the overloaded **Keep()** method to retain all temp data variables. On the other hand, we can use the peek method to get the item stored in temp data without marking it for deletion as shown in following code:

```
public class UserController : Controller
{
        public IActionResult Index()
        {
            if (TempData.Peek("SelectedDataId") != null)
            {
            int selectedDataId = Convert.ToInt32(TempData.
Peek("SelectedDataId"));
            }
            return View();
        }
```

}

There are some ways to implement **TempData**. If the data stored in **TempData** is small in size, then we can use the cookie-based **TempData** provider, but if it is not small in size and we use the session store, then we can use the session for temp data. We configure it in the **ConfigureServices** method in the Startup class by the **AddSessionStateTempDataProvider** method as shown here:

```
public void ConfigureServices(IServiceCollection services)
{
        services.AddSession(options =>
        {
            options.IdleTimeout = TimeSpan.FromMinutes(20);
            options.Cookie.HttpOnly = true;
            options.Cookie.IsEssential = true;
        });

        services.AddControllersWithViews()
                .AddSessionStateTempDataProvider();
}
```

- **Items dictionary in HttpContext**: We can use the Items dictionary in **HttpContext** for storing and accessing data across the lifetime of the request. For example, it can be handy to store some data in a middleware and get it after in an action method. The data in it will be wiped out after the request is ended.

ASP.NET Core authentication and identity management

For the new starters, authorization and authentication can be confused with each other. Authorization is what the user is authorized to do. For example, it can be used on the following:

- An action method or an entire controller.
- A block of code specified by an if statement in a business service called from the controller action method or a service called from another service.
- Making some part of the user interfaces visible (buttons for example).

- Determining the user interfaces that the user is authorized to view (in enterprise projects, the application menu is created or filtered by the user's authorization).

- Making some columns of a table selectable at the database level.

The list can go on. We explained the authorization methods ASP.NET Core offers in *Chapter 8, Dependency Injection and Action Filters in ASP.NET Core*. We can authorize action methods by authorization filters but the other methods previously mentioned can also be achieved easily.

Authentication means checking if the user allowed to access the system at first. It also contains managing the way a system recognizes the user. Technically, authorization depends on authentication first.

There are many different authentication types ASP.NET Core supports such as cookie, ldap, Azure Active Directory, Identity Server (Single sign on, federation gateway, access control, authentication as a service), multi factor or custom-made authentication, whatever suits our needs.

We can configure the cookie-based authentication with the **AddAuthentication** extension method of the **IServiceCollection** interface and **AddCookie** method of the authentication builder as shown in the following code:

```
public void ConfigureServices(IServiceCollection services)
{
        services.AddAuthentication("CookieAuth")
        .AddCookie("CookieAuth", config =>
        {
                config.Cookie.Name = "AuthCookie";
                config.LoginPath = "/User";
                config.ExpireTimeSpan = TimeSpan.FromMinutes(30);
        });


        services.AddControllersWithViews()
        .AddSessionStateTempDataProvider();
}
```

It takes a delegate with a parameter which has type **CookieAuthenticationOptions**. It contains the **Cookie** property which we can use to configure cookie options. We can also set the **LoginPath** and **LogoutPath** properties. When the cookie expires, the framework redirects to **LoginPath** automatically. We can redirect an already logged in user to the logout path to remove and invalidate the cookie. The following code shows how to implement a simple login:

```
[HttpPost]
public async Task<IActionResult> Login([FromForm] UserIdentityModel
model)
{
        //check if the user name and password is correct and set the
users claim.
        var defaultClaims = new List<Claim>
        {
            new Claim(ClaimTypes.Name,"Kemal Birer"),
            new Claim(ClaimTypes.Email,"admin@allemandesoftware.com"),
            new Claim("UserId","15671"),
        };
        var defaultIdentityprovider = new ClaimsIdentity(defaultClaims,
"default");
        var userPrincipal = new ClaimsPrincipal(defaultIdentityprovider);
        await HttpContext.SignInAsync(userPrincipal);
        return Redirect("/Home");
}
```

Then, we can use the **Authorize** attribute to make action methods enforce the authentication. It is possible to access claims of the authenticated user with the User property of Controller as shown here:

```
[Authorize]
public class HomeController : Controller
{
    private readonly ILogger<HomeController> _logger;

    public HomeController(ILogger<HomeController> logger)
    {
      _logger = logger;
    }

    public IActionResult Index()
    {
      ClaimsIdentity identity = User.Identity as ClaimsIdentity;
      Claim userNameClaim = identity.Claims
        .FirstOrDefault(c => c.Type == ClaimTypes.Name);
      String userName = userNameClaim.Value;
```

```
    return View();
    }
}
```

ASP.NET Core also offers an identity API that provides easy management of login, creating or modifying user profiles, registering a user, applying password policies, emailing confirmation, the other groundwork for identity management, etc. It uses the SQL Server as the backend storage by default and other storage types are community maintained and configurable. The source code is also accessible from GitHub at **https://github.com/dotnet/AspNetCore/tree/main/src/Identity**.

Microsoft also offers Azure solutions to secure web APIs and identity servers which are advanced and flexible OAuth2.0 and OpenID connect-enabled solutions. It provides **single sign on (SSO)** from different kinds of applications, **authentication as a service (AaaS)**, and many built-in ready to use solutions. It can be checked out from the website **https://duendesoftware.com/**.

We will show you how to set up and configure it by a new project. Let's create a new project by starting Visual Studio and pressing the **Create New Project** button. Now, we select the web app template and in the **Additional information** step, select **Individual Accounts** as the authentication type as shown in the following screenshot:

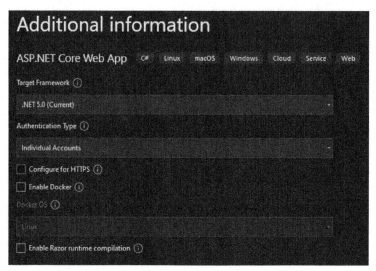

Figure 9.9: Selecting the authentication type

ASP.NET Core identity is a ready-to-use solution. It contains the required Razor components and database tables for us already. We can set the connection string, run migrations and the identity database is going to be created for us. We will cover migrations in *Chapter 10, Introducing Accessing Data with ASP.NET Core*. The following figure shows the scaffolded identity database:

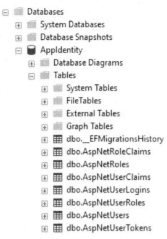

Figure 9.10: ASP.NET Core identity tables

We must also configure identity services at the **Startup** class. We can define a password policy, and enforce some rules such as a required length, specific number of digits and an uppercase letter, define a username policy, configure when the user is going to be locked out, and arrange cookie settings by the extension methods of the identity API as shown in the following code:

```
public void ConfigureServices(IServiceCollection services)
{
        services.AddDbContext<ApplicationDbContext>(options =>
            options.UseSqlServer(
            Configuration.GetConnectionString("DefaultConnection")));
            services.AddDatabaseDeveloperPageExceptionFilter();
            services.AddDefaultIdentity<IdentityUser>(options =>
options.SignIn.RequireConfirmedAccount = true)
                .AddEntityFrameworkStores<ApplicationDbContext>();

        services.Configure<IdentityOptions>(options =>
        {
            options.User.AllowedUserNameCharacters = "1234567890";
            options.User.RequireUniqueEmail = false;

            options.Lockout.DefaultLockoutTimeSpan = TimeSpan.
FromMinutes(5);
            options.Lockout.MaxFailedAccessAttempts = 5;
            options.Lockout.AllowedForNewUsers = true;

            options.Password.RequireDigit = true;
```

```
        options.Password.RequireLowercase = true;
        options.Password.RequireNonAlphanumeric = true;
        options.Password.RequireUppercase = true;
        options.Password.RequiredLength = 6;
        options.Password.RequiredUniqueChars = 1;

});

services.ConfigureApplicationCookie(options =>
{
        options.Cookie.HttpOnly = true;
        options.ExpireTimeSpan = TimeSpan.FromMinutes(15);

        options.LoginPath = "/Identity/Account/Login";
        options.AccessDeniedPath = "/Identity/Account/AccessDenied";
        options.SlidingExpiration = true;
});

services.AddRazorPages();
}
```

We can scaffold the identity user interfaces and modify their markups later. We will right click on our project and select the **Add** | **New Scaffolded** item. Then, we need to select the **Identity** option from the opened add new scaffolded item dialog box, select the required entity framework context, or create a new one. At the end, Razor views are added to our project automatically as shown in the following screenshot:

***Figure 9.11**: Scaffold identity user interfaces*

We must also add the authentication middleware by calling the **UseAuthentication** method. The following figure shows a scaffolded user registration razor page. Notice how ASP.NET Core simplifies things for us:

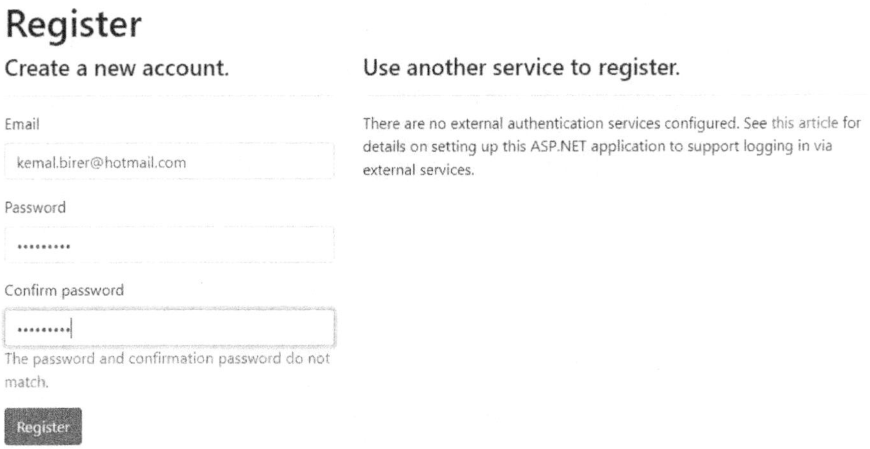

Register

Create a new account.

Email

kemal.birer@hotmail.com

Password

·········

Confirm password

·········

The password and confirmation password do not match.

Register

Use another service to register.

There are no external authentication services configured. See this article for details on setting up this ASP.NET application to support logging in via external services.

Figure 9.12: Ready to use identity management user interfaces with functionality

Finally, we added the identity management functionality to our project with user interfaces that have validation inside them as we configured them at the Startup in just a few minutes. The following figure shows the scaffolded razor pages:

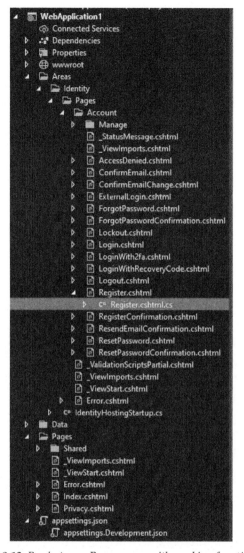

Figure 9.13: Ready to use Razor pages with working functionality

We can modify the added razor pages as we desire and add more business logic to the added action methods. ASP.NET Core really does a good job that features an easily configurable, ready-to-use identity framework and saves us from a lot of groundwork.

Conclusion

We learned that the session, state, identity management, and how ASP.NET Core helps us to manage identity with minimal coding and configuration as possible. We will cover accessing data in the next chapter.

Questions

1. We do not want cookies of our application modifiable from the JavaScript. How can we achieve that?

2. Our application is behind NLB and in a cluster with many servers that run it. How can we configure session storage and why?

3. How can we manage identity in an ASP.NET Core application?

CHAPTER 10

Introducing Accessing Data with ASP.NET Core

Introduction

We covered session state management and how to authorize and authenticate in ASP.NET Core in the previous chapter. We will cover data access with ASP.NET Core in this chapter Every enterprise software project at every scale accesses and persists data somehow and this makes accessing data a fundamental pillar of the backend development. We will explain using the entity framework and how to manage data operations.

Structure

In this chapter, we will discuss the following topics:

- Introduction to SQL and Ado.NET
- Introduction to Language Integrated Query
- Introduction to ORM, Entity Framework Core, and development approaches
- Configuring DbContext for ASP.NET Core
- Understanding querying data, lazy loading, eager loading, and change tracking
- Introduction to the Repository design pattern

- Transaction management

Objectives

After reading this chapter, you should be able to understand and implement data management in ASP.NET Core with Entity Framework Core. You can still benefit the knowledge explained here by applying them to the other type of .NET projects. We assume you have some knowledge about SQL and relational databases.

Introducing SQL and Ado.NET

There are several relational database management systems (RDMS) out in the market. From open-source PostgreSQL, MySQL to commercial SQL Server, Oracle, DB2, and so on. The language that relational databases understand is **Structured Query Language** (**SQL**). We query, manipulate data, define data objects, such as tables and views in RDMS with SQL. Whatever data access framework or programming language we use, the final stage is generating SQL statements and running them on RDMS.

When the .NET framework was first born, it came with a framework named Ado. NET. It has the fundamental classes required for independent database development. It has abstract classes, such as **DbConnection**, **DbCommand**, and **DbDataReader,** and for every RDMS, they have implementations like **SqlConnection**, **SqlCommand**, and **SqlDataReader** as shown in the following code snippet:

```
using (DbConnection connection = new
SqlConnection("Server=(local);Database=AppIdentity;Trusted_
Connection=True;MultipleActiveResultSets=true"))
{
    DbCommand command = connection.CreateCommand();
    command.CommandText = @"SELECT [Id]
                          ,[UserName]
                          ,[NormalizedUserName]
                          ,[Email]
                          ,[NormalizedEmail]
                          ,[EmailConfirmed]
                          ,[PasswordHash]
                          ,[SecurityStamp]
                          ,[ConcurrencyStamp]
                          ,[PhoneNumber]
                          ,[PhoneNumberConfirmed]
```

```
                             ,[TwoFactorEnabled]
                             ,[LockoutEnd]
                             ,[LockoutEnabled]
                             ,[AccessFailedCount]
                        FROM[AppIdentity].[dbo].[AspNetUsers]";


 DbDataReader dataReader = command.ExecuteReader();
while (dataReader.Read())
{
 string id = dataReader[0].ToString();
 string userName = !dataReader.IsDBNull(1) ? dataReader["UserName"].
ToString() : "";
}
 dataReader.Close();

}
```

One of the best practices is to create **DbConnection** and create **DbCommand** from it. We can specify the SQL command text or stored procedure and execute a data reader from it. We can use the read method of **DbDataReader** by calling it in a loop until it returns the false value. It is important we close it when we are done with it. We can use the index or alias name of columns in the **select** statement.

We can call the **ExecuteNonQuery** method of **DbCommand** for manipulating data. It returns the number of rows affected as shown in the following code snippet:

```
using (DbConnection connection = new
SqlConnection("Server=local;Database=AppIdentity;Trusted_
Connection=True;MultipleActiveResultSets=true"))
{
        DbCommand command = connection.CreateCommand();
        command.CommandText = @"insert into AspNetUsers (Id
                                    ,UserName
                                    ,NormalizedUserName
                                    ,Email
                                    ,NormalizedEmail
                                    ,EmailConfirmed
                                    ,PasswordHash
                                    ,SecurityStamp
                                    ,ConcurrencyStamp
                                    ,PhoneNumber
```

```
                                    ,PhoneNumberConfirmed
                                    ,TwoFactorEnabled
                                    ,LockoutEnd
                                    ,LockoutEnabled
                                    ,AccessFailedCount)
                            VALUES (......)";
        Int numOfAffected=command.ExecuteNonQuery();
}
```

The Ado.NET framework is the fundamental framework of data access in .NET. Whether you use the Entity Framework Core or nHibernate or any high-level data access framework, the generated SQL is executed by using the Ado.NET framework.

Although it provides features enough for database independent development, using it is cumbersome and error prone. We must map data reader values to objects and set parameters of SQL statements manually. Programming dynamic SQL can also be a painful work. Concatenating strings based on dynamic conditions and setting parameters depending on the generated dynamic SQL can be tedious. The need for better data access frameworks arose to solve all these problems and simplify database access for developers, so they can focus their attention to business of the projects instead of dealing with the complicated data access code.

Introducing to Language Integrated Query (LINQ)

LINQ is the name of querying capabilities and technologies integrated into C# language. We used to write SQL queries in strings. There was no strong typing and making dynamic queries were difficult. LINQ was developed to query by C# code and we can query different data sources by using it as follows:

- Databases
- XML documents
- Collections of objects
- Active directories
- Many data sources having a LINQ provider

We can achieve this with a single interface and extension methods with lambda expression paramteters. Let's assume we have a class like the following:

```
public class UserInformation
{
    public int Id { get; set; }
```

```
    public string UserName { get; set; }
    public string Email { get; set; }
}
```

We can query a collection of the **UserInformation** objects by a given username like the following:

```
public void OnGet(string userName)
{
  IEnumerable<UserInformation> users = new List<UserInformation>();
  UserInformation user = users.Where(u => u.UserName == userName).
FirstOrDefault();
}
```

The where extension method takes a predicate (a lambda expression returns a Boolean) and the **FirstOrDefault** method returns the first object matching the criteria in the where predicate.

We can also query the file system like the following. In this example, we query files in a directory with creation date less than the given date:

```
public void OnGet(DateTime fileCreationDate)
{
    DirectoryInfo directory = new DirectoryInfo("C:\\some_path");
    List<FileInfo> files = directory.GetFiles()
                .Where(file => file.CreationTime < fileCreationDate).
ToList();
}
```

We can also query an XML document. The following example shows selecting concatenated names and surnames. Let's say we have an XML document like the following:

```
<?xml version="1.0"?>
<Users>
  <UserInformation CreationDate="2005-11-08">
    <Name>John</Name>
    <Surname>Doe</Surname>
    <Address>
      <Zip>78484</Zip>
      <Country>USA</Country>
    </Address>
  </UserInformation>
```

```
<UserInformation CreationDate="2014-12-02">
  <Name>Jane</Name>
  <Surname>Doe</Surname>
  <Address>
    <Zip>45645</Zip>
    <Country>UK</Country>
  </Address>
</UserInformation>
</Users>
```

We can list the entire concatenated name and surname pairs like the following query:

```
public void OnGet()
{
  XElement xmlData = XElement.Load("some path to a xml");

  IEnumerable<string> nameSurnames = from item in xmlData.
Descendants("UserInformation") select item.Element("Name").Value + " " +
item.Element("Surname").Value;
}
```

We can write LINQ statements in the following two ways:

- **LINQ queries**: They have a similar syntax to SQL as shown here:

  ```
  from {alias} in {collection name} where {criteria with using
  alias} select {alias.property}.
  ```

- **Object methods (lambda expressions)**: They use extension methods and lambda expressions to form queries as shown here:

  ```
  {collection}.Where(c=> {criteria}).Select(alias=> alias.{property
  to select})
  ```

We can use any of them depending on the coding standards we would like to apply to our project.

Introduction to the Entity Framework Core and development approaches

Object relational mapping (ORM) is a programming paradigm for converting data between sides which have incompatible forms of data. From the .NET perspective, we can say mapping data reader values to .NET objects and mapping property values in .NET objects to SQL statement parameters.

The Entity Framework Core is an open-source, cross-platform version of the previous entity framework developed for .NET. It helps taking care of most of the data access code and allow developers to create database queries by LINQ.

The Entity Framework Core performs data access and persistence on models. A model consists of dB sets which are a collection of entities. Entities are C# classes which are equivalent of database tables. A model can be generated by different approaches with the Entity framework as follows:

- **Database First**: As the name implies, we develop the database first by a database tool, generate entities and context by the tool named **dotnet-ef**. It is used from dotnet cli. To be able to use it, we must install it by using the CLI command:

```
dotnet tool install --global dotnet-ef
```

We must also add the NuGet package **Microsoft.EntityFrameworkCore.Design** to our project.

We can then generate entities and context classes by running the following **dotnet ef** command:

```
dotnet ef dbcontext scaffold "connection string" Microsoft.
EntityFrameworkCore.SqlServer -o {output folder}
```

- **Code First:** The code first approach allows you to define entities first on the code and generate and migrate changes to the database later. Let us create a simple model for our phonebook application by code first. Assume we would like to store contacts (name, surnames, birth date) and their phone numbers (phone number, mobile phone). Contacts have a one-to-many relationship to phones. We can define an entity class for contacts as follows:

```
[Table("tblContactInformation")]
public class ContactInformation
{
    [Key]
    [Column("colID")]
    [DatabaseGenerated(DatabaseGeneratedOption.Identity)]
    public int Id { get; set; }

    [Column("colName")]
    [StringLength(50)]
    [Required]
    public string Name { get; set; }
```

```
    [Column("colSurname")]
    [StringLength(50)]
    [Required]
    public string Surname { get; set; }


    [Column("colDateOfBirth")]
    [Required]
    public DateTime? Dob { get; set; }


    public ICollection<ContactPhone> PhoneNumbers { get; set;
}


    }
```

It is a simple class with properties having accessors and mutators. We notice the **Table**, **Key**, **DatabaseGenerated**, and **Column** attributes. We can define the name of the table by the **Table** attribute, its primary key column by the **Key** attribute, how the primary key column will be generated by the **DatabaseGenerated** attribute, and column names by the **Column** attribute.

> **TIP:** The DatabaseGeneratedOption enum specifies how the primary key is generated. It can be None if we would like to set the primary key by ourselves; it can be a globally unique identifier for example. Identity if we would like the database to generate the primary key (identity column in SQL Server for example). Computed if we would like to specify the way how a database generates the primary keys. Also, you can define a composite primary key by putting the Key attributes on top of multiple properties.

If we do not use the **Table** and **Column** attributes, the entity framework will generate tables and columns with the same name of the entity class and its properties. We use the data annotations to define mandatory columns (**Required**) and length of the string columns (**StringLength**). The data annotations validate the entities and define the properties of the columns of the database tables. We also define one-to-many relations with the **ICollection** which has the generic type to the other end of the relation. Now, let's define that other end by the **ContactPhone** class as shown here:

```
    [Table("tblContactPhone")]
    public class ContactPhone
    {
        [Key]
        [Column("colID")]
```

```
        public int Id { get; set; }


        [Column("colContactInformationId")]
        [ForeignKey(nameof(ContactInformation))]
        public int ContactInformationId { get; set; }


        public ContactInformation { get; set; }


        [Column("colPhone")]
        public string Phone { get; set; }


        [Column("colIsMobilePhone")]
        public bool IsMobilePhone { get; set; }
    }
```

Since **ContactPhone** is the other end of the one-to-many relation from **ContactInformation**, we have a many-to-one relation from **ContactPhone** to **ContactInformation**. We must define two properties, the foreign key property (**ContactInformationId**) and the other property which is the actual property to the other end of the relation (**ContactInformation**). We then define the foreign key by the **ForeignKey** attribute.

In the Entity framework, the **PhoneNumbers** property in the entity **ContactInformation** and **ContactInformation** property in the **ContactPhone** entity are called navigational properties. It allows us to traverse the relations between tables just like accessing the object graph in C# by the properties.

We must define a database context class. It is a class derived from the **DbContext** class that contains **DbSet** of entities. DbSets are the properties that are considered as queryable tables by the entity framework. When we want to query a table, we use a LINQ query or lambda expression on DbSets in the **DbContext** object and the entity framework converts those queries into SQL, runs it on the database, receives, and maps them to the entities (materialization). Let's define a sample database context named **PhoneBookContext** as follows:

```
public class PhoneBookContext : DbContext
{
    public PhoneBookContext()
    {
```

```
    }

    public DbSet<ContactInformation> ContactInformations { get;
set; }

    public DbSet<ContactPhone> ContactPhones { get; set; }

    protected override void OnConfiguring(DbContextOptionsBuilder
optionsBuilder)
    {
        optionsBuilder.
UseSqlServer(@"Server=(local);Database=PhoneBook;Integrated
Security=True");
    }
}
```

NOTE: Notice how we named Db Sets for entities ContactInformation, ContactPhone with plural naming ContactInformations and ContactPhones. This naming convention is one of the best practices for the entity framework. This way we can distinguish Db Sets since they represent the entire database table for an entity.

We must add the entity framework provider of the database we want to use as the NuGet package to our project. In our example, it is the SQL Server provider.

NOTE: The entity framework is database independent. A provider for the underlying database must be used. They are vendor specific and can be checked from the following URL https://docs.microsoft.com/en-us/ef/core/providers/?tabs=dotnet-core-cli.

The code first approach is used when usually developers design the database, and they want to design the entities at the same time to quickly set up a new project with the database and manage database changes (called migrations in the entity framework) from the code.

The database first approach is used when a skilled database administrator or an expert specific to the database of the project designs the database with dba tools. A fine-tuned database for the project is designed first, and entities are created from it later.

The **DbContext** object must be supplied with the connection string. It can be done from the OnConfiguring method of the base **DbContext** class. When we want to create or modify changes made to the database in the code first approach, we can open the Package Manager Console in Visual Studio, select the .Net project that contains the database context, and type **Add-Migration** {a unique migration name}. This is going to create a migration class. Let's run the **Add-Migration InitialCommit** command to create the initial database from our model in PhoneBook. A migration class is automatically generated as follows:

```
public partial class InitialCommit : Migration
{
    protected override void Up(MigrationBuilder migrationBuilder)
    {
        migrationBuilder.CreateTable(
            name: "tblContactInformation",
            columns: table => new
            {
                colID = table.Column<int>(type: "int", nullable:
false)
                    .Annotation("SqlServer:Identity", "1, 1"),
                colName = table.Column<string>(type:
"nvarchar(50)", maxLength: 50, nullable: false),
                colSurname = table.Column<string>(type:
"nvarchar(50)", maxLength: 50, nullable: false),
                colDateOfBirth = table.Column<DateTime>(type:
"datetime2", nullable: false)
            },
            constraints: table =>
            {
                table.PrimaryKey("PK_tblContactInformation", x =>
x.colID);
            });

        migrationBuilder.CreateTable(
            name: "tblContactPhone",
            columns: table => new
            {
                colID = table.Column<int>(type: "int", nullable:
false)
                    .Annotation("SqlServer:Identity", "1, 1"),
```

```
                colContactInformationId = table.Column<int>(type:
"int", nullable: false),
                colPhone = table.Column<string>(type:
"nvarchar(max)", nullable: true),
                colIsMobilePhone = table.Column<bool>(type:
"bit", nullable: false)
            },
            constraints: table =>
            {
                table.PrimaryKey("PK_tblContactPhone", x =>
x.colID);
                table.ForeignKey(
                    name: "FK_tblContactPhone_
tblContactInformation_colContactInformationId",
                    column: x => x.colContactInformationId,
                    principalTable: "tblContactInformation",
                    principalColumn: "colID",
                    onDelete: ReferentialAction.Cascade);
            });

        migrationBuilder.CreateIndex(
            name: "IX_tblContactPhone_colContactInformationId",
            table: "tblContactPhone",
            column: "colContactInformationId");
    }

    protected override void Down(MigrationBuilder
migrationBuilder)
    {
        migrationBuilder.DropTable(
            name: "tblContactPhone");

        migrationBuilder.DropTable(
            name: "tblContactInformation");
    }
}
```

There are **Up** and **Down** methods in every migration class that defines how the changes are applied and how the changes are reverted. Since this is our initial database creation, the **Up** method contains the method calls that generate tables from the dB sets inside the database context, data annotations, and other attributes in the properties of entities. The **Down** method drops the tables defined by the dB sets in the database context by the nature of the initial migration that creates the database for the first time.

We can apply migrations by the **Update-Database** command from the Package manager console in Visual Studio. It applies the migrations to the database. When we open the database with a tool, we notice an extra table named **EFMigrationsHistory** is created. It tracks the version of the database and applies the migrations by the last migration information inside it. The following figure shows a database with the initial migration applied:

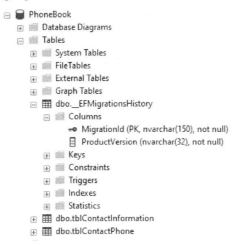

Figure 10.1: *A database created by the Code First approach*

Now, let's suppose we would like to add a column to the **tblContactPhone** table to hold country codes of the phone numbers. We can add an integer property **CountryCode** to the **ContactPhone** entity. We must add a new migration to apply the new column addition to the table by running **Add-Migration CountryCode**. We notice the Up method contains the code for adding a new column and the **Down** method contains the code to drop that column as shown here:

```
public partial class CountryCode : Migration
{
    protected override void Up(MigrationBuilder migrationBuilder)
    {
        migrationBuilder.AddColumn<int>(
            name: "colCountryCode",
            table: "tblContactPhone",
            type: "int",
```

```
            nullable: false,
            defaultValue: 0);
    }

    protected override void Down(MigrationBuilder migrationBuilder)
    {
        migrationBuilder.DropColumn(
            name: "colCountryCode",
            table: "tblContactPhone");
    }
}
```

Configuring the database context for ASP. NET Core

It is time to explain how we will use the database context in our code. The entity framework uses the entity framework provider of the database, and the provider eventually uses ADO.NET and ADO.NET uses the driver of the database in the end. The database context also manages sensitive resources, such as the underlying database connection, transactions, and the lifetime of the database context must be managed carefully. An entity framework database context lifetime can be considered as the following order:

- Creating the context
- Opening the database connection
- Querying
- Loading data
- Tracking changes made to the loaded data
- Reflecting changes to the database
- Disposal and closing the database connection

> NOTE: The concept explained above is named Unit of Work. It is basically tracking changes that must be reflected to the database in a single business transaction.

The entity framework database context is not thread safe; it must open a database connection, perform the unit of work, close the database connection, and be disposed. Therefore, it must be short lived.

In the case of ASP.NET, of course, dependency injection is used to configure the lifetime of a database context. The context must be configured as scoped in the dependency injection container, so it has the same lifetime as the request. A new context is created when it is needed in a request and disposed when the request is ended and closes the database connection while disposed. We covered dependency injection in *Chapter 8, Dependency Injection and Action Filters in ASP.NET Core*. The following code registers the database context as configured scoped lifetime in the di container:

```
public void ConfigureServices(IServiceCollection services)
{
    services.AddControllersWithViews();
    services.AddDbContext<PhoneBookContext>(options => options.
UseSqlServer("connection string of the database"));
}
```

> **NOTE: You can also inject IConfiguration into DbContext and read the connection string from there or read the connection string in Startup.cs. This way you can benefit the reading connection string from the configuration files in different environments.**

Now, we can inject and use the database context in our controllers or other business objects like the services registered in di.

Querying data, lazy loading, eager loading, and change tracking

We can perform many query operations in SQL, if the entity framework provider of the database can interpret and convert them to SQL. **IQueryable<>** is the fundamental interface of the entity framework for querying data. We can start querying from DbSets themselves (which implements the **IQueryable<>** interface also), chain, and compose queries using the extension methods in this interface.

We can filter the tables with the **Where** extension method. It takes a predicate which is a lambda expression that results in a Boolean. For example, we can query contacts with names that start with **"So"** as shown here:

```
public class HomeController : Controller
{
    PhoneBookContext _dataContext;

    public HomeController(PhoneBookContext dataContext)
    {
        _logger = logger;
```

```
        _dataContext = dataContext;
    }

    public IActionResult Index()
    {
        var query= _dataContext.ContactInformations.Where(ci => ci.Name.
StartsWith("So"));
    }
}
```

We can query contacts whose names start with So and contain surnames with more than 3 characters with the logical and (**&&**) operator of the C# as follows:

```
var query= _dataContext.ContactInformations.Where(ci => ci.Name.
StartsWith("So") && ci.Surname.Count() > 3);
```

We can achieve the same purpose by calling an another where of the first query. The **Where** method also returns the **IQueryable<>** interface and when chained, it applies logical AND:

```
var query= _dataContext.ContactInformations.Where(ci => ci.Name.
StartsWith("So"));
query = query.Where(q=> q.Surname.Count() > 3);
```

Writing predicates are like writing if statements; we can also use the OR (| |) operator to generate the SQL criteria with or clauses.

We can generate criteria using in clauses with the **Contains** method of the C# collections. For example, we have a phone numbers array like the following, and we want to get the name and surname of the people having those phone numbers:

```
public IActionResult Index()
{
  string[] phones = new string[3] { "5558889965", "5558889964",
"5558889963" };

  var query = _dataContext.ContactPhones
  .Where(cp => phones.Contains(cp.Phone))
  .Select(ci => ci.ContactInformation.Name + " " +
ci.ContactInformation.Surname);

  .

  .

}
```

The preceding query uses the **Contains** method of the array in the where predicate to generate an in SQL clause, and uses the navigation property **ContactInformation** in the **ContactPhone** entity to reach the filtered contact information in the select method. When we use navigation properties between entities this way, entity framework generates an SQL with inner join between tables.

The **Select** extension method allows us to write lambda expressions that project and shape the result. We can specify specific columns as properties or related entities with navigation properties.

We can also compose queries with the **Contains** method. Let's say we would like to list the names and surnames of the people having phone numbers with the country code of India as follows:

```
public IActionResult Index()
{
    IQueryable<int> phoneQuery = _dataContext.ContactPhones
        .Where(cp => cp.CountryCode == 91)
        .Select(t => t.ContactInformationId);


    _dataContext
      .ContactPhones
    .Where(cp => phoneQuery.Contains(cp.Id))
    .Select(ci => ci.ContactInformation.Name + " " +
ci.ContactInformation.Surname);

    .

    .

}
```

In the preceding query, we write a query for **ContactPhones** having the country code 91 and select the foreign key property **ContactInformationId** in the select method and assign it to the **phoneQuery** variable having type **IQueryable<int>** since it has **ContactInformationId** selected which is an integer property Then we compose and intersect two queries by the contains method. The **IQueryable** interface is derived from **IEnumerable,** and we can use the contains method in the same way as previously done.

> **TIP: The preceding code shows one of the many ways to compose queries. Writing a huge query with complicated logic can be very hard to read and understand. Try to break down large queries into smaller ones and compose them. You can also reuse them this way.**

While we are preparing IQueryable queries, they are not run on the database yet. To execute an entity framework query on the database, we can call the following methods of the IEnumerable interface:

- **ToList, ToArray**: These methods execute the query and return the results as a list or an array.

- **First, FirstOrDefault**: The first method returns the first element in the query or throws an exception if the query has no elements. The `FirstOrDefault` method works in the same way like First, but it returns the default type of the result of the query if it does not have any elements (null for reference types, 0 for integers, and so on).

- **Any**: It generates exists or similar SQL statement and returns a Boolean variable depending on whether the query has a result or not.

- **Count**: It returns the count of elements in the query.

- **Max**: It returns the maximum of the elements in the query.

- **Min**: It returns the minimum of the elements in the query.

These are the most used ones, and they also have async versions. We can identify them as having the same method names but ending with the Async suffix.

The preceding methods materialize the query. The results are mapped to the entities or custom classes projected with select. After this stage, the entities are tracked for changes made to them until the database context is disposed of or the `SaveChanges` method is called. We can also load entities by lazy loading. Let us assume we would like to load the phone contact with the ID that equals to some number coming from the user interface. We then need to load phones of that contact if the user is authorized as shown in the following code snippet:

```
public IActionResult Index(int id)
{
    ContactInformation contact = null;
    contact = _dataContext.ContactInformations
            .Where(ci => ci.Id == id).FirstOrDefault();

    if (/*check if authorized to get phones*/)
    {
        var phones = contact.PhoneNumbers;
    }
}
```

We query the contact with the primary key property equals to the **id** parameter of the **Index** method. We then check whether the user is authorized to access contact phones and then call the navigation property as if it is filled with phones already. This is called **lazy loading**. We do not have phone numbers of the contacts at the initial stage, but when we need it, we use the navigation property (simply, it is an accessor C# property). The entity framework runs a query immediately and loads the phone numbers with **ContactInformationId** equals to the ID parameter and assign it to the variable used (phones variable in our case).

> TIP: Lazy loading can degrade performance of the database if used carelessly. Developers may forget and duplicate the queries made to the database. For these reasons, lazy loading is usually considered harmful and disabled from the database context in many software projects.

We can also optimize our queries and load entities together with their navigational properties. Let's assume we would like to load a phone number along with the contact information together at once as shown here:

```
public IActionResult Index(string phoneNumber)
{
    ContactPhone phone = null;
    phone = _dataContext.ContactPhones.
                    Include(cp => cp.ContactInformation)
                    .Where(p => p.Phone == phoneNumber)
                    .FirstOrDefault();
}
```

We filter the **ContactPhones** dB set with the given phone number parameter by the **Where** method and use the **Include** method to specify the navigation property in the lambda expression. This will create an SQL statement with a left outer join and loads the **ContactPhone** and **ContactInformation** if exists (in our example, it exists already). This technique is called **eager loading**.

> NOTE: Be advised, if you fetch so much data with so many related entities to them with eager loading, the performance of the query may degrade. The generated SQL statements for eager loading may not be database friendly. Use eager loading with keeping this in mind.

After querying and materializing data, they are attached to the database context and change tracked. Let us assume we would like to load a **ContactInformation** with the given **id** parameter. We set its **Dob** parameter with today's date and add a new contact information as shown here:

```
public IActionResult Index(in id)
{
    ContactInformation contact = null;
    contact = _dataContext.ContactInformations
                .Where(ci => ci.Id == 10).FirstOrDefault();
    contact.Dob = DateTime.Now;
```

```
ContactInformation newContact = new ContactInformation()
{
    Name = "John",
    Surname = "Doe"
};


_dataContext.ContactInformations.Add(newContact);
_dataContext.SaveChanges();


int newContactId = newContact.Id;
}
```

We modified an entity's **Dob** parameter and add a new entity by simply adding the new entity to the **db** set of the database context. The database context has an entity to update and a new entity to insert into the database. We reflect those changes to the database by the **SaveChanges** method of the database context. The primary key values of the entities are automatically mapped back to the new inserted entities (the properties having key and **[DatabaseGenerated(DatabaseGeneratedOption. Identity)]** attributes).

Introducing the Repository pattern

We use the common database operations for many entities in a project. We delete them by their primary key, select them by their primary key, query them, and so on. We can abstract these common operations in a generic interface as shown in the following code snippet:

```
public interface IRepository<T> where T: class
{
    T SelectById(object id);
    IEnumerable<T> SelectAll();
    void Delete(object id);
    void AddNew(T obj);
    void Update(T obj);
}
```

And we encapsulate them in an implementation as shown here:

```
public class BaseRepository<T> : IRepository<T> where T: class
{
```

```
    DbContext _context;
    DbSet<T> _set;
    public BaseRepository(DbContext context)
    {
        this._context = context;
        this._set = context.Set<T>();
    }
    public virtual void AddNew(T obj)
    {
        this._set.Add(obj);
    }


    public virtual void Delete(object id)
    {
        T existingEntity = SelectById(id);
        this._set.Remove(existingEntity);
    }

    public virtual IEnumerable<T> SelectAll()
    {
        return this._set.ToList();
    }

    public virtual T SelectById(object id)
    {
        return _set.Find(id);
    }

    public virtual void Update(T obj)
    {
        EntityEntry<T> entry = _set.Attach(obj);
        entry.State = EntityState.Modified;
    }
}
```

We can then derive a repository for an entity from the base repository as shown here:

```
public class ContactInformationRepository :
BaseRepository<ContactInformation>
```

```
{
    public ContactInformationRepository(PhoneBookContext context) :
base(context)
    {

    }
}
```

We can override virtual methods in the base repository and add some validation or extra stuff for the current entity at hand (which is **ContactInformation** in our example).

> NOTE: The Repository design pattern is widely used in many software projects but considered anti pattern by some part of the software community because it does not comply with S.O.L.I.D. principles.

Transaction management

The database transactions are units of work done at the database level. They are used when it is desired that multiple database operations are completed successfully or failed all together if one of the operations fails or a condition is unsatisfied. We use transactions in .NET with **using** blocks. We can begin a transaction by calling the **BeginTransaction** from the database context's **Database** property as shown in the following code:

```
using(var transaction = _dataContext.Database.BeginTransaction())
{
    if (/*some condition*/)
    {
        transaction.Rollback();
    }
    else
        transaction.Commit();
}
```

Transactions must be completed or rolled back. We use using blocks to guarantee it is rollbacked automatically when there is an exception inside the using block. We can rollback transactions if we like and entire modified, deleted or added entities with the **SaveChanges** method is not applied to the database.

> NOTE: Database transactions can lock database tables and degrade performance. It is best to keep them short.

Conclusion

In this chapter, we learned setting up the entity framework and using it in ASP.NET Core. The entity framework is a large topic with many more features and these are out of the scope of this book. In the next chapter, we will cover optimization of ASP. NET Core applications.

Questions

1. How do we model databases with the entity framework and what are the differences, advantages, and disadvantages between them?

2. How can we register and use a database context in ASP.NET Core?

3. Can a database context be registered as a singleton? If not, explain why?

4. How can we compose queries in the entity framework and why we should do it?

5. Explain the differences between lazy and eager loading.

CHAPTER 11

Optimizing ASP.NET Core Applications

Introduction

In the previous chapter, we covered how to access data in ASP.NET Core, and now we will cover optimization of ASP.NET Core applications in this chapter. Optimization is an important aspect of any software project that must be able to provide a better end user experience and save server resources. We will also cover some of the techniques that can be applied to the other types of .NET applications.

Structure

In this chapter, we will discuss the following topics:

- Introduction to response caching
- Using Cache tags
- Content bundling and minification
- Using event counters
- Other optimization techniques

Objectives

After reading this chapter, you will be able to optimize ASP.NET Core projects easily. We will cover response caching, minification, bundling, and how to measure the performance of your code by using event counters.

Introduction to response caching

Response caching allows us to cache some of the resources on the server or client browser; so, the server does not execute requests for those resources and returns cached responses directly to the client. The response cache can be implemented at the server, proxy, or the browser. It is controlled by http headers, query strings, and ASP.NET Core allows us to easily configure caching by different parameters such as headers, query string parameters, and so on. There are caching standards in HTTP and ASP.NET Core honours them.

Caching depends on the Cache-Control request header which can have the following values:

- **no-cache**: This forces the server to handle the request and returns fresh responses.
- **max-age**: Clients invalidate responses whose age is older than the value in seconds specified in here.
- **public**: This response can be cached by any store.
- **private**: This response is not to be stored in a shared cache.
- **no-store**: This specifies cancelling the store of requests or responses.

ASP.NET Core controls those headers by the response cache filter. Its parameters are described as follows:

- **VaryByHeader**: The response is cached by the value of the request header specified with this parameter.
- **VaryByQueryKeys**: The response is cached by the value of the query string keys specified with this parameter. This parameter is an array of strings.
- **Duration**: This is the lifetime of the cached response in seconds.
- **NoStore**: This denotes that the response should not be stored. If the Location property is None, then the duration is ignored and response will not be cached.

To use response caching, we must register the response caching services and add middleware, as shown in the following lines of code:

```
public void ConfigureServices(IServiceCollection services)
```

```
{
    services.AddResponseCaching();
    services.AddControllersWithViews();
    services.AddDbContext<PhoneBookContext>(options => options.
UseSqlServer("connection string of the database"));
}
public void Configure(IApplicationBuilder app, IWebHostEnvironment env)
{
    if (env.IsDevelopment())
    {
        app.UseDeveloperExceptionPage();
    }
    else
    {
        app.UseExceptionHandler("/Home/Error");
    }
    app.UseStaticFiles();
    app.UseResponseCaching();

    app.UseRouting();

    app.UseAuthorization();

    app.UseEndpoints(endpoints =>
    {
        endpoints.MapControllerRoute(
            name: "default",
            pattern: "{controller=Home}/{action=Index}/{id?}");
    });
}
```

Let us consider we would like to cache the JSON result of our service for ten minutes by the query string parameter named **type**. We put the **ResponseCache** filter attribute on top of our action method as shown here:

```
[ResponseCache(VaryByQueryKeys = new string[1] { "type" }, Duration =
600)]
public IActionResult GetData([FromQuery] string type)
{
```

```
return Json(new
{
    Name = "some name",
    Surname = "some surname"
});
}
```

We specify the response cache of this resource (an action method for this case) that depends on the query string parameter **type** and for a duration of 600 seconds. This means when a request is issued like **GetData?type=contact,** the response is cached for the query string parameter type equals to the **contact** for 600 seconds. When the request is issued for the first time, it will run the action method but for subsequent requests with the same parameter value, the response will be read from the cache and the action method will not be executed. If another request with **GetData?type=phones** is issued, the action method will be run for the first time for the **phones** query string parameter and the response will be cached for 600 seconds also.

We can observe and check response caching by using developer tools of our browser. The following image shows the response headers when the request is issued for the first time. The **ResponseCache** filter sets the Cache-Control response header appropriately:

Figure 11.1: Cache-Control header set for the first time of access

This will make the subsequent requests cached for 600 seconds. You can check that if you put a breakpoint in the beginning of the **GetData** action method, it will not be hit before the cache expired. It can be noticed (from disk cache) next to the status code indicator in Chrome's developer tools, as shown in the following figure:

Figure 11.2: Cached response in developer tools

> **NOTE:** Caching can be disabled in developer tools and hitting the Ctrl+F5 key combination also instructs the browser to invalidate the cache. These factors can make you think cache is not working while you try it.

We can also create commonly used cache profiles in the service registration at the Startup, as follows:

```
public void ConfigureServices(IServiceCollection services)
{
  services.AddResponseCaching();
  services.AddControllersWithViews();
  services.AddDbContext<PhoneBookContext>(options => options.
UseSqlServer("connection string of the database"));
  services.AddMvc(mvcSetupOptions =>
  {
    mvcSetupOptions.CacheProfiles.Add("Api20Min", new CacheProfile()
    {
      Duration=1200,
      VaryByQueryKeys=new string[1] { "type" }
    });
  });
}
```

Then, reuse them by setting the **CacheProfileName** parameter of the **ResponseCache** filter, as shown here:

```
[ResponseCache(CacheProfileName = "Api20Min")]
public IActionResult GetData([FromQuery] string type)
{
    return Json(new
    {
```

```
            Name = "some name",
            Surname = "some surname"
    });
}
```

Response caching can be of great performance improvement if used correctly. It is commonly used for login and home pages come after login because these are the pages most demanded to be rendered fast by the end users.

Using cache tags

ASP.NET Core also simplifies caching Razor pages or views partially by the **cache** tag helper. It can be used as follows:

```
<cache expires-on="@DateTime.Now.AddMinutes(15)" vary-by-
query="type,id">
    <form method="post">
        <div class="container-fluid">
            <div class="row m-2">
                <div class="col-sm-2">
                    Name:
                </div>
                <div class="col-sm-4">
                    <input class="form-control" asp-for="Detail.Name" />
                </div>
                <div class="col-sm-2">
                    Surname:
                </div>
                <div class="col-sm-4">
                    <input class="form-control" asp-for="Detail.Surname"
/>
                </div>
            </div>
            <div class="row m-2">
                <div class="col-sm-2">
                    Adress:
                </div>
                <div class="col-sm-10">
                    <textarea class="form-control" asp-for="Detail.
```

```
Address">
                </textarea>
            </div>
        </div>
        <div class="row m-2">
            <div class="col-sm-2">
                Country:
            </div>
            <div class="col-sm-4">
                <input class="form-control" asp for="Detail.Country"
/>
            </div>
            <div class="col-sm-2">
            </div>
            <div class="col-sm-4">
                <input type="submit" value="Save" />
            </div>
        </div>
    </div>
</form>
</cache>
```

We can control the expiration date and time using the **expires-on** attribute and caching using query string parameters by the **vary-by-query** attribute. It also supports many other parameter sources to cache like headers, cookies, and so on. The cache tag helpers can greatly help caching dynamically created parts of razor pages or views.

> NOTE: If you would like to cache the entire HTML output of a Razor page or MVC View, consider using the response cache filter.

Content bundling and minification

A web application does not consist of just the server-side code. It contains many JavaScript, CSS, and other types of static files. It is a best practice to make a JavaScript and a CSS file for every Razor view or page and keep script codes and style sheets specific to them in a chosen standardized location for every view. We also include common JavaScript and CSS files to every view or page in the layout pages. This forces browsers to make a request and download these files every time, thus reduces the performance.

To reduce the number of requests made to the server for asset files, we can use the technique called **bundling**. It is simply concatenating JavaScript and CSS files into one file for each of them. Instead of downloading a lot of files, the browser downloads one or two files. Combined with caching, this can greatly improve performance.

The servers hosting our project also serve these files to the browsers accessing it. Browsers make requests for every JavaScript, CSS, and image files needed and download them. It is no different downloading a file from the Internet. Even when we use caching, loading performance of our application can be poor for the first-time if we have long script files. Many users would like to have pages, especially the login and home pages, come up and appear quickly. We can use a technique called **minification** to solve these problems.

Minification means removing white spaces such as new lines, tabs, comments from asset files, and shortening the variable names in the JavaScript files. Consider the following JavaScript file:

```javascript
// the explanation of the JavaScript function
function DoSomeWork_With_A_Long_Method_Name(someVeryLongVariable1,
someVeryLongVariable2) {
    var someObjectWithVeryLongVariableName = {
        SomeVeryVeryLongPropertyName: someVeryLongVariable1 *
someVeryLongVariable2
    };
    return someObjectWithVeryLongVariableName;
}


window.Somefunction = DoSomeWork_With_A_Long_Method_Name;
```

When we apply minification to this JavaScript file, it is going to be like the following:

```javascript
function DoSomeWork_With_A_Long_Method_Name(o,e)
{return{SomeVeryVeryLongPropertyName:o*e}}window.
Somefunction=DoSomeWork_With_A_Long_Method_Name;
```

Notice the parameter variable names are shortened to one character long and comments are removed along with the white spaces. The minification process is smart and does its job as it detects the usage of variables, functions and performs renaming for every occurrence, just like the rename feature of Visual Studio.

We can use these techniques to greatly improve the speed of the first-time load of our projects if we apply both minification and bundling. The browsers download asset files with smaller sizes (thanks to minification) and fewer requests are made (thanks to the bundling).

TIP: Of course, these methods should be employed at the production environment because they are going to complicate development. You must also have a good knowledge of JavaScript logging and error management. If you encounter JavaScript errors at only the production environment, it is going to be hard to open developer tools of the browser, understand and debug the minified JavaScript code.

Bundling and minification can be applied easily to our ASP.NET Core project by using an open-source side project called **WebOptimizer** (**https://github.com/ ligershark/WebOptimizer**). The predecessor versions of ASP.NET provided a built-in solution to minification and bundling, but unfortunately ASP.NET Core does not provide a native solution.

NOTE: There are automation tools like gulp and grunt which can automate bundling, minification, and many other automated tasks. You can integrate them to your continuous integration and deploy your application with bundled and minified assets, but keep in mind that these can make your deployments take a longer time depending on the number of your asset files.

If you decide to use automation tools to create minimized bundles, ASP.NET Core provides the environment tag to use in Razor pages or MVC views. For example, we can have several JavaScript files in our development environment like the following:

```
<environment include="Development">
    <script src="~/lib/jquery/dist/jquery.js"></script>
    <script src="~/lib/bootstrap/dist/js/bootstrap.js"></script>
    <script src="~/js/global.js"></script>
</environment>
```

We can specify the combined and minified file by setting the include attribute of the environment tag, as shown in the following code. It checks the value stored in **ASPNETCORE_ENVIRONMENT** variable and applies the contents based on that condition. We can include the minified script bundle for our application in the Production environment like the following:

```
<environment include="Production">
    <script src="~/lib/bundle.js"></script>
</environment>
```

TIP: You can also consider content delivery networks (CDN) to serve your static assets and bundled files. This way you delegate serving those to the CDN provider (a cloud computing platform) instead of serving them in your application server.

Using event counters

Event counters are provided by ASP.NET Core to gather performance metrics for events that occur frequently. They are used for measuring performance and monitoring certain parts of an application.

We expect these kinds of tools to log performance statistics fast, so they do not bring overhead to the application by themselves. Event counters measure statistics inside the process and write logs between specified periods. This brings very less overhead to the system as much as possible. We can install the global performance counters tool by running the following cli command:

```
dotnet tool install --global dotnet-counters
```

Now, we can run the following command and learn our applications process that can be monitored:

```
dotnet-counters ps
```

This outputs a table with columns consisting of IDs of the processes and their names in a table with three columns - **`Process id`**, **`hosting server`**, and **`path`** of the executable, as shown in the following figure:

```
C:\Windows\System32>dotnet-counters ps
       900 iisexpress C:\Program Files\IIS Express\iisexpress.exe

C:\Windows\System32>
```

Figure 11.3: Processes that can be monitored

Now, we can use this process ID with the **`monitor`** and **`--process-id`** parameters as shown here:

```
dotnet-counters monitor --process-id 900
```

This will list the default metrics like the CPU, working set, heap size, and so on as shown in the following output:

```
[System.Runtime]
    % Time in GC since last GC (%)                                   0
    Allocation Rate (B / 1 sec)                                      0
    CPU Usage (%)                                                    0
    Exception Count (Count / 1 sec)                                  0
    GC Fragmentation (%)                                           NaN
    GC Heap Size (MB)                                               13
    Gen 0 GC Count (Count / 1 sec)                                   0
    Gen 0 Size (B)                                                   0
    Gen 1 GC Count (Count / 1 sec)                                   0
    Gen 1 Size (B)                                                   0
    Gen 2 GC Count (Count / 1 sec)                                   0
    Gen 2 Size (B)                                                   0
    IL Bytes Jitted (B)                                        277.681
    LOH Size (B)                                                     0
    Monitor Lock Contention Count (Count / 1 sec)                    0
    Number of Active Timers                                          0
    Number of Assemblies Loaded                                    139
    Number of Methods Jitted                                     3.466
    POH (Pinned Object Heap) Size (B)                                0
    ThreadPool Completed Work Item Count (Count / 1 sec)             0
    ThreadPool Queue Length                                          0
    ThreadPool Thread Count                                          1
    Working Set (MB)                                                88
```

Figure 11.4: Monitoring default event counters

Now, let us assume a simple and widely used scenario. We would like to gather statistics of requests made to an action method. We can create a custom event source like the following:

```
[EventSource(Name = "TestEventSource")]
public class TestEventSource : EventSource
{
  public static TestEventSource Instance = new TestEventSource();
  private EventCounter eventCounter;
  private int eventId = 1;

  private TestEventSource()
  {
    eventCounter = new EventCounter("processing time", this)
    {
        DisplayName = "Processing Time",
        DisplayUnits = "ms"
    };
  }

  public void RecordRequestMetric(string url, long elapsed)
  {
    WriteEvent(eventId, url, elapsed);
    eventCounter.WriteMetric(elapsed);
  }

  protected override void Dispose(bool disposing)
  {
    eventCounter?.Dispose();
    base.Dispose(disposing);
  }
}
```

We derive a class from **EventSource** and set its alias by the **EventSource** attribute, which is **TestEventSource** in our example. Custom event sources must define an event counter which describes the display information of them. We would like to log the elapsed time of action methods by their URL. We make a public method for it to call the **WriteEvent** method in it.

We can simply use it in an action method like the following with a stopwatch calling the method from our instance:

```
public IActionResult Index()
{
    Stopwatch stopWatch = new Stopwatch();
    stopWatch.Start();
    var result = View();
    Thread.Sleep(10);
    stopWatch.Stop();

    string url = HttpContext.Request.Path;

    TestEventSource.Instance.RecordRequestMetric(url, stopWatch.
ElapsedMilliseconds);

    return result;
}
```

This will start gathering metrics for a custom event source. We can then use **--counters** flag with our event source alias to monitor our custom event source, as shown here:

```
dotnet-counters monitor --process-id {id of process to monitor}
--counters {event source alias}
```

This will display our custom event source metrics as shown in the following figure:

Figure 11.5: *Monitoring custom event source*

> **TIP: You can create action filters or middleware to use these kinds of event sources and avoid putting measurement code in the action methods themselves. Keep in mind what is measurable can be improved, make use of event counters in your application that may require optimization.**

The .Net Core framework also presents additional diagnostic tools to analyse dump and view traces of a .Net Core process:

- **dotnet-trace**: It is a cross platform tool to collect the traces of a .Net Core process and it is integrated into the framework. It can be installed from the command line like the following.

  ```
  dotnet tool install --global dotnet-trace
  ```

We can use it to generate trace files in the output format for **PerfView** **nettrace**, **speedscope json** or **chromium**. It has flags for many features and can be used like the following in a simple form:

```
dotnet-trace collect -p {process id of the .net core application}
--format Speedscope
```

It starts generating the trace file until it is stopped. Then, the trace file can be viewed with Perfview or a browser by speed scope plugin.

We can gather so much diagnostic data like garbage collection, loading libraries, threading, status of the heap, CPU stacks, and so on These can be enabled from the **- -clrevents** flag of the tool.

- **dotnet-dump**: It is a cross-platform tool to collect and analyse dump files of .Net Core applications without a debugger. It can be installed with the command like the following code:

```
dotnet tool install --global dotnet-dump
```

Then, we can collect the dump of the process with the following command:

```
dotnet-dump collect -p {process id}
```

Then, we can use the following command to analyse dump files. It starts an execution environment in the shell and allows us to enter dump commands:

```
dotnet-dump analyze {path to the dump file}
```

We can gather info about unhandled exceptions, status of the threads, and many other things.

> **TIP: Event counters, trace, and dump tools are powerful diagnostic tools. They can be a life saver if you run your application in a container where you do not have direct access to the container environment.**
>
> **Imagine you are using Kubernetes to run your application and it starts slowing down, crashing without a solid reason. You can install these tools into a sidecar container and use them to find the root of the problem.**

Other optimization techniques

There are other types of optimization tricks that can be applied to the ASP.NET Core projects and other .NET project types also.

Compression of the response

We have already discussed bundling and minification; despite these measures, our asset files can still be large. We can compress the http response by using several algorithms like Brotli or Gzip. The algorithms are issued by the browsers in the

Accept-Encoding header to ask the server to compress them. Browsers are also made aware to decompress the responses automatically by their built-in features and no extra coding in the client side is required.

Keep in mind that running those algorithms also increase overhead. You should not compress small sized assets because it is not worth to compress them for a tiny amount of reduction in size. Also, compressing natively compressed asset types (for example, JPEG files) are not worth of the compression because they are already compressed enough.

To use response compression, we must register the service with the extension method **AddResponseCompression** and register the middleware by the extension method **UseResponseCompression**. The compression algorithm that the server is going to support, and the compression rate can be specified from the middleware.

We can use fiddler proxy to observe the compression behavior. Suppose we configured the compression middleware and ran our application. We can observe that the browser sends multiple values in the Accept-Encoding header in priority. In this example, the server will check whether it supports gzip, deflate, or br (Brotli) algorithms in order and use the supported one first:

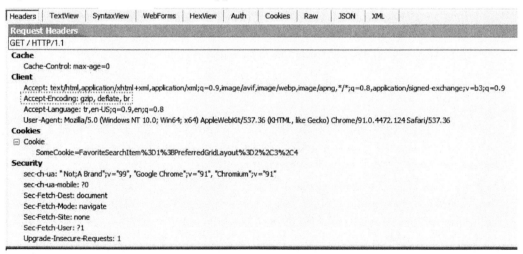

Figure 11.6: Accept-Encoding header to specify preferred compression algorithms in order

Then, we can check the response in the **Raw** tab of fiddler to view the compressed response, the algorithm and server used to compress the response. It is specified in the Content-Encoding header of the response, as shown here:

Figure 11.7: Compressed response and Content-Encoding header

Reducing roundtrips made to the database

We must watch out and try to reduce multiple queries made to the database. For example, consider the following lines of code:

```
[HttpPost]
public async Task Query([FromBody] int[] idArray)
{
    ContactInformation contact = null;
    List<ContactInformation> contacts = new List<ContactInformation>();

    foreach(int id in idArray)
    {
        contact = await _dataContext.
        ContactInformations.FirstOrDefaultAsync(t => t.Id == id);
        contacts.Add(contact);
    }
}
```

Instead of querying every single item in an array, we can use **Contains** to create an In SQL clause and query database only once, as shown here:

```
[HttpPost]
public async Task Query([FromBody] int[] idArray)
{
    List<ContactInformation> contacts = new List<ContactInformation>();
    contacts = await _dataContext.ContactInformations
                        .Where(ci => idArray.Contains(ci.Id))
                        .ToListAsync();
}
```

The contains statement is just one of the many examples that can be applied to the data access code.

> **NOTE: While trying to reduce data access round trips to the database, avoid writing unreadable and hard to maintain code. Instead of writing a huge Entity Framework Core query, it must be separated into smaller queries.**

Reduce roundtrips made to the server

Instead of making a lot of requests to the server, try to pack them into a post request and send them all together to the server. This can greatly improve performance and end-user experience.

Use server-side paging for large data sets

Instead of querying and returning hundreds of data rows to the browser at once, paginate the results from the server side. This will reduce the network usage of the server and highly increase database performance. If we display too much data in the browser (tables and grids for example), the end user experience is going to degrade greatly. We just cannot assume every user has a high-end computer.

We can use a class to carry the number of pages and partial paged data like the following:

```
public class PagedResult<T>
{
    public List<T> Data { get; set; }
    public int NumberOfTotalPages { get; set; }
}
```

Then, we can use it to carry our paginated data. We must also somehow set the number of pages when querying is reset; in our example, this is accessing the first page:

```
[HttpGet]
public async Task<PagedResult<ContactInformation>>
QueryWithPaging([FromQuery] int pageIndex, [FromQuery] int pageSize)
{
    PagedResult<ContactInformation> result = new
PagedResult<ContactInformation>();
    if (pageIndex == 0)
    {
        result.NumberOfTotalPages = Convert.ToInt32(_dataContext.
ContactInformations.Count() / pageSize);
```

```
    }
    result.Data = await _dataContext.ContactInformations.
        OrderBy(ci=> ci.Name).
        Skip(pageIndex*pageSize).
        Take(pageSize).
        ToListAsync();

    return result;
}
```

Notice the extension methods **Skip** and **Take** used here. We first order by some columns and use the **Skip** method to skip the amount of record which is page index multiplied by page size and take records with an amount of page size. The entity framework will convert the **Take** and **Skip** methods to a SQL statement with ranking instructions.

Using asynchronous programming

ASP.NET Core is designed to execute many requests simultaneously. To get the advantage of it, asynchronous programming should be employed and used wisely.

The .NET framework uses the pooling technique for the threads. It spawns many threads in the pending state and keeps them in a pool since creating threads from scratch is costly. When we would like to use threading, it tries to allocate a pending thread for us. Using and blocking threads carelessly or using too much synchronous API (even for an action method which is written using synchronous API, a thread is allocated to execute its request) can lead to thread pool starvation. It means there is no pending thread in the thread pool to handle an asynchronous code.

We should also avoid putting locking constructs in common places; for example, a middleware or an action filter which every request passes through them.

We should also not await a running task after creating it immediately. The request is handled in a thread already and creating a **Task.Run** will ask another thread from the pool. If an API contains the asynchronous version, we must prefer using it instead of wrapping it in a **Task.Run** and awaiting it. Doing that does not magically create an asynchronous version of a synchronous API.

We should also keep the entire call stack asynchronous starting from the action method to the bottom and execute potential long running tasks in parallel, especially if we have long-running code in common code paths. This will make our application scalable and when we deploy it to a server with more CPU cores, we will benefit from them without changing code.

Keep the common code for every request and response with less overhead

The common code paths consist of middleware, widely used action filters, and base controllers that other controllers derive. Since these are run at every request and response, they must execute fast without blocking.

For example, model binding is not ready at the middleware and intercepting post requests and deserializing body to check for something is not beneficial and increases the overhead of the server. Instead, we must create an action filter that has the model that is already bound and make our checks there.

Throw exceptions wisely

As their name implies, exceptions are rare conditions, and they should not be used to control the execution flow. Throwing and catching exceptions are costly processes. Let us assume we have a data access class like the following:

```
public class SomeDataAccessObject
{
  public List DoSomeDatabaseWork()
  {
    if(/*domeCondition*/)
    {
      throw new Exception("some exception");
    }
  }
}
```

We check some condition and throw an exception if it is true. Then, let us assume we have a business object that uses this data access object like the following:

```
public class SomeBusinessObject
{
  public List DoSomeWork()
  {
    try
    {
      SomeDataAccessObject dao = new SomeDataAccessObject();
      return dao.DoSomeDatabaseWork();
    }
```

```
        catch(Exception e)
        {
            throw ApiException(e);
        }
    }
}
```

We catch if an exception is thrown in the data access object, and we throw another exception. This brings overhead to the heap management of the .NET Core framework, and it is not garbage-collector friendly. Instead of controlling the execution flow with exceptions, we can use conditional statements and avoid exception throwing like the following:

```
public class SomeBusinessObject
{
  public ApiResult<List> DoSomeWork()
  {
    ApiResult<List> result=new ApiResult<List>();

    SomeDataAccessObject dao=new SomeDataAccessObject();
    if(dao.CheckSomeCondition())
    {
      result.Error="your error message";
    }
    else
    {
      result.Data = dao.DoSomeDatabaseWork();
    }

    return result;
  }
}
```

> **NOTE:** Also, try to avoid throwing exceptions in middleware and some type of action filters. They already have properties and methods for setting an error that returns 500 responses. Throwing exception in these may cause abnormal behaviour and other errors.

Cache data in TempData before redirecting

The temp data dictionary is great if you want to cache data before redirection and access it later. It is memory efficient since it is wiped out when accessed after the second request. It can be handy for master detail scenarios.

Let us assume we have a table of records and when we select a row, we would like to send the selected row data to an action method, do some work, and redirect the response to another controller's action method. We can use the ID of the selected row in a route parameter of the redirect URL, as shown here:

```
[HttpPost]
public IActionResult SelectData([FromQuery] int id)
{
    //do some work
    return Redirect($"Data/Open/{id}");
}
```

We can then access the selected row again from the database using the route parameter, as shown here:

```
[HttpGet("Data/Open/{id}")]
public IActionResult OpenData([FromRoute] int id)
{
  //access data by id;
  return View();
}
```

Instead we can cache the selected row data into **TempData** in the first request and access it on the redirected action method, as follows:

```
[HttpPost]
public IActionResult SelectData([FromBody] ContactInformation data)
{
  TempData["SelectedData"] = data;
  return Redirect($"Data/Open");
}
```

It will be wiped out when accessed, as follows:

```
[HttpGet("Data/Open")]
public IActionResult OpenData()
{
  ContactInformation selectedcontact = null;
```

```
    selectedcontact = TempData["SelectedData"] as ContactInformation;
    return View();
}
```

Use diagnostic tools to analyse performance metrics

Visual Studio also provides a built-in diagnostic tool, Application Insights, which can automatically collect the rate data from successful and failed responses. It also allows logging many kinds of metric data. These tools can greatly help us to determine poor performing parts of our applications.

Conclusion

We learned response caching, bundling, minification, and event counters in ASP. NET Core and common optimization techniques. There are so many optimization techniques that cannot be covered in one chapter and most of them are specific to the project we are working on. We can combine and mix the techniques described here to optimize our application. We will discuss the security of ASP.NET Core applications in the next chapter.

Questions

1. How can we monitor our application and gather metrics in ASP.NET Core?

2. Is response compression beneficial for assets with small size? Why?

3. How can we redirect to another action method and access data from the previous action method without database loading, and so on.?

4. Is accessing http post requests body with large payloads in middleware a good idea? Why?

5. We want to cache partial region of a Razor view instead of the entire view. How can we do it?

6. How can we improve the performance of the loading time of pages?

CHAPTER 12
Securing ASP.NET Core Applications

Introduction

We covered how to optimize ASP.NET Core applications in the previous chapter. We will describe common attacks and see how to handle security for ASP.NET Core applications in this chapter.

Structure

In this chapter, we will discuss the following topics:

- Introducing SQL injection attacks and how to avoid them
- Introducing cross-site request forgery attacks and how to avoid them
- Introducing server-side evaluation
- Introducing man-in-the-middle attacks and hypertext transport secure
- Introducing cross-site scripting (XSS) attacks and how to avoid them
- Introducing open redirect attacks
- Introducing data protection

Objectives

After reading this chapter, you should be able to handle the most common security attacks in ASP.NET Core projects. Security is one of the most important aspects of a software project in its lifetime and ignoring common or basic security may cost a lot. It affects end user experience or satisfaction directly or indirectly. It is also one of the criteria that a software project is chosen to be bought or not.

The reader can apply the techniques described here to fend off most of the attacks so a mere person cannot hack the projects of the reader easily.

> **NOTE: Kali Linux is a Linux distribution specialized for security. It comes with so many security tools installed and ready to use. It is widely used and you can use it by running it as a virtual machine in your computer. You can check it out by the following link https://www.kali.org/.**

Introducing SQL injection attacks and how to avoid them

The description of SQL injection, in short, is a malicious user that can enter potentially harmful SQL statements to user interface elements such as HTML inputs, query string parameters, or invoke an API with SQL statements embedded into payload data.

This kind of attack is even more dangerous when the attacker has information about the database of the project. The attacker can send harmful SQL statements specific for the brand of the database like the ones that return the names of the tables.

There are several ways to exploit this vulnerability. For example, we would like to query information of active contacts. We have a textbox to enter the country name to search; we can construct a SQL query like the following:

```
Select * from ContactPhones where Country='India' and Active=1
```

The attacker can enter the phrase **India'--** in the textbox and send a name ending with a single quotation mark and a double dash. It results with the following SQL query:

```
Select * from ContactPhones where Country='India'-' and Active=1
```

The double dash is a single line comment in many databases, and it will ignore the rest of the statement, resulting in both active and passive data to return.

Other than making database to ignore some parts of the statement, it can add an additional result set returned from the database. If the attacker knows the table name, it can send a union statement to the query and can convert the following query by the country statement:

```
Select * from ContactPhones where Country='India'
```

Here is the following code:

```
Select * from ContactPhones where Country='India'' union select * from ContactPhones
```

And this returns the entire table. If there is a lot of data in the table, this can lock down the server and rocket the memory and CPU usage; it is not necessary that the server returns the entire data to the client.

If the attacker knows the brand of the database, it can inject database administration statements and learn about the current sessions, list of tables, database users, and so on.

This attack can affect if raw SQL queries are used in the project. Raw SQL queries can be constructed by ADO.Net by default or the entity framework and other ORM frameworks. The following SQL query shows a common dynamic SQL scenario. If the name criteria come as a parameter, we will add those criteria to the SQL statement by concatenating strings:

```
public IActionResult PostFormData([FromForm] ListPageCriteriaModel criteria)
{
    string sql = "select * from tblContactInformation ";
    if (!String.IsNullOrWhiteSpace(criteria.Name))
    {
        sql += "where colName like '" + criteria.Name.ToString() + "%'";
    }
    using (var connection = new SqlConnection("connection string"))
    {
        DbCommand command = connection.CreateCommand();
        command.CommandText = sql;
        connection.Open();
        command.ExecuteReader();
        .
        .
    }
}
```

We can also use the entity framework and the **RawSql** method of DbSet collections for the same purpose. The entity framework will handle the database connection for us:

```
public IActionResult PostFormData([FromForm] ListPageCriteriaModel criteria)
{
    string sql = "select * from tblContactInformation ";

    if (!String.IsNullOrWhiteSpace(criteria.Name))
    {
        sql += "where colName like '" + criteria.Name.ToString() + "%'";
    }

    var result = _context.ContactInformations.FromSqlRaw(sql).ToList();
    .
    .
    .

}
```

Both approaches are open to the attacks described previously. Earlier, we had to check and control the strings if they would contain database commands or SQL statements. Fortunately, parametrized queries are developed for handling security and parameter support for executing raw SQL queries.

ADO.Net API supports writing parametrized queries. We put parameters inside the SQL string (starts with **@** sign for **SqlServer** and may differ for other database vendors) and then we can call the **CreateParameter** method of **DbCommand** and set the parameter's name and value like the following:

```
public IActionResult PostFormData([FromForm] ListPageCriteriaModel criteria)
{
    string sql = "select * from tblContactInformation ";
    if (!String.IsNullOrWhiteSpace(criteria.Name))
    {
        sql += "where colName like '@name%'";
    }
    using (var connection = new SqlConnection("connection string"))
    {
        SqlCommand command = connection.CreateCommand();
        command.CommandText = sql;
        SqlParameter parameter = command.CreateParameter();
        parameter.ParameterName = "@name";
        parameter.Value = criteria.Name;
        connection.Open();
```

```
        command.ExecuteReader();
        .
        .
        .
    }
}
```

The entity framework **FromSqlRaw** method also supports specifying parameters in curly braces similar to the **string.Format** or **FromSqlInterpolated** method, which supports string interpolation syntax of C# and saves us from the complicated ADO.Net API like the following:

```
var result = _context.ContactInformations
    .FromSqlRaw("select * from tblContactInformation where Name like
'{name}%'", criteria.Name)
    .ToListAsync();

var result = _context.ContactInformations
    .FromSqlInterpolated($"select * from tblContactInformation where
Name like '{criteria.Name}%'")
    .ToListAsync();
```

> **NOTE: Lambda expressions and LINQ queries also generate parametrized queries by default. The entity framework takes care of the SQL injection vulnerability by default. You do not need to do or configure anything special.**

When parametrized queries are used the .NET provider and the driver of the database checks whether the parameters contain any threat to the database and raise exception if that is the case.

> **NOTE: Whatever is the size and scale of the project or using parametrized queries or not, you should never use database admin user accounts in connection strings for the production environment. You need to create a user account in the database with only needed privileges for running the application. For example, if you are developing a reporting application and you do not need to insert, update, delete any data, you should create a database account that can execute select queries only.**

Introducing cross site request forgery attacks and how to avoid them

Cross site request forgery (CSRF) is an attack that a malicious web site can trick the logged in user to send a harmful request to the trusted web site. Let us assume we host our web site with the URL, www.phonebooktest.com. The execution of the CSRF attack can be as the following in a sketchy description:

1. The user logs in to the **www.phonebooktest.com**, and the authorization and session cookies are returned to the client browser.

2. The user opens another tab in the browser and visits a malicious web site (this usually happens by clicking on links in emails or a series of redirections from one malicious site to another).

3. The malicious web site contains a markup like the following:

```
<form          action="http://www.phonebooktest.com/contacts/save"
method="post">
          <input type="hidden" name="Name" value="some contact
name">
     <input type="hidden" name="Phone" value="555-444-4444">
     <input type="submit" value="Click to execute">
</form>
```

Notice the action attribute of the form contains an address from the trusted application. When the user clicks on the submit button, the browser issues the request using the cookies that comes from the previously authenticated trusted application in another tab.

> **NOTE: This is by design since we can open multiple pages of the same web application with different tabs. Therefore, cookies are shared across tabs of the browser. CSRF attacks mainly target web sites which use cookie-based authentication.**

The same malicious request can be made with AJAX from malicious web sites also. ASP.NET offers the anti-forgery token to prevent CSRF attacks.

The anti-forgery token is a hidden field with a hash value specific to the user, injected between form tags. The HTML helpers responsible for creating forms also create the anti-forgery token. The following razor markup with **Html.BeginForm** creates an anti-forgery token automatically:

```
@using (Html.BeginForm(FormMethod.Post))
{
    <div class="container-fluid">
        <div class="row m-2">
            <div class="col-sm-2">
                Name:
            </div>
```

```
            <div class="col-sm-4">
                @Html.TextBoxFor(t => t.Criteria.Name)<br />
                @Html.ValidationMessageFor(t => t.Criteria.Name, null,
new { style =                   "color:red" })
            </div>
            <div class="col-sm-2">
                Surname:
            </div>
            <div class="col-sm-4">
                @Html.TextBoxFor(t => t.Criteria.Surname)<br />
                @Html.ValidationMessageFor(t => t.Criteria.Surname,
null, new { styl  e = "color:red" })
            </div>
        </div>
        <div class="row m-2">
            <div class="col-sm-2">
                Birth Year:
            </div>
            <div class="col-sm-4">
                @Html.TextBoxFor(t => t.Criteria.BirthYear, new { type =
"number" })<br />
                @Html.ValidationMessageFor(t => t.Criteria.BirthYear,
null, new { style = "color:red" })
            </div>
            <div class="col-sm-2">
            </div>
            <div class="col-sm-4">
                <input type="submit" value="Search" />
            </div>
        </div>
    </div>
}
```

When we look at the generated markup, we see the hidden HTML field for the anti-forgery token is generated:

```
... ▼<form action="/contacts" method="post" novalidate="novalidate"> == $0
    ▼<div class="container-fluid">
      ▼<div class="row m-2"> (flex)
         <div class="col-sm-2"> Name: </div>
       ►<div class="col-sm-4">…</div>
         <div class="col-sm-2"> Surname: </div>
       ►<div class="col-sm-4">…</div>
       </div>
     ►<div class="row m-2">…</div> (flex)
     </div>
     <input name="__RequestVerificationToken" type="hidden" value="CfDJ8Fo_-IMUln1Dg
  </form>
```

Figure 12.1: Anti-forgery token

The anti-forgery token is unique and unpredictable. As a hidden field in a form tag, it travels with the post data and ASP.NET Core checks whether it is equal to the authorized users' identity and rejects the request if so. We need the anti-forgery token for specified controllers or action methods with the **ValidateAntiForgeryToken** attribute. We can also require this token at application wide level with middleware.

If we are using Ajax, we can also inject a token into our page with the method by calling **Xsrf.GetAndStoreTokens(Context).RequestToken**. We can inject it into a hidden field or a JavaScript variable, and then we add this token into an Ajax request header and check it on the server side.

> NOTE: You can also check for the Referrer header of the request. It must have the same URL or IP with your application. It will contain malicious web sites address in case of CSRF.

Introducing server-side evaluation

There are built-in counter measures provided by ASP.NET Core, but they are not enough for enforcing security rules required by the business rules of the applications.

Let us consider a simple scenario. We list contacts in a table containing the name, surname, phone number, and we have a location check service specific to India. This service takes a phone number, and we need to display a button in the row for phone numbers that start with the country code of India, 91. When this button is pressed, we send this phone number by an Ajax request to the backend and then to the service mentioned. We can achieve this by the following Razor markup:

```
@using Phonebook.MVC.Models;

@model List<ListPageModel>

@if (Model != null && Model.Count > 0)
{
```

```
<table style="width:100%">
    <thead>
        <tr style="border-bottom: 1px solid gray">
            <td>
                NAME
            </td>
            <td>
                SURNAME
            </td>
            <td>
                Phone Number
            </td>
            <td>

            </td>
            @if (ViewBag.RenderActionColumn)
            {
                <td>
                </td>
            }
        </tr>
    </thead>
    <tbody>
        @foreach (var contactData in Model)
        {
        <tr style="border-bottom: 1px solid red">
            <td>
                @contactData.Name
            </td>
            <td>
                @contactData.Surname
            </td>
            <td>
                @contactData.PhoneNumber
            </td>
            <td>
```

```
                    <button style="display:@(contactData.PhoneNumber.
StartsWith("91")?"block":"none")" onclick="checkLocationInIndia(@
contactData.PhoneNumber)">Check Location</button>
                </td>
                @if (ViewBag.RenderActionColumn)
                {
                    <td>
                        <a href="/Detail/@(contactData.Id)">Edit
Contact</a>
                    </td>
                }
            </tr>
            }
        </tbody>
    </table>
}
```

Notice how we set the style attribute. We set the display property to block and show the button if the number starts with 91 and hide the button by setting the display to none in a row by a C# conditional statement. The button registered its onclick JavaScript event and calls the **checkLocationInIndia** function which makes the Ajax request. The following figure shows the output of the Razor markup:

NAME	SURNAME	Phone Number	
Last Contact Name 1	Last Contact Surname 1	4896415365	
Last Contact Name 2	Last Contact Surname 2	1645685643	
Last Contact Name 3	Last Contact Surname 3	9181656532	Check Location
Last Contact Name 4	Last Contact Surname 4	1231685445	

Figure 12.2: Hiding and showing buttons based on a condition in UI

We then call the service in one of our action methods:

```
[HttpGet]
public IActionResult CheckPhoneLocationForIndia([FromQuery] string
phoneNumber)
{
    //call the location service by the given phone.
    return Json(true);
}
```

The problem here is the hidden button in rows (which are the rows with the phone numbers that do not start with the 91 code) can be so easily made visible by opening developer tools of the browser and changing their display property to block. The solution is of course to make a validation at the backend:

```
[HttpGet]
public IActionResult CheckPhoneLocationForIndia([FromQuery] string
phoneNumber)
{
    if (phoneNumber.StartsWith("91"))
    {
        //call the location service by the given phone.
        return Json(true);
    }
    else
    {
        return Json(false);
    }
}
```

> NOTE: For the software security in client server architectures; the server is the essential part. The front-end is never to be trusted. Validations in the front-end are also important because it prevents sending data to the server which, we already know is going to fail. But the front-end can be manipulated easily. It can be done by developer tools of browsers or a malicious user can log in to your site with a browser equipped with extensions for hacking. It can even be done by attaching a debugger to the front-end and alter variables in memory if your backend is an API and the front-end client is a desktop application.

These kinds of vulnerabilities are common pitfalls and there is nothing ASP.NET Core or any other framework can provide a built-in solution for them. You must determine those pitfall points and keep them in mind while developing your application.

> NOTE: Of course, this scenario is a very rough example, and we can choose not to render the button by the razor markup at all but doing that way does not make the server-side evaluation unnecessary.

Introducing man-in-the-middle attacks and hypertext transport secure

Man-in-the-middle attacks allows attackers to monitor data secretly between the client and server, and even alter them or make fake requests and messages. It is an ordinary attack to make if the attacker has access to routers, unencrypted Wi-Fi access points, and so on. The following figure explains its mechanism and logic:

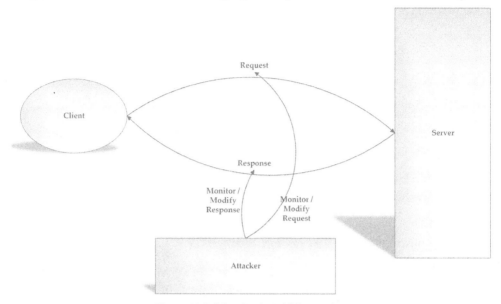

Figure 12.3: *Man-in-the-middle attack*

To avoid man-in-the-middle attacks, we can use tamper detection methods. Tamper detection methods can be handshake algorithms between the client and server. For example, let us assume we would like to detect if the request body is altered on the way to the server. We can use one-way hashing algorithms like MD5, SHA256, SHA512, and so on, to generate HMAC (hash-based message authentication code) and use it as a common handshake criterion on the server side.

TIP: MD5 is outdated, so try to use a stronger algorithm to generate HMAC.

We determine a common key to generate HMAC through any SHA algorithm. These keys are usually called **secrets** because they are known only by the client and server and must not be shared with anyone else. Assume we have a request body to be sent like the following:

```
{
    "Name":"John",
    "Surname":"Smith",
    "PhoneNumber":"5555555555"
}
```

We can take the whole JSON data as a string and pass it across the SHA512 algorithm and generate a unique HMAC hash. Then, we can send the generated HMAC hash in a place agreed by the server and client (a request header for example) to the server.

Then, on the server, we apply the same handshake algorithm. We read the request body, use the secret to generate the hash from the JSON string in the request body, and compare the generated hash with the hash that has arrived from the client. If they are not the same, then this means the request is tampered. The following figure explains the process:

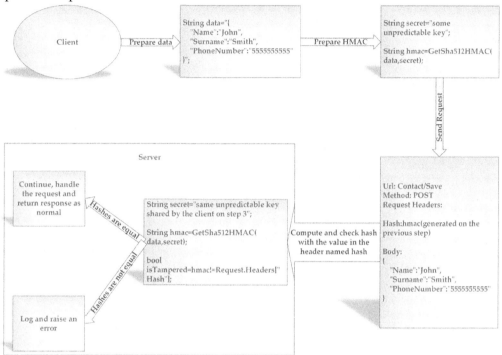

Figure 12.4: A handshake algorithm to prevent man in the middle attack

> **TIP: This kind of counter measure is popular among APIs. There are authorization protocols with open standard. O-Auth is a popular one. You can check out the 1.0 version from https://en.wikipedia.org/wiki/OAuth.**

Https is an extension of the hyper-text transfer protocol that allows secure communication between clients and servers by using bidirectional encryption. It encrypts data prior to sending from the client browser, decrypts data on the server side and vice versa. It offers protection against man-in-the-middle attacks, which the following figure explains:

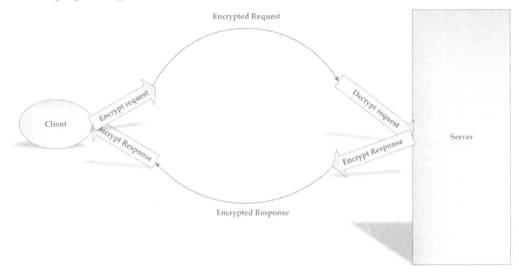

Figure 12.5: SSL in action

We can force our application to redirect requests with http authority to https by registering its middleware by calling the **UseHttpsRedirection** method in the **Configure** method of the **Startup** class.

> TIP: Use https whenever possible. It is the best and easy to implement way to avoid man in the middle attacks.

Introducing cross site scripting (XSS) attacks and how to avoid them

Cross site scripting (**XSS**) attack is a security flaw that allows an attacker to send JavaScript codes into applications. JavaScript code is stored as string data in application database, and when it is loaded as content and rendered in HTML, the JavaScript is injected into the page and runs automatically.

The following figure shows an example of performing a XSS attack. Notice the address field contains an alert statement inside script tags:

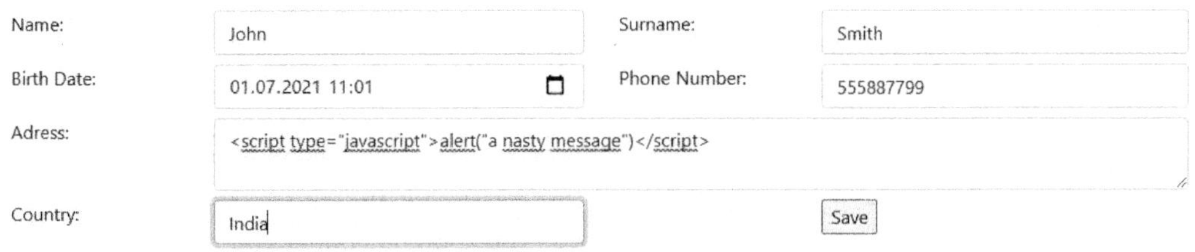

Name:	John	Surname:	Smith
Birth Date:	01.07.2021 11:01	Phone Number:	555887799
Adress:	<script type="javascript">alert("a nasty message")</script>		
Country:	India		Save

Figure 12.6: A XSS Attack example

The attacker hopes it can inject a JavaScript code that can be executed when the saved string data is loaded on another page as shown in the following figure:

NAME	SURNAME
<script type="text/javascript">alert("a nasty message")</script>	Last Contact Surname 1
Last Contact Name 2	Last Contact Surname 2
Last Contact Name 3	Last Contact Surname 3
Last Contact Name 4	Last Contact Surname 4

Figure 12.7: Injected script in XSS Attack

This is a very simple example. Attackers occasionally cause a forever loop with a JavaScript on the clients' browser. This greatly reduces the end user experience because it makes the CPU usage of their browser increase rapidly. Attackers can also inject hidden iframes which target malicious sites that can leave a Trojan or a worm on the end users' system.

The ASP.NET Core Razor engine automatically encodes HTML tags, which prevents XSS attacks. There is no extra effort needed. Using the @ directive as it is, as shown in the following code, generates the output of the previous figure:

```
@using Phonebook.MVC.Models;
@model List<ListPageModel>

@if (Model != null && Model.Count > 0)
{
    <table style="width:100%">
        <thead>
            <tr style="border-bottom: 1px solid gray">
                <td>
                    NAME
                </td>
                <td>
                    SURNAME
```

```
        </td>
        <td>
            Phone Number
        </td>
        <td>
        </td>
        @if (ViewBag.RenderActionColumn)
        {
            <td>
            </td>
        }
    </tr>
</thead>
<tbody>
    @foreach (var contactData in Model)
    {
        <tr style="border-bottom: 1px solid red">
            <td>
                @contactData.Name
            </td>
            <td>
                @contactData.Surname
            </td>
            <td>
                @contactData.PhoneNumber
            </td>
            <td>
            </td>
            @if (ViewBag.RenderActionColumn)
            {
                <td>
                    <a href="/Detail/@(contactData.Id)">Edit
Contact</a>
                </td>
            }
        </tr>
```

```
        }
    </tbody>
</table>
}
```

When we inspect the response HTML, we can see the less than (**<**) character is converted to **<**, greater than character (**>**) is converted to **>**, and the quotes(**"**) are converted as **"**. This is called **HTML encoding**.

> **TIP: ASP.NET Core handles encoding automatically, and it is safe as long as you do not do something to reverse the encoding. There is also a class named HtmlString that provides writing raw string values; use it with caution.**

The following figure shows the HTML encoded content:

```
</LiIcau>
<tbody>
            <tr style="border-bottom: 1px solid red">
                <td>
                    &lt;script&gt;alert(&quot;a nasty message&quot;)&lt;/script&gt;
                </td>
                <td>
                    Last Contact Surname 1
                </td>
                <td>
                    4896415365
                </td>
```

Figure 12.8: HTML encoded content

We can also inject the encoders to controllers or services and use them before saving the database. This may come in handy in the case of security while developing an API. The following code shows injecting and using the **HtmlEncoder** class. We can use the encoder to HTML encode any string variable we would like:

```
public class HomeController : Controller
{
    private readonly ILogger<HomeController> _logger;
    PhoneBookContext _dataContext;
    HtmlEncoder _htmlEncoder;

    public HomeController(ILogger<HomeController> logger,
        PhoneBookContext dataContext,
        HtmlEncoder htmlEncoder)
    {
        _logger = logger;
        _dataContext = dataContext;
        this._htmlEncoder = htmlEncoder;
    }
```

```
[HttpPost]
public IActionResult SaveData([FromBody]ContactInformation
information)
    {
        string encodedSafeName = _htmlEncoder.Encode(information.Name);
        return Json(true);
    }
}
```

Introducing open redirect attacks

Open redirect attacks target web applications that redirect the request by the URL located in the query string. Attackers can change the redirect URL in the query string with an address of a malicious web site.

To explain this with a simple example, let us assume the user is not authenticated and wants to access the contacts page. User types **{url of application}/Contacts**, we check for authentication, and if the user is not authenticated, then we redirect the user to the login page with a query string parameter to remember the page user wants to access (for example, **{url of application}/Login?RedirectUrl=/ Contacts**). Once the action method handles authentication, we check whether the **RedirectUrl** parameter exists and on successful authentication, we redirect to **{url of application}/Contacts** after a successful login.

This is a comfortable way to handle redirecting users directly to the page they desire and it is nearly a standard for every web application. But what if an attacker tricks the user by sending a login link with the redirect URL of a malicious web site **{url of application}/Login?RedirectUrl={address of a malicious web site}**. A careless person can log in and will be redirected directly to the malicious site.

> **TIP: For a solid security perspective, consider every end user is ignorant, careless, and capable of attempting every mischief while using your application.**

ASP.NET Core fortunately provides an easy way to handle open redirect attacks. It provides the **LocalRedirect** controller method. It takes the redirect URL as a parameter and throws an exception if it does not point to a resource inside the application:

```
public class LoginController : Controller
{
    public IActionResult Login([FromBody] LoginInformation
userNameAndPassword,
```

```
    [FromQuery] string redirectUrl)
    {
        //check user name and password and authenticate
        //if successfull redirect to the parameter in the redirectUrl
        return LocalRedirect(redirectUrl);
    }
}
```

Introducing data protection

We sometimes need to send additional sensitive data to the client, and we would like to have them encrypted, expire after a period of time, and be tamper proof. We can send this kind of data in cookies or query string parameters. Especially encrypted query strings are common in web applications. There are a lot of approval algorithms that consist of sending a link to the user via an email and tell them this link is going to expire in a certain period of time. You can notice that these kinds of links contain encrypted query strings. The encrypted query string contains the expiration date along with relevant data inside.

As for the system and server protection, we also would like to protect data in configuration whether they are stored in environment variables or **appconfig.json** files. Therefore, if we deploy our project in a common server which is shared by other deployed applications (this means different people have access to the server), we must be able to encrypt data in our applications configuration.

ASP.NET Core offers the protection API for these kinds of scenarios. It is very easy to use and efficient in security.

We must register protection services and make them ready for dependency injection. We call the extension method **AddDataProtection** at the **Startup** class, as follows:

```
public void ConfigureServices(IServiceCollection services)
{
    services.AddDataProtection();
    services.AddResponseCaching();
    services.AddResponseCompression();
    services.AddControllersWithViews();
    services.AddDbContext<PhoneBookContext>(options => options.
UseSqlServer("connection string of the database"));
    services.AddMvc(mvcSetupOptions =>
    {
        mvcSetupOptions.CacheProfiles.Add("Api20Min", new CacheProfile()
```

```
            {
                Duration=1200,
                VaryByQueryKeys=new string[1] { "type" }
            });
        });


}
```

We can then inject **IDataProtectionProvider** into our controllers or service classes and use it like the following:

```
public class HomeController : Controller
{
    IDataProtectionProvider _provider;

    public HomeController(IDataProtectionProvider provider)
    {
        this._provider = provider;
    }

    public IActionResult Index(int id)
    {
        String purposeString = "Some string";
        IDataProtector protector = _provider.
CreateProtector(purposeString);
        string protectedString = protector.Protect("sensitive data");
        Response.Headers.Add("Protected", protectedString);
        .


        .

    }
}
```

We determine a purpose string, create an **IDataProtector** from it, and create an encrypted string. We can then return it to the client in a cookie, query string, or any other similar way.

We can use the same purpose string to decrypt data by the **Unprotect** method of the **IDataProtector** interface. Decryption works only by using the same purpose string or purpose string array. ASP.NET Core manages all the underlying encryption and decryption by data protection keys, and we do not really need to do anything else. It uses the data protection API to handle authentication tokens and session cookies as well.

NOTE: There is a concept of rotation in security which means changing passwords, keys, certificates in a regular period of time. The data protection API manages the rotation process automatically and it has 90 days by default. This means the protected data will not be decrypted by using the same purpose key for encrypting it after the data protection keys are rotated.

The purpose keys allow us to derive child keys from the parent keys. Usually, the same key is used to encrypt and decrypt the query string of password reset links, user profile data, and so on. Using only one key for encrypting everything can make the encryption key predictable and create vulnerabilities. We can create an array of strings to increase a variety of purpose strings. We can, for example, create **UserAccount** as a base purpose string for user account operations and create the child purpose key for encrypting user preferences by **Preferences** or encrypt the password reset link by **Reset**. The **CreateProtector** method takes an array of strings and we can use our hierarchical strings in an array as a parameter:

```
public class HomeController : Controller
{
    IDataProtectionProvider _provider;

    public HomeController(IDataProtectionProvider provider)
    {
        this._provider = provider;
    }

    public IActionResult Index(int id)
    {
        String purposeString = "UserAccount";
        string preferencesPurposeString = "Preferences";
        IDataProtector protector = _provider.
CreateProtector(purposeString, preferencesPurposeString);
        string protectedString = protector.Protect("sensitive data");
        Response.Headers.Add("Protected", protectedString);
        .
        .
    }
}
```

This will make it harder to guess purpose strings. We can also enforce expiration by using the **ITimeLimitedDataProtector** interface. We can get an instance by calling the **ToTimeLimitedDataProtector** method of the **IDataProtector** interface. We can then give the date time offset parameter to the protect method:

```
public IActionResult Index(int id)
{
    String purposeString = "UserAccount";
    IDataProtector protector = _provider.CreateProtector(purposeString);
        string protectedString = protector.ToTimeLimitedDataProtector()
                .Protect("sensitive data", TimeSpan.FromDays(5));
    Response.Headers.Add("Protected", protectedString);

        .

        .

}
```

The **Unprotect** method will throw an exception automatically when the encrypted data is expired.

Conclusion

We covered the common security attacks and learned how to avoid them in ASP.NET Core. The framework offers many easy-to-use counter measures against attacks. You need to use the right method for the right scenario and analyze common pitfall points to apply server-side evaluation and validation. We will cover architectures and designs using ASP.NET Core in the next chapter.

Questions

1. We want to send a link via an email to the users of our application, and we would like to send sensitive data in the query string that must not be understandable to them. We would also like the link to expire after a certain period of time. How can we achieve that?

2. What are the different ways to avoid SQL injection attacks?

3. How can we avoid cross-site request forgery for incoming AJAX requests?

4. We fetch the user's authorization data to the client and store it on the JavaScript side. We show, hide some buttons that make requests based on that authorization data to prevent the user from making unauthorized requests. Is that enough? Why?

CHAPTER 13

Introducing Software Architectures

Introduction

We covered how to secure ASP.NET Core applications in the previous chapter. We will cover software architectures, command query responsibility segregation, and asynchronous message queue processing.

Structure

In this chapter, we will discuss the following topics:

- Defining architecture in software projects
- Introducing monolithic architecture
- Introducing layered architecture
- Introducing service-oriented architecture
- Introducing microservices architecture
- Introducing command query responsibility segregation
- Introducing eventual consistency
- Introducing the API gateway
- Introducing backend for frontend

Objectives

After reading this chapter, you should be able to understand what software architecture is, learn about the popular architectures around, and how to decide the right architecture for the projects. This chapter will be about software design. It is quite important to start a project with the right architecture.

The definition of architecture in software projects

Architecture in the IT industry has many meanings by various sources. It is a process done consciously that involves analysing the IT environment, technical requirements of the project, and dividing the software project into sub systems that interact with each other and at the end, delivering a method for building the system for the software project.

The meaning can change depending on the perspective; it can be a network architecture if we think by the perspective of the hardware and their relationships between them. It can be a data architecture if we are building a business intelligence project and defining the components that process data and relations between them, or it can be a software architecture that defines sub systems of a software project. The list can go on.

The definition changes by the aspect and perspective, but they all have one thing in common. Architecture defines the method of building something. For the software world, we can roughly say architecture is the strategy of the development of software components, organizing hardware, and maintaining applications.

There are constantly occurring processes in a software project such as development, design additional modules, deployment, maintenance, and so on. The aim of a good architecture is to make those processes easy to implement and keep their lifetime short.

The same principles of strategy and planning apply to software design too. It can be very difficult to cover a poor strategy with tactical moves which can only save the day. If your architecture (technology strategy) is poorly designed, your project's maintenance, development or any other technical process that results with a deliverable will suffer or making additional changes can be a nightmare.

Introducing monolithic architecture

A monolithic architecture aims to create self-contained applications which contain domain-specific business services, data transfer objects, data access objects, presentation, and UI classes in the same project. It is deployed as everything in one place application. The following figure describes a sample monolithic application:

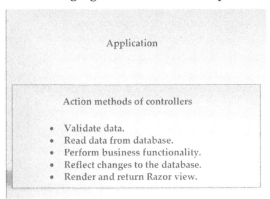

Figure 13.1: Monolithic application with a simple workflow

We can consider it as we access data directly inside the action methods, perform business logic, arrange model objects from entities, and send model objects to Razor views, and return the rendered HTML as a response. We can make our application scalable by putting it behind a NLB proxy and add new servers that contain it if necessary. Since the application is self-contained, every part of it is scaled automatically.

> **TIP: You can still benefit from cloud native tools for monolithic applications. Container orchestrators can scale up and down monolithic applications just like a microservice.**

The following figure describes a typical scalable monolithic application. A load balancer, which is a reverse proxy, is set up and different clusters, which are deployable units, are introduced in the configuration of the load balancer. The load balancer can then be configured to route requests among them in a sequential order (round robin) or send requests with the same IP address to the same cluster (sticky session). We can configure the clusters to reside in an Intranet network, configure

NLB to reside in Internet, and access the system with the IP or DNS of the NLB. The load balancer then takes care of the rest and routes the request to the clusters:

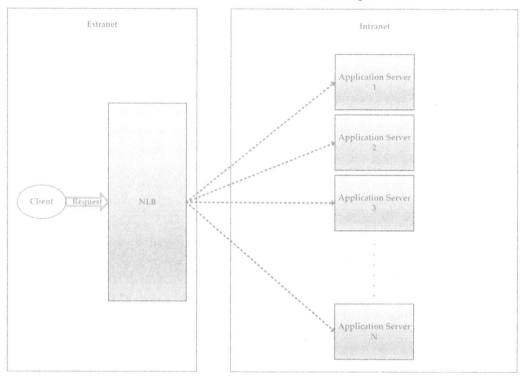

Figure 13.2: Scalable monolithic application

We explained these concepts in *Chapter 3: Running, Debugging and Deploying ASP. NET Core Applications*.

It is easy to notice the following points:

- **No separation of concerns**: Everything is put into one place. Controllers are responsible for sending data to the Razor view and return the HTML response or response with other formats (JSON, XML, and so on). Accessing data has nothing to do with them. After a certain point, the code will become spaghetti and developers will be lost in the project.

- **No code reuse**: Let us assume we have written the saving contact information code in an action method. We have a workflow like validating data, checking the uniqueness of phone number, and saving the data to the relevant database tables. Then, we are presented another requirement. We need to create and expose a service that does the same thing, saving contact information with different parameters. Or we are asked to create a scheduled task to fetch new contacts from a remote data source (a web service, for example) at the end of every day. We must rewrite (copy-paste) the same code at different places where we need to maintain and add extra business rules or workflows to the same functionality. We need to apply the changes to the different places we copied and pasted.

To avoid these problems, layers are introduced to the software community.

> **NOTE: The monolithic architecture is not bad or outdated; it is still widely used. You do not consider a microservices architecture for an application with a few user interfaces, limited functionality, and user capacity.**

Introducing layered architecture

A layered architecture is used for achieving code reuse, separation of concerns, maintainability by grouping by placing code in respective places, and creating highly cohesive, loosely coupled components that depend on to the next layer like a ring connected to the next one in a chain. Layers are encapsulated black boxes that allow coherent and loosely coupled software design. The following figure describes a simple layered architecture. The number of the layers can vary as the requirements, but there are occasionally three layers: presentation, application, and data access. To achieve separation of concerns and cohesion, a layer should only know the layer it uses. For example, it is an anti-pattern to access data from the presentation layer:

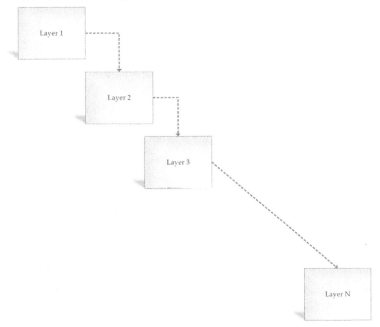

Figure 13.3: Layered architecture

Layers are not just logically separated codes in a single web project like having the following folder/namespace structure:

- Phonebook solution

  ○ Phonebook.Web (ASP.NET Core web project)

    ▪ Controllers (Presentation layer)

    ▪ Views

    ▪ Application (Application layer)

    ▪ Data (Data layer)

Layers must also be separated physically; instead of putting everything in a single project, every layer must have its own .NET project like the following:

- Phonebook solution

  ○ Phonebook.Web (ASP.NET Core project)

    ▪ Controllers (presentation layer)

    ▪ Views

  ○ Phonebook.Application (.NET Core class library project)

  ○ Phonebook.Data (.NET Core class library project)

This provides modularity and high cohesion. Let us suppose we are asked to create a task scheduler application that runs some of the functionality (for example, sending emails) in application layer between a certain period. We can create a console project that schedules this task and invokes some code in the application layer (because we may not want to bring additional overhead to the web application by sending requests to it). We can achieve this by adding the application layer and data layers as references to the scheduler project we created and use the application layer objects from there. The projects in a solution can look like the following:

- Phonebook solution

  ○ Phonebook.Web (ASP.NET Core project)

    ▪ Controllers (presentation layer)

    ▪ Views

  ○ Phonebook.Scheduler (.NET Core console project)

  ○ Phonebook.Application (.NET Core class library project)

  ○ Phonebook.Data (.NET Core class library project)

The following figure displays layer dependencies:

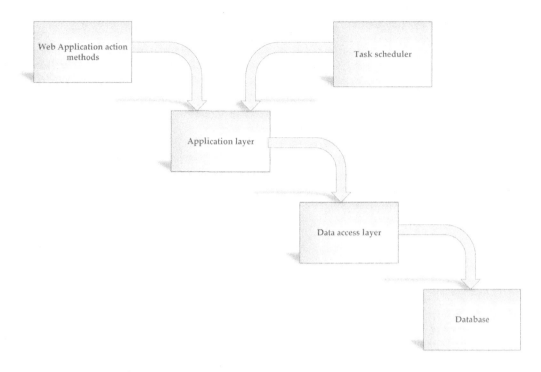

Figure 13.4: Layers in a project

Therefore, layering an application physically provides modularity. We can take a layer and plug it to another layer with the rest of the dependent layers.

In a typical ASP.NET Core application, the layers can be established as follows:

- **Presentation**: The presentation layer is responsible for calling the necessary object methods from the application layer and shaping, projecting the data returned from them into model objects (or data transfer objects), passing them to renderer (Razor engine), rendering, and returning the view as a response. They correspond to the action methods in ASP.NET Core MVC or Razor pages. If we are developing a service API, we can call this layer, API layer also. The presentation layer is about triggering the relevant application layer object methods and preparing data for display. It only knows the application layer and has no idea about the layers that the application layer depends on (we should not perform database operations here).

- **Application layer**: An application layer performs business functionality. It validates data, loads data by invoking relevant data access object methods, checks data by applying business rules, persists data, and returns data or information that the operation is successful or not. The application layer has no idea about the layer that depends on it (in our case presentation layer). It performs business logic by using data access layer objects. This layer also does not connect to the database directly.

- **Data access layer**: The data access layer is responsible for managing database connections, transactions, querying, and persisting data. The queries are occasionally written in a reusable way. Again, the data access layer has no idea about the layer that depends on it (in our case, the application layer). Objects that comply with the repository design pattern are an example for data access layers.

- **Database**: If we are developing a database sensitive application and require faster database operations, we can use stored procedures. If the stored procedures contain workflows, business functionality like the application layer, the database can be considered as a layer also.

> NOTE: Stored procedures are compiled and therefore fast working routines that reside in the database. If your application requires fast operations on a large amount of data, you can choose to write stored procedures. But keep in mind that stored procedures are hard to develop, debug, and maintain.

Introducing service-oriented architecture

A service-oriented architecture is splitting the application into loose coupled, cohesive, reusable services and creating a design that is easy to integrate, scale, and maintain. The application is analyzed by its domain and decomposed into smaller parts that require to be scaled, maintained, and developed independently from other parts. It is like a class design. We decompose our code into coherent, loose coupled, and reusable classes. We apply the same principles to the higher-level service design at the application scope.

Service oriented architecture (SOA) allows the following benefits:

- We can decompose an application into smaller services and assign different teams, resources for developing them.

- We can maintain and deploy services without breaking entire application. It is separation of concerns principle applied at a higher level.

- We can scale specific services, if necessary. Sometimes, a part of our application requires handling more requests and we can scale up necessary services.

The following figure explains a typical SOA architecture. Notice the UI presentation is also considered as a service. We can also configure services for cross-origin resource sharing to allow easy usage from web browsers:

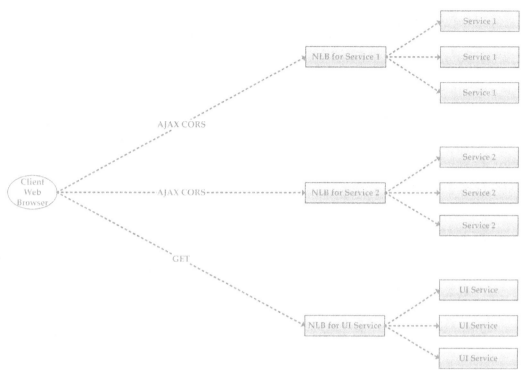

Figure 13.5*: Service Oriented Architecture*

SOA brings some dynamism to the large enterprise projects. The key to success in SOA is to make services loosely coupled and coherent. This allows scaling part of the application and assigning resources for its development and maintenance. We consider the domain and parts of the application require to be integrated by the other applications while separating the application into services.

Introducing microservices architecture

A microservices architecture is done by separating a server application into a smaller set of microservices, which have certain domain boundary, independent of each other, have data sovereignty by itself (having separate databases or separate schemas in a database). The application is designed by fine-grained microservices, which are independent, have business capability by themselves alone and have no information about each other directly.

NOTE: The name micro has nothing to do with the size of the microservice. The service must be developed, deployed, and scaled independent of other services, thus providing granularity for the application. The main principles of SOA apply to microservices. Some part of the software community accepts that microservices are SOA perfected.

Since the microservices are independent, they do not communicate directly with each other, they use events with messages. A microservice design uses a message broker and a protocol like **asynchronous message queuing protocol (AMQP)**. The protocol must support asynchronous message processing and microservices require a broker to utilize it.

Message brokers provide event-driven programming. A service does not consume another service; it sends an event with a message to the broker asynchronously and that message is delivered to the necessary service by the broker. This also avoids blocking the system because the messages must be sent asynchronously.

Asynchronous message queue protocols are message-oriented protocols that guarantee each message is delivered:

- **At least once**: A message is guaranteed to be delivered once but may be delivered more than once.

- **Exactly once**: A message is guaranteed to be delivered only once.

- **At most once**: A message is guaranteed to be delivered once or never.

> **TIP: RabbitMQ and Apache Kafka are popular message brokers. They support many languages and platforms. You can check them out from https://www.rabbitmq.com/ and https://kafka.apache.org/, while RabbitMQ is good for low message traffic and adjustable routing Kafka is great for a huge amount of messages.**

If the system is stopped or interrupted, the message broker must also guarantee to store messages and continue to send them when the system is back online.

Let us assume one of the microservices must notify another microservice. It must send a message to the broker, and it is delivered to the respective microservice by it. The following figure displays how to deliver messages by a broker:

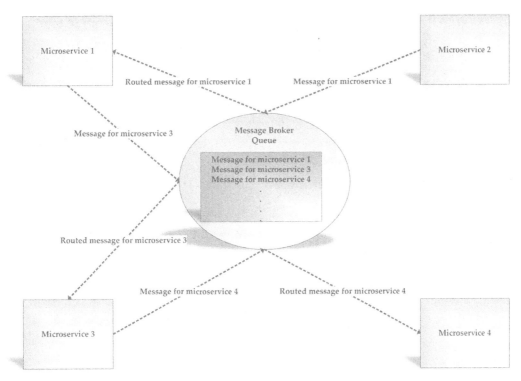

Figure 13.6: *Message broker in a microservices architecture*

If we are to explain principles for microservices, we have IDEALS principles to follow, just like we have SOLID principles for the class design:

- **Interface segregation**: Different types of clients (mobile, web, desktop) of the application must be able to interact with microservices for their specific needs. For example, a mobile client must gather less data compared to a web client through the same service call. We benefit from the backend for frontend pattern for this which we will explain later in this chapter.

- **Deployability**: Since we can have as many microservices as we require, we need to take into consideration deploying, packaging, and monitoring microservices. This is the part DevOps comes in and these must be designed along with the application.

- **Event-driven**: A microservice should not consume another microservice directly; instead, it must send asynchronous events with messages.

- **Availability over consistency**: The microservices architecture favors availability over consistency. We will explain eventual consistency later in this chapter.

- **Loose coupling**: Microservices should be loosely coupled with their internals as much as possible. A service has a contract and some capabilities. It must complete its tasks without the consumer knowing the technology or internal business logic. The API gateways detaches consumers from microservices and provides great flexibility. We will explain them later in this chapter.

- **Single responsibility**: A microservice should contain just enough functionality in the perspective of the domain-driven design, no more or no less. Thus, the microservices in an application must be coherent.

Now, let us compare the monolithic architecture and microservices architecture to better understand microservices.

The pros of the monolithic architecture are as follows:

- Simply designed and developed.

- Easy to deploy, many monolithic applications are shutdown and restarted while deploying.

- Additional concerns of the application such as logging, monitoring, testing, debugging are easier since everything is in one place.

The cons of the monolithic architecture are as follows:

- It is scaled entirely and hardware resources can be wasted. Monolithic applications do not have independent parts.

- Since everything is written by the same technology, it can be very hard to add new components with a new technology.

- Availability can easily become a problem, depending on the number of users and requests.

The pros of the microservices architecture are as follows:

- Different parts (services) of the application can be scaled independently of other parts. This way we save hardware resources and not enforce to scale services that are not in demand.

- Concerns are separated. Microservices are designed as coherent, loose coupled components and this allows easy developing, understanding, and deploying without shutting down the entire application.

- Services with different technologies can easily be added to the application as needed. The microservices are loosely coupled components; they are unaware and not interested of the other microservices internal technology. For example, one microservice in a system can be developed by ASP.NET Core, another Python, and so on.

- Microservices are more fault tolerant. If a microservice fails, other microservices allow the application to continue functioning, thus allowing the other parts of the application to be available.

The cons of the microservices architecture are as follows:

- Deployment strategy of the application must be dealt with at the design stage and can become complicated.
- Microservices are hard to design and develop. Architects must separate the application into loosely coupled and coherent services; developers must achieve challenging core tasks such as the API gateway and eventual consistency.
- Microservices are hard to maintain.

To give a solid real-world example of microservices, we will introduce the CQRS design pattern.

Introducing command query responsibility segregation

CQRS is an architectural design pattern that separates command and querying. In a typical application, we insert, update, delete data (commands) in a database and generate reports (queries) from the data we inserted. CQRS allows you to scale command and querying independently of each other. Let us assume we have an online shopping application, and we insert orders such as bought products then we query and generate reports from them to view daily, monthly income, and so on. The following figure describes how it is done in a monolithic application:

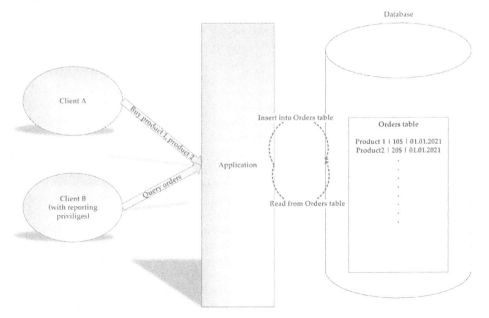

Figure 13.7: Command and query from the same API and the same database

Clients buy products and we insert them into an Orders table, and we query the same table for income reports for a given period. Let us assume there is a period that sales are increased and a lot of data is inserted to the Orders table simultaneously by different clients and therefore the accounting department started to generate reports more frequently. The following problems are noticeable in this monolithic architecture.

- We must be able to scale the part of the application for clients that buy products (commands) and scale the part of the application for report generation (queries). But it is not possible in a monolithic application because it is entirely self-contained. We should be scaling parts independently and satisfy every type of user.

- Performing huge amounts of writing and reading on the same database and tables is not a database friendly way and a lot of writing will affect the performance of the database for reading because of the locks in transactions.

- Reporting and ordering must share the same database tables and therefore, they must share the same data models that may have no meaning to one another. We may need to include columns specific to reporting which has no meaning to ordering.

- When we would like to update the code for the ordering part of the service, we must also deploy the reporting part of our application together; even that is unnecessary, and this blocks the users who generate reports. The reverse of this is also true; when we deploy the reporting part of the application, we must also deploy the ordering part of the application.

We can overcome these pitfalls by applying CQRS and microservices. We take the command part (buying products) and querying part (generating reports) as separate concerns and encapsulate them into microservices. When an order is given, we send a message to the reporting microservice through the broker with the amount of sale. Each of the services are independent and can be scaled up and down without affecting each other. We also keep reporting and orders as separate databases which increase the overall database performance also. The following figure displays this CQRS scenario:

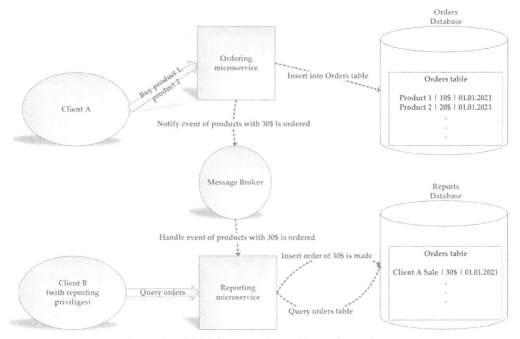

Figure 13.8: *CQRS for separating writing and querying*

Notice how we notify the reporting microservice. We send an asynchronous event with a message from the order microservice and save the total amount in the reporting service. We can shape the data in the message as we desire before or after sending. In our example, we sum and take the total price of the orders since we are interested in the income and not the sold products.

In a monolithic application, this must be done in a database transaction because it is an atomic operation and called strong consistency. The data must be inserted in the Orders table in the Orders database and orders table in the Reporting database both successfully. Failing in inserting one of them will result in inconsistent data. This is achieved by eventual consistency in microservices.

Introducing eventual consistency

The microservice architecture contains separate services with their own business capability and database. A microservice does not consume another microservice. It sends an event to the message broker asynchronously and forgets the rest. The microservice which handles the event can fail to process the message after it receives it. We cannot do it in a transaction since they have different databases.

This is the architecture of applications that can handle huge amounts of requests simultaneously. We simply can't achieve this by a single service behind a load balancer that employs a single atomic transaction (strong consistency). The application is divided into loosely coupled services and they have databases of their own. A service can handle a part of the job by a transaction, notify another service by events for the rest of the job, and it handles its own part in another transaction, etc. Since we do not complete the job in a single transaction, we must provide a safe mechanism that the job is completed eventually.

Eventual consistency is completing distributed transactions or jobs by processing messages, eventually. The message broker is the key in achieving eventual consistency. The broker must be configured to provide a mechanism that can satisfy the following requirements:

- The broker must supply the replay function and resend failed messages. This is necessary for failover scenarios also if the respective microservice crashes for some reason. The broker must achieve this by saving messages to the disk or some durable place and keep them until they are processed successfully.

- The broker should send events in the order it received them. Some messages can be handled more than one microservice and handling the order can be important.

- The broker should keep track of the failure times, failure reasons, and information about the microservice failed processing the event. This is essential for debugging microservices.

When we use a message broker with these functionalities, the processing of the messages will be completed eventually, even if something goes wrong.

> **NOTE: Eventual consistency is the key to performance in microservices. The fintech, online trading, or similar applications architected by microservices and provide handling millions of simultaneous requests by users with combining microservices architecture together with cloud computing.**

The microservices architecture must also provide an easier way for clients to consume them together. Since there can be many different microservices in a system, the clients must be able to communicate with them together instead of one by one.

Introducing the API gateway

The API gateway is the entry point of a system with the microservices architecture. The microservices reside in an Intranet network and they are not accessed directly from outside. The API gateway handles the following:

- **Security**: The API gateway handles authentication and authorization. After the request passes these checks, it is redirected by the API gateway to the respective microservice. The microservices reside in Intranet and usually do not check for authentication or other security concerns. We can also apply other security measures such as rate limiting for denial-of-service attacks, whitelist authentication at API gateways, and so on.

- **Decouples clients and microservices**: There can be many microservices at the server and API gateways provide single entry points for them; so clients do not need to configure and manage every IP address, DNS, and port information of every microservice separately.

- **Request aggregation**: A client may need to send multiple requests to several different microservices at the same time. API gateways allow clients to send a onetime composed request. The API gateway then routes the parts of the request to the respective microservices. To give an example of the request aggregation, let us assume we have two action methods in two different microservices. One of them has a **/Contacts** route that is run by the **HttpGet** method, as shown here:

```
public class Contact
{
    public string Name { get; set; }
    public string Surname { get; set; }
}


[ApiController]
public class ContactsController : ControllerBase
{
    [HttpGet]
    public IEnumerable<Contact> Contacts()
    {
        List<Contact> list = null;

        .

        .

        .

        .

        return list;
    }
}
```

The other action method has a route by /Numbers that is run by the http get method again, as shown here:

```
public class PhoneNumber
{
```

```
        public string CountryCode { get; set; }
        public string Number { get; set; }
    }

    [ApiController]
    public class NumbersController : ControllerBase
    {
        [HttpGet]
        public IEnumerable<PhoneNumber> Numbers()
        {
            List<PhoneNumber> list = null;

            .

            .

            .

            return list;
        }
    }
```

They return different objects as a response in the JSON format. We can configure the API gateway and when it receives a request with the route **/ContactsAndNumbers**, it decomposes it and sends it to the microservices. Then, it aggregates the responses of the two requests and returns them as a single response, as shown in the following JSON sample:

```
{
    "Contacts":
    [
        {
            "Name":"John",
            "Surname":"Smith"
        },

        .

        .

        .

    ],
    "Numbers":
    [
        {
```

```
        "CountryCode":"91",
        "Number":"5555555555"
      }
   ]
}
```

The following figure illustrates the aggregation of requests in an API Gateway:

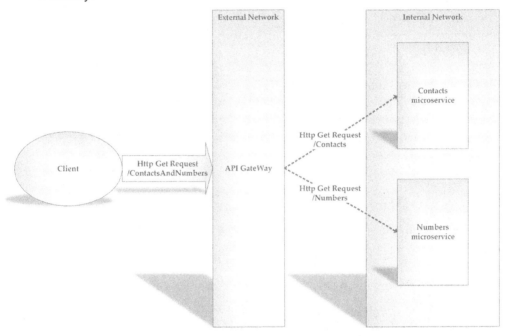

Figure 13.9: Request gateway in API Gateway

Request aggregation is a handy feature that reduces server roundtrips greatly. We can send many requests to the different microservices at once.

- **Backend for frontend**: The clients of a server designed with microservices can be different types of clients. Many applications today have at least two clients, web, and mobile (native or responsive web). Their frontends may need different data and mobile applications have a network speed and bandwidth disadvantage compared to their web counterparts because of the cellular network.

  API gateways present a solution to this problem. We can have different gateways to shape and tailor data as we desire for the client's needs. We can add a separate gateway for mobile clients and separate for web clients and scale them independently.

NOTE: Ocelot is an open source API gateway framework for the .NET framework. It supports almost every functionality an API gateway must support. It can be checked from its Git Hub page at https://github.com/ThreeMammals/Ocelot.

Conclusion

The backend architecture is certainly a fundamental aspect of a server application. It affects the project team and operations directly and eventually end users indirectly. Choosing it depends on projects' technical requirements, your team's knowledge, experience, and willingness if you think about microservices. A wrong architecture choice may lead to failure of a software project.

NOTE: As explained in this chapter, microservices are no joke. You should consider it if you need to handle so many concurrent requests and scale different parts of the applications dynamically as needed and there are strong operation specialists who have experience about maintenance of cloud or cloud-native environments.

Questions

1. What are the requirements of a good architecture? Explain with examples.

2. What are the disadvantages of a monolithic architecture?

3. Should layers in an architecture be logical only? Explain with reasons.

4. What points should we consider while implementing SOA?

5. Explain CQRS and its advantages.

Chapter 14
Landing a Job

Introduction

We explained various architectures of software projects in the previous chapter. We will cover how to prepare developer job interviews in this chapter. We will explain general concepts and give answers to the questions we gave at the end of every chapter which are possible interview questions.

Structure

In this chapter, we will discuss the following topics:

- Preparing for coding challenges
- Achieving technical assignments
- Answers to questions at the end of each chapter and their variations that you may encounter at interviews

Objectives

After reading this chapter, you should be ready for job interviews that requires ASP. NET Core knowledge.

Preparing for coding challenges

A job application contains several processes. A coding challenge may be the first or the second step after the introduction. Coding challenges are online assignments that are to be completed in a short period of time (in 20 or 40 minutes likely), and you must complete a task by coding it with using the relevant programming language. It is usually done by writing code for a single method that takes parameters and returns the expected output.

These challenges are presented by online coding editors that counts down time and allows you to write and submit your code. It also runs your solution by passing different parameters that vary in size and compares your solution's output with the expected output and refuses your submission if they are not equal.

These tasks have short descriptions which are a few paragraphs long and they are about implementing an algorithm. Although one or more algorithms are asked to be implemented, they do not ask directly about implementing an algorithm, they describe a story in the description that requires an implementation of an algorithm.

A short story is given at the description that you must grasp and choose the relevant algorithms to be implemented to solve the task. There can be different algorithms for solving the problem and they will grade the applicants by choosing the right and most optimal algorithm, considering time and space complexity.

To achieve these kinds of challenges, we can suggest some advice as follows:

- There are several web sites that you can train yourselves. They have the same features like online code editors, countdown timers, and so on. They allow you to solve various tasks that are like the ones asked in job applications and they also describe and train you for the various solutions of these tasks.

  It may be shocking if you need to implement an algorithm that you never heard of or you have learned years ago while in the university. You should sign up to some of those sites and train yourselves by solving and studying tasks in a regular basis. This will also give you confidence.

- Do not rush into coding with the very first thing comes to your mind. It can be the brute force way of solving the problem. Keep a pencil and a sheet of paper in front of you and try to figure out your options by thinking about the task by running your solution step by step. This way you can figure out a different and better way for solving the problem by using recursive or dynamic programming instead of brute force.

  These assessment tools also calculate your solution's time and space complexity, and the applicants are graded by their solution's time and space complexity.

- Try to write clean code. Applicants are also graded by their coding. Make indentations, be careful with the name of your variables, and write auxiliary methods for code reuse. These kinds of challenges are occasionally about just coding a method. Do not bother design patterns, SOLID principles, dependency injection, and so on, unless it is asked of you or else you will lose precious time.

> **NOTE: You may be presented with a problem that requires an algorithm you have never heard of before and it can appear as nonsense such as is there any usage of this algorithm in real life. Keep in mind tech recruiting itself has become an industry and companies are usually looking for the best talent through recruiters. They think the best way to eliminate thousands of applicants by coding challenges or other types of assignments.**

Achieving technical assignments

Some companies prefer giving assignments to the applicants. They are real-life coding assignments like implementing a small application. They occasionally contain developing the UI part also. The point in these kinds of assignments is to grade applicants by their frontend and backend development skills. Compared to the coding challenges more time is given to the applicant like a few days or a week.

The evaluation may be done by taking into consideration the following points, may be more or less:

- Are the SOLID principles applied? The classes must be loosely coupled and coherent.

- Is the right architecture chosen? For layered architectures are there any physical layers present?

- Is dependency injection used for the parts having a potential to change with the right lifetime?

- Is validation present at both frontend and backend?

- If an API needs to be developed for the assignment, are the rest principles used?

- Is there any repeating code present? Is the code structured properly for reuse?

- Is there any coding style present? Is there a convention for variable, class, method names?

- How the methods are structured? There should not be methods with too many lines of code.

- Is there any code that can lead to security vulnerability?

- Are there unit tests present with the right purposes they should have?
- Are the database queries efficient? For example, is there a loop that makes a database query multiple times that can be achieved by a single or fewer database queries?
- Are the CSS is structured well and as minimal as possible?
- Is the UI consistent across different browsers?
- Are the features specific to the JavaScript or Typescript used properly in the right places?
- Questions about the front-end framework (Angular, React, Vue.js, and so on) specific to the job that is applied.

For these kinds of assignments, it should be enough to apply the principles and techniques presented in this book.

Now, let us review every chapter, discuss what kind of questions you can encounter about the information presented at them, and give answers to the questions at the end of them.

Chapter 1 - Introduction to ASP.NET Core

You may be asked theoretical questions about features in ASP.NET Core or .NET framework itself. For example, how garbage collection works in .NET Core. The difference between old .NET frameworks and .NET Core frameworks.

The answers to the questions are as follows:

1. If we are starting a new project, when should we prefer using ASP.NET Core?

    ASP.NET Core is a unified way of making web applications. We can use Razor engine to embed server-side logic into HTML and add dynamism to the generated HTML with using C#.

    It is cross platform and not only works in Windows platform as its predecessors only worked on Windows. We can get the advantages specific to Linux, and we can host our applications on different web servers instead of IIS. We can also develop ASP.NET Core applications on different platforms.

    It is open source, and we can always check for its source code in any case we need it.

    It comes with a built-in dependency injection framework. This also encourages testable code.

    It is easy to configure routing. We can simply apply route patterns to our action methods.

2. When should we use reverse proxy for deploying our ASP.NET Core applications?

   In Linux, Kestrel can be used for both development and production environment. If we decide to use it for production, we should consider putting it behind a reverse proxy because it is vulnerable to many kinds of attacks.

3. Where do we configure our applications service container and request pipeline?

   We configure middleware pipeline in the **Configure** method and the DI container the **ConfigureServices** method in the **Startup** class.

4. What could we use for intercepting and modifying requests?

   We can intercept requests at middleware or action filters.

Chapter 2 - Setting Up the Development Environment

You may encounter some questions about your preference between Visual Studio or Visual Studio Code. Usually, there is not only one right answer to these kinds of questions, and the person you are interviewing with would like to learn about your familiarity to integrated development environments.

We prefer Visual Studio for backend development and Visual Studio Code for front end development (like JavaScript, Typescript, and HTML) because Visual Studio Code is fast, lightweight and can handle compilation of many script files together.

The answers to questions are as follows:

1. When should we use dotnet CLI?

   Visual Studio provides every functionality .NET CLI provides but in case of Visual Studio Code in the Linux environment, you need to use .NET CLI to create new projects from templates or adding references to projects.

   Before deploying projects to the production or test servers, you can use .NET CLI to install and configure the environment. There is usually no need for an IDE installed in the production environment.

2. Why should we use an IDE or editor for development?

   Integrated development environments contain many enhancements for coding such as renaming variables, autocomplete, peeking, or viewing the definition of a class in a library. These are must have tools for a professional developer.

But for example, if you deploy your application without publishing and need to make a quick fix to a Razor cshtml, then you can use the default text editor installed on the server.

3. What can we do for increasing the building performance of the Visual Studio?

There can be tens of projects in a solution which degrades the Visual Studio performance. It tries to load them all, prepare IntelliSense with the classes, methods, properties in every project and does the same with the added references.

We can prefer using Visual Studio Code. It is lightweight and has fewer features compared to Visual Studio, but it has essential features like autocomplete, show errors in code before compilation, and so on. These can be enough for many development scenarios.

We can split the entire solution into smaller solutions with related projects together. For example, we can have an API solution, web client solution, desktop client solution. We can use the same common projects between them also (projects that contain data transfer objects, models, utility classes, and so on).

We can unload the projects in a solution which we do not need at that time and does not affect compilation. For example, we can unload unit test projects until we need unit testing. Visual Studio is going to remember our unloaded projects and is not going to attempt loading them again on start-up unless we reload them again.

4. How do we manage launching order of projects for debugging in Visual Studio, Visual Studio Code and why should we manage it?

We can use the solution property dialog in Visual Studio and the **launch.json** file in Visual Studio Code.

If we are developing a client and server application, we need the server (API) project to start debugging before the client project.

Chapter 3 - Running, Debugging, and Deploying ASP.NET Core Applications

Occasionally, developers are responsible for development only but if the job you are applying also requires responsibility about the servers or features of the server that application is deployed, you may be asked questions about configuring servers.

The answers to the questions are as follows:

1. Why and when should you use reverse proxies?

   Reverse proxies are essential for security. It is common that server applications reside at the internal network (intranet) and they have an IP address valid for intranet network only. A reverse proxy server is configured to reside at internet and routes requests to the application servers at intranet. Users access applications with the IP address, port, or DNS name of the reverse proxy server.

   Reverse proxy servers are protective shields against several security attacks. They present many options that you can configure them to prevent security attacks, so they get the punishment instead of your application servers.

   We can also configure reverse proxy as **network load balancer (NLB)** to route requests to the application servers and scale the application.

   We can also cache some static content such as image, CSS, HTML files directly at proxy server so our application servers do not bother with caching them.

2. Is using Kestrel as a production server exposed directly to Internet a good idea?

   No. Kestrel is originally a development server, but it can be safely used under the wings of a well configured reverse proxy server.

3. Suppose you are getting errors from your application in the production servers, and you do not encounter them when you debug your code; where it is related to the origin of the error. What should you do?

   We can deploy our application with debug configuration and use remote debugging.

4. You deployed your application to IIS, but it fails to start. Even the code of the entry point of your application does not run. What should you do?

   IIS logs many events to windows event logs. It is a good place to start.

Chapter 4 - Introduction to HTTP, HTML, CSS, and JavaScript

If you are applying for full-stack development jobs that are based on ASP.NET Core, they occasionally would like to ask about the framework used for front-end like Angular, React, and so on, but sometimes, you may encounter general questions about JavaScript or HTML.

The answers to the questions are as follows:

1. For which purposes, can we use the user-agent header?

   We can detect the browser of the client whether it is mobile or not and render the UI according to that information.

2. Assume you are writing a service that downloads a pdf file. How do you automatically open the pdf file in the browser when it is downloaded?

   We can set the Content-Type header of the response to application/pdf.

3. Assume you are in a team that you are coding the backend and another developer coding the front-end. You have written a service, but its HTML page user interface is not ready. How can you test and debug your service?

   We can use clients like postman to craft web requests, send them to the server, and inspect the response in detail.

4. You want to collect data from the user and redirect it to another website or page. Which method should be used?

   We can use Http 302 temporary redirect. If we use Http 301 permanent redirect, the browser can cache response and instead of hitting our action method that makes redirection, it can go to the URL at the response directly next time.

Chapter 5 - Developing ASP.NET Core Web Applications with Razor

If the job you apply for does not require a front-end framework directly like Angular and requires Razor, you can be asked a question about Razor or principle of MVC, routing, and so on.

The answers to the questions are as follows:

1. Suppose you are developing a web page and you coded the necessary validation by JavaScript. Is this enough? If not explain reasons.

   Putting validation to JavaScript is necessary but it is not enough. We also must apply the same validation at server-side. Validation code at front-end can be bypassed.

2. Suppose you are developing a web page and you coded the necessary validation in the backend server side. Is this enough? If not explain the reason.

   Validation at the backend is mandatory for protecting the operation that is done with the data arrived at server, but it is not enough. We also apply validations at frontend, so we avoid unnecessary server calls.

3. Let us assume you are developing a web application with many pages. Some of the pages require a menu on the top and some of the pages require menu on the left. How do you handle this without rendering menu on every page?

We can create a layout page with conditional rendering logic which renders top or left menu depending on the route, or we can create two layout pages responsible for generating left and top menu, respectively.

4. Let us assume you redirect your user to another page in your application, but you want to carry a small amount of data. How can you achieve it in a simple way?

We can use the **TempData** dictionary or a query string parameter. The data in **TempData** is going to be wiped out after it is accessed.

5. You are asked to create a web application with four or five UI pages. Should you use MVC or Razor pages?

It may be more convenient to use Razor pages since MVC is more structured and suitable for handling more user interfaces.

Chapter 6 - Developing Restful Services with ASP.NET Core

If you are applying for a job that requires ASP.NET Core knowledge, there is going to be API development for sure and you will be asked questions about it. They can be about rest principles, differences of ASP.NET Core MVC action methods, and API controller action methods.

Here are the answers to the questions:

1. Assume you start a new project that has a web client, Android client, IOS client and many potential third-party applications that would like to integrate to your application. Should you separate your UI rendering part and API part? Why?

UI rendering and service API must be separated if there are multiple front-end clients. The data format and its scope may change for web clients and mobile clients.

2. You have common configuration variables that is the same for every runtime environment. Where do you include them? Why?

We can keep them in the **appsettings.json** file. It is common and independent of the value in the **ASPNETCORE_ENVIRONMENT** environment variable.

Chapter 7 - The Async/Await Pattern and Middleware in ASP.NET Core

The Async/await pattern is one of the very useful features of ASP.NET Core. It makes writing asynchronous code comfortable, easy to understand, and maintain. You may be asked why we should use asynchronous code, how to parallelize execution of partial code, and so on.

If you are applying for an ASP.NET Core job, middleware knowledge is also a must, and you can be asked a question that is directly about middleware pipeline or the answer to that question may be handled at the middleware stage.

Here are the answers to the questions:

1. Assume you have an action method that takes a long time. You decided to move your server to another server that has the same clock speed of the previous server's CPUs but more CPU cores. You action method still takes a long time. What is it that you miss?

   You should use asynchronous programming with the async/await pattern and run independent codes in parallel (you can try optimizing action method, but it is assumed there is no asynchronous programming used).

2. Assume you need to log certain types of response for application level. What should you do?

   Middleware is a good place to log responses in global. It can be a fire and forget asynchronous code in one of the outer middleware.

3. Assume you have some middlewares and you need developers to execute them in the order of you want. What should you do?

   We can create an extension method and register grouped middlewares by order inside of it. Then, the extension method can be called at the Startup class.

4. Assume you need to check a request by a specific header value and redirect it to a different action method. What should you do?

   We can add a middleware to the pipeline and use URL rewriting.

Chapter 8 - Dependency Injection and Action Filters in ASP.NET Core

Software companies do care for making change proof and testable code. Dependency injection is one of the keys for achieving those. Most likely you might receive a question about DI or an assignment that is required to use DI, if you are applying for an ASP.NET Core job. The question can be about lifetimes of instances too. Especially, the singleton design pattern.

Action filters are the features of ASP.NET Core for aspect-oriented programming. You can receive questions when to use them, differences between middleware and action filters, or a question that the answer consists of using an action filter.

Here are the answers to the questions:

1. Assume you have a non-changing static data that can be very hard to load, and it is accessed across your project frequently. What is one of the strategies you can do with a pure ASP.NET Core solution?

   We can create a class, load data in its constructor, and register it in DI with a singleton lifetime.

   We can also use response caching if possible.

2. You need to modify the request body for certain routes that receives post requests in your project. Is writing a middleware for this a good choice?

   This is not a good choice; middlewares are common code paths that every request passes through and deserializing JSON is a costly process, especially if it is large. We can use action filters at a later stage and modify any property we like by using some reflection. Model is already bound and deserialization will be complete at the action filters stage.

3. You want to register an interface and its implementation in the DI container, and you want it to be a new instance every time it is injected. Which lifetime should you choose?

   Transient lifetime.

Chapter 9 - State Management in ASP.NET Core

At job interviews, recruiters may need to know about how you manage state in ASP. NET Core. The questions may be about using the right state management technique, how to deal with storing session for multiple clusters, and so on.

Here are the answers to the questions:

1. We do not want cookies of our application modifiable from the JavaScript. How can we achieve that?

   Making cookie http-only at the server side.

2. Our application is behind NLB and in a cluster with many servers that run it. How can we configure the session storage and why?

We can use different session storage providers such as Redis, SQL Server, NCache, and so on. This will provide putting the same session data in a common place between clusters.

3. How can we manage identity in an ASP.NET Core application?

    We can use scaffolding and modify the generated default code and Razor UI or provide custom authentication methods.

Chapter 10 - Introducing Accessing Data with ASP.NET Core

If you are given an assignment and it consists of database access with the entity framework, you will be evaluated with how effective you write your queries, do you write queries that are easy to read and maintain. You can also be asked about the code-first approach and managing migrations. Also, the repository pattern is popular amongst software companies, and it should not be a surprise if they would like to know your knowledge about it.

Here are the answers to the questions:

1. How do we model databases with the entity framework and what are the differences, advantage, and disadvantages between them?

    We can model databases with code-first or database-first approaches. In the code-first approach, we use **plain old CLR objects** (**POCO**) which are simply C# classes and attributes with properties to manage database changes, table, and column names.

    In the database-first approach, we design the database with a tool and scaffold POCO classes with .net CLI.

    The difference between them is that the code-first approach presents a quick setup, easy migration (though can be troublesome sometimes), and can be used by developers. The database-first approach is used by database administrators or experts which requires careful database design and special tools.

2. How can we register and use database context in ASP.NET Core?

    We can configure DI at the startup class to inject context for us by the **AddDbContext** method.

3. Can a database context be registered as a singleton? If not, explain why?

    It should not be registered as a singleton. The database context is not thread safe and runtime errors will occur for concurrent requests using the same context instance at the same time.

4. How can we compose queries in the entity framework and why we should do it?

    The entity framework and LINQ allow us to compose queries easily. It makes our code maintainable and readable.

5. Explain the differences between lazy and eager loading.

    Lazy loading allows us to load connected data to an entity when needed by navigational properties. Eager loading allows us to load connected data in navigational properties at once.

Chapter 11 - Optimizing ASP.NET Core Applications

You can encounter optimization questions at interviews. It will be good to have knowledge of the techniques together with options and what to use when to use.

Here are the answers to the questions:

1. How can we monitor our application and gather metrics in ASP.NET Core?

    We can use event counters with default events of an ASP.NET Core application along with custom events we create.

2. Is response compression beneficial for assets with small size? Why?

    It is not. Compression algorithms are not efficient for files with small sizes. They are not worthy of compression.

3. How can we redirect to another action method and access data from previous action method without database loading, and so on?

    We can use **TempData** for quick storage and removal along with a redirect response.

4. Is accessing http post requests' body with large payloads in middleware a good idea? Why?

    No. Middlewares are common code paths that many or every request passes through. The payload is already going to be model bound at a later stage in action filters.

5. We want to cache partial region of a Razor view instead of the entire view. How can we do it?

    By cache tag helpers.

6. How can we improve the performance of the loading time of pages?

We can use response caching together with bundling and compression.

Chapter 12 - Securing ASP.NET Core Applications

Whether you are given an assignment or making an interview, your assignment will be evaluated whether you implemented security measures in your code or not and you should expect at least one question about security. No one wants to employ a developer that has no idea about basic security vulnerabilities and how to counter them.

Here are the answers to the questions:

1. We want to send a link via an email to the users of our application, and we would like to send sensitive data in the query string that must not be understandable to them. We would also like the link to expire after a certain period of time. How can we achieve that?

   We can use data protection API to create encrypted strings easily. We can also put expiration date inside the encryption.

2. What are the different ways to avoid SQL injection attacks?

   LINQ and object queries generate parametrized query by default. We can also use raw queries with calling the **FromSqlRaw** and **FromSqlInterpolated** methods of the Entity Framework Core.

3. How can we avoid cross-site request forgery for incoming AJAX requests?

   We can inject an anti-forgery token string into the page and send it along with Ajax requests, or we can check the referrer header value. It must have the same DNS or IP address with our application.

4. We fetch user's authorization data to the client and store it on the JavaScript side. We show, hide some buttons that make requests based on that authorization data to prevent the user from making unauthorized requests. Is that enough? Why?

   It is not enough because it is very easy to make a hidden button visible by developer tools. Server-side evaluation must be present for validating authorization.

Chapter 13 - Introducing Software Architectures

Even if you are not applying for a software architect job, you are mostly required to answer some questions about architectures and system design. The same is true for assignments also; the job owner may ask you to implement a certain architecture in your assignment.

Here are the answers to the questions:

1. What are the requirements of a good architecture? Explain with examples.

    There are certain repeating processes that occur in a software project. At the end of them, occasionally a deliverable is produced.

    The design phase ends with a full design document or a partial document (if additional modules or features to the application are being made). If additional modules are to be made, the current architecture must allow adding them as flawlessly as possible.

    The development phase is the implementation of the architecture. Wrong architecture will prolong this phase and incorporating changes since change is one of the facts of the software world.

    The deployment phase ends with a product ready to be tested and deployed. The right architecture allows easy deployments or rolling back deployments.

2. What are the disadvantages of a monolithic architecture?

    Every part of the project is in one application. It is scaled up or down entirely; it is very hard to roll out new deployments without shutting down the entire system (you must stop requests coming from NLB to a cluster, wait for the cluster to finish requests, then deploy the new version to the cluster and enable that cluster to accept the request from NLB again. We repeat this process for the other clusters).

    Also, there is not any separation of concerns. View rendering, application logic, data access, all of them are in one project, and this leads to no code reuse.

3. Should layers in an architecture be logical only? Explain with reasons.

    Not if it is not a very small application. We may need to take one layer and use it in another application. Layers provide code reuse and separation of concerns.

4. What points should we consider while implementing SOA?

    We must split the application into loosely coupled and coherent services.

5. Explain CQRS and its advantages.

Command query responsibility segregation allows separating commands (business logic that involves manipulating or inserting data) and querying (fetching data) which allow scaling and maintaining them separately.

Conclusion

The information presented in this book should be enough to make the reader gain self-confidence and know enough to start with ASP.NET Core. Software development requires practise along with theoretical knowledge. We believe that the reader is going to be prepared to apply for ASP.NET Core jobs by the techniques and knowledge explained in this book. Good luck with your journey into the software world.

Index

Printed in Great Britain
by Amazon

81543387R00201